In Africa's Forest and Jungle

RELIGION AND AMERICAN CULTURE

Series Editors
David Edwin Harrell Jr.
Wayne Flynt
Edith L. Blumhofer

In Africa's Forest and Jungle

Six Years Among the Yorubas

R. H. STONE

EDITED BY BETTY FINKLEA FLOREY

The University of Alabama Press
Tuscaloosa

Copyright © 2010
The University of Alabama Press
Tuscaloosa, Alabama 35487-0380
All rights reserved
Manufactured in the United States of America

Typeface: Bell MT
Designer: Kaci Lane Hindman
Original photographs circa 1859–1861

∞

The paper on which this book is printed meets the minimum requirements of
American National Standard for Information Sciences-Permanence of Paper for
Printed Library Materials, ANSI Z39.48-1984.

Library of Congress Cataloging-in-Publication Data

Stone, Richard Henry.
  In Africa's forest and jungle : six years among the Yorubas / by R. H. Stone ;
edited by Betty Finklea Florey.
       p. cm. — (Religion and American culture)
  Includes index.
  ISBN 978-0-8173-5567-8 (pbk. : alk. paper) — 978-0-9183-8446-3 (electronic)
1. Stone, Richard Henry. 2. Missionaries—United States—Biography.
3. Missionaries—Nigeria—Biography. 4. Baptists—Missions—Nigeria.
5. Yoruba (African people)—Nigeria—Religion. I. Florey, Betty Finklea. II. Title.
  BV3625.N6S76 2010
  266´.6132092—dc22
  [B]

                                                              2009018499

Contents

Acknowledgments

I wish to thank Professor Toyin Falola, an inspiring and articulate historian, who generously provided poignant information, pertinent texts, and creative suggestions.

I also wish to thank Dr. Lekan Ayanwale, former Department Head of Veterinary Medicine at the University of Ibadan and the first African Vice-President of the World Veterinary Association, who, as a native of Ijaye, enthusiastically shared many aspects of the Yoruba culture with me.

Additionally, I wish to thank Dr. David Mathews, President of the Kettering Foundation, who initiated communication with several prominent Nigerian and America educators; Dr. Chapman Greer, a dedicated scholar, who helped me with the initial editing; Ana Schuber who provided an interesting perspective on cultural history; Fred Anderson and Darlene Slater Herod of The Virginia Baptist Historical Society for introducing me to my great-grandfather's handwritten journal and artifacts; Edith M. Jeter, Archivist of the International Mission Board of the Southern Baptist Convention, who spent hours researching, photocopying, and mailing me the handwritten letters of R. H. Stone; Arlette Copeland and Susan Broome of the Jack Tarver Library of Mercer University, who scoured the records and found articles and references to Stone in *The Christian Index* and Henry A. Tupper's book; Elizabeth C. Wells, Special Collections Archivist, Samford University; Kiki Karatheodoris, who worked by my side to put the book together; Ed Florey, who encouraged me; and the professional staff of The University of Alabama Press.

Introduction

Richard Henry Stone was among the Americans who felt called as missionaries in Africa during the nineteenth century. As a representative of the Southern Baptist Convention, he spent his years in Africa with the Yoruba-speaking people in what is now Western Nigeria. He lived in Ijaye, Abeokuta, and Lagos; and traveled to Ibadan, Lahlookpon, Ewo, Ogbomishaw, and Oyo. Stone observed the Ijaye wars and wrote detailed accounts of the battles while he and his wife, Susan Broadus Stone, cared for wounded soldiers and conveyed war orphans to Abeokuta. The reports and letters that he sent to his administrators as well as his book, *In Afric's Forest and Jungle or Six Years Among the Yorubans*, provide valuable eyewitness accounts of Yoruba life and culture.

Stone's chronicle is a rare, respectful, and positive one from a Western perspective, and despite his missionary status, most of his observations are of the people and culture he encountered. Moreover, Stone's narrative fills a gap in the Ijaye time line as T. J. Bowen's *Adventures and Missionary Labors in Several Countries in the Interior of Africa From 1849 to 1856*, ends where Stone's begins in 1859. Toyin Falola cites Stone's book in his *The Military in the Nineteenth Century Yoruba Politics* (1984) and *Yoruba Warlords of the Nineteenth Century* (2001),[1] further demonstrating the lasting importance of the topics discussed in Stone's work.

Stone was stationed in West Central Africa between 1859 to 1863 and 1867 to 1869. He created his narrative by relating his adventures as described in his comprehensive journal and letters. Stone published his book in 1899 and included many of the same subjects as Bowen's. However, while Bowen's includes a comprehensive section on language and uses a scientific approach to the study of culture, Stone's is a narrative that concentrates on the personalities of the Yoruba leaders, the Yoruba people, and the religious personnel with whom he interacted.

In spite of Richard Stone's account of his African adventures, he remains an enigma. While it is clear that he was a devout Christian, he makes a distinction between American and African slaveries, never addressing the inherent contradiction. Although Stone saw slavery firsthand in America, he chose not to see the connection to the Africans to whom he went to minister. Neither did he make the connection when he witnessed firsthand the dispensing of Yoruba prisoners of war into slavery. In a letter to James B. Taylor, corresponding secretary of the Southern Baptist Convention Foreign Mission Board, he wrote, "it would require but short residence in this country to make anyone detest the slave trade." In this same letter, Stone agonized over the fate of children and said he could not imagine "that the Lord will permit them to be carried away from us by violent hands and carried into captivity & slavery." Yet he wrote in another letter to Taylor that if war came in America, "Georgia will do her duty," implying Georgia's obligation to maintain a heritage created and sustained by slave labor. After risking Susan's and his lives to return to Lagos with two hidden war orphans, Stone traveled to Liverpool, England, where he felt the anti-slavery pressure of the British. He later stated: "In England a southern man has to contend with many difficulties and discouragements. As a general thing, people have been educated to regard slavery as the 'sin of all villainies,' and think it heresy in a Christian to give 'aid and comfort' to anyone who sympathizes or is connected with this institution in any way." When Stone and his wife returned from England to attend to Susan's gravely ill mother, they were held at City Point, Virginia, which was under Union control and pressured to take the oath of allegiance to the Union. They refused on behalf of their Southern loyalties.[2] At length, G. W. Samson, a ministerial colleague, assisted them in securing from the secretary of war in Washington, "an unconditional permit to visit their kindred in their native State of Virginia, and when prepared to resume missionary efforts, to return by way of the North to their field of labor."[3]

After reaching their home and attending the funeral of Susan's mother, Susan Gaines Broadus, Richard Stone went to Georgia as a missionary agent of the International Mission Board to collect money to support the missions' efforts.[4] He sent detailed and interesting accounts to Susan about the affairs of the church and of the war. While there, Stone received devastating news of Susan's wound from a spent bullet[5] and of the deaths of his brothers, Peter Conway and John William, all direct results of the Civil War. Upon returning to Culpeper, Virginia, and finding Susan's wound healed, Richard joined the Confederate Army in Petersburg as a volunteer chaplain, joining Robert E. Lee's forces at Petersburg. He stayed until the fall of Richmond in 1865, taking his rations at General Gordon's headquarters, and staying with the Georgia troops as much as possible because, he said, "Georgia paid my way to Africa."[6]

As he headed homeward, Stone described the last days of the war. While anxious to return to Ijaye, Stone wrote to Taylor: "My father's plantation was swept away with the besom of destruction, and a recent destructive fire has left him, my mother, and two sisters destitute for the present,"[7] requiring that Stone remain to care for them. In 1867, Stone returned to the Baptist mission at Lagos where he wrote a passionate letter "To the Colored Baptists" asking the recently freed southern slaves to send money for the spiritual redemption of their "close relatives." In 1868, after contracting brain fever, Stone returned to Culpeper, where he established the first African American normal school in the area.[8] Despite several attempts, Stone was never able to find a way to continue his missionary work in Africa. As late as 1888, at the age of fifty, Stone petitioned to be sent back. He wrote the Rev. H. A. Tupper from Culpeper saying, "I have never forgotten the language, the people have never forgotten me, and wish me to return." Instead, the last years of his life were spent as a principal in the Culpeper Public Schools, a minister of Lael Baptist Church, and a director of the African American normal school he had established.[9] Stone's 1899 publication of *In Afric's Forest and Jungle*, describing his experiences in the land he loved, was perhaps an acceptance that his African adventures were at an end. In the final paragraph of this book, he wrote, "The author . . . will often in imagination revisit the scenes so hallowed by precious memories."[10]

Some of Stone's paradoxical actions may be illuminated by examining his background. He was born the son of Jane Payne Kelly and John [Jack] Stone, a planter who owned 1,300 plus acres, a mill, and a coach in the county of Culpeper, Virginia, on Mountain Run.[11] And according to the 1860 Census, John Stone had thirteen slaves and two white overseers. The Stones had three sons and two daughters whom they raised at Paoli Mills, the Stones' family plantation.[12]

As a boy at Paoli, Richard Stone seems to have relished the countryside, for in a letter written while at sea he spoke wistfully of his boyhood days. He described a beautiful "butterfly" flying about the ship: "The sight of this companion of my childhood in the sunny meadows of summer caused a thrill of pleasure to dart through my heart." Yet Stone was drawn to a life of greater adventure than that afforded him in Virginia. When he was only twenty-one years old, he wrote James B. Taylor, saying, "The finger of God's providence points me to Africa, and I do hope to spend the first part, if not all my life, in that benighted country." In addition to an intense desire to travel to Africa, Stone, an accomplished equestrian, was equipped with a somewhat classical education in which he attended a boarding school conducted by Albert G. Simms and, later, Kemper's University School at Gordonsville. Following his school years, Richard's letters indicate that his father and he planned for him to attend the University of Virginia until Richard felt called to "put on Christ" and become a missionary. Stone noted the obvious tension between his father and him: "Through the mistaken kindness of my parents, however, I was prevented from doing so until the summer of '56, when I had the inexpressible happiness of being 'buried' with my Savior, and of uniting myself with those whom I believed to be the true church."

In a letter to Taylor, Stone tells about his conversion and his reasons for wanting to become a missionary. He explained that while contemplating and praying in his room at Paoli, he was given a magazine that advertised for a missionary in Africa. He "shouted, 'I am going; I am going!'" He was just twenty years old. Jack Stone obviously relented; in a letter dated October 20, 1858, Richard told Taylor that in preparation for his imminent journey to his West African mission appointment, his father had given him $150 to purchase goods. In this same letter Richard Stone announced his coming marriage to Susan James Broadus: "I expect to be married tomorrow night. I am at home now but will go up tomorrow." Susan, the daughter of James and Susan Gaines Broadus, was known in Culpeper as "one of the smart Broadus girls." When her only brother, James, died at a young age, her father closed himself in the library and did not come out until three days had passed. As he entered the hall he said, "My son had to die to teach me my wrong. Girls have minds as well as boys. I have given all to my son and neglected my daughters. I shall make amends."[13] As a result of their brother's death, Susan and her sisters were given the classical education that would have been his due. Consequently, Susan Stone, at age twenty-four, was well equipped to teach her missionary work when she and Richard sailed on their honeymoon to West Africa. Richard, too, was properly qualified because, prior to their marriage, he had attended a missionary training school in Sparta, Georgia.

Susan and Richard Stone went down to the wharf in a hack to Baltimore, Maryland, to board a steamer that would take them to the *Mary Caroline Stevens* downstream. Stone described how "the ladies were lifted and the men climbed rope ladders." There were fireworks and cannons and streams of smoke. The missionaries gathered on deck and began to sing "From Greenland's Icy Mountains," [the missionary farewell]; Stone said the hymn sounded "discordant" because the guns were so noisy. In spite of the discordance, Stone took the title of his book from one of the phrases in the song: "from Afric's sunny fountains."

In his account, Stone listed fellow religious personnel and described other people on board. He quickly overcame his seasickness due to his excitement and fascination with the sea, the activities, and the people on board.

According to Stone, zealous missionaries practiced their techniques on the sailors; however, the sailors had learned to deflect the constant missionary conversion tactics. Stone further described the activities on board: meetings, talks, and Yoruba studies.

When Scottish doctor/explorer Mungo Park first saw the city of Segu on the Niger River in July of 1796, he wrote, "The view of this extensive city . . . the numerous canoes upon the crowded river; the crowded population; and the cultivated state of the surrounding country, formed altogether a prospect of civilization and magnificence, which I little expected to find in the bosom of Africa."[14] More than half a century later, Stone was likewise dazzled by his first sight of an African city. After ascending a "lofty granite boulder" overlooking Abeokuta, he too had an important moment of revelation:

> What I saw disabused my mind of many errors in regard to this part of Africa. The city extends along the bank of the Ogun for nearly six miles and has a population approximating 200,000 . . . souls. The view of the surrounding country . . . is both picturesque and beautiful. . . . Here are the homesteads, the winding river, the browsing cattle, azure hills, lofty trees, and green, far-extending plains.
>
> The outward condition of the people . . . was as great a revelation to me as the appearance of the country. Instead of being lazy, naked savages living on the spontaneous productions of the earth, they were . . . dressed with comparative decency and were industrious enough to provide everything their physical comfort required.

Stone had come to the "Dark Continent" to convert Africans to Christianity. Although he continued to believe his mission was to save the people from their "gross spiritual darkness," revelations like the one above freed him to deal with Africans on another level. He came to admire Yoruba culture, especially appreciating the skills and industriousness he saw employed in the daily lives of those individuals whom he lived among.

Stone's records today provide a rare, firsthand account of Yoruba life and culture in the mid-nineteenth century. He was a good observer and provided a surprisingly objective record of what he saw. He was also in a position to become acquainted with some of the key players in the tribal affairs in the area. Shortly after arriving in Ijaye, Stone and his wife were taken to meet the local chief, Areh [a.k.a. Kumee, Kurumni of Ijaye], "one of the most venerable and historic figures in Yoruba history" as according to scholar Samuel Johnson.[15] Stone's description of this meeting with the Yoruba chief clearly indicated the cultural similarities and differences between the Americans and the Africans but also depicted Areh as possessing comfortingly recognizable traits, such as a sense of humor. As the drummers announced, "Areh, oyinbo day" [Areh, the white man has come], Stone and his wife saluted the chief and "the venerable men . . . sitting on his left." Areh, in excellent humor, chatted and joked with the Stones throughout the interview. Noticing Stone tightly holding Susan's hand, Areh laughingly exclaimed, "'Why are you holding your wife's hand? I am not going to take her away from you. Put her hand down.'" After Stone became more closely acquainted with Areh, with whom he interacted throughout his residence in Ijaye, he noted that the chief could appreciate and reward "excellence of character and nobility of conduct" but sometimes, when he thought necessary, Areh could be "haughty" or "cruel." Stone further described Areh's skill as a leader and strategist in his chapters on the Ijaye wars.

Areh's receptiveness to missionaries, particularly to R. H. Stone and A. D. Phillips, both stationed at Ijaye, seems both personal and political. Stone believed Areh wanted the white men to live in his town because he thought their presence would facilitate trade; the chief promised "personal protection" to missionaries and white men who would follow him. He would not, however, assure protection from persecution to native Christian converts. Falola, in his book, *The History of Nigeria*, expands Stone's theory by giving reasons why indigenous rulers might have been receptive to Christian doctrine or missionaries. Falola believes that "the Yoruba rulers [hoped] . . . the missionaries would help them win their wars and procure arms and ammunition."[16]

Falola also discusses the motives that prompted missionaries like Stone to have a heightened interest in spreading Christianity in Nigeria in the mid-1850s. Many missionaries, including Richard Stone, believed that "Christianity would aid in stamping out slavery . . . because a new set of converts would be morally equipped to avoid slavery . . . and adopt new ethical codes drawn from Christianity."[17] While in Nigeria, Stone helped to train African men and women as missionaries who could recruit and educate native Christians. Among his trainees was an Abeokuta orphan, Moses Ladijo Stone, who worked as a missionary in Ogbomishaw and later signed himself "Native Pastor of the First Baptist Church of Lagos."

Stone shared enough of this nineteenth-century Western perspective to title a chapter on Yoruba religion "Superstitions" and to write, "The gospel of Jesus Christ is the only cure for the ills which afflict the victims of spiritual darkness." And he remained dogmatic about his mission in Africa, continuing to believe in the superiority of not just Christianity but also of the Baptist denomination among the Christian sects. However, despite Stone's filtering every person and event he encountered through Western cultural lenses, his fascination with and appreciation of the individuals, flora, fauna, and geography permeate his account of his experiences in Africa.

Although Stone never questioned his assumptions about Christianity's elevation above indigenous religions, he did not consider all things Western to be superior. Nigerian novelist Chinua Achebe explains that "one of the great problems the missionaries had was their inability to see the language as music."[18] Stone, however, did not share this condition. His memoir includes praise of the Yoruba language he heard and came to speak. Disturbed by the pidgin English he heard in Lagos, he said, "I much preferred to hear their own musical language and did not encourage them to speak a mutilated form of my own." Stone learned most of the native language from children, and he often reported his level of proficiency in his letters back to the United States. He explained that Susan and he learned the language from the children because "they spoke it more plainly than the other people did." However, in spite of the informal tutoring, the Stones both had trouble pronouncing the accent on the right syllable, a necessity of tonal language. Stone reported that "One morning at breakfast the children were convulsed with laughter by my wife saying there was a *horse* in her cup of coffee." Nonetheless, Stone became proficient enough in Yoruba to preach his sermons in this language, and told A. M. Poindexter, the Assistant Corresponding Secretary of the Foreign Mission Board of the Southern Baptist Convention, in a letter from Abeokuta, "When I preach, the people affirm they distinctly hear and understand every word I say."

Stone's life in Yoruba would come to encompass much more than the missionary duties he performed. One of his more exciting adventures came when Areh, counseled by the oracle of Efa, purchased a white Arabian horse and persuaded Stone to buy his former mount, "the largest horse in all that country," and known by all as "Areh's war horse." The horse, so unmanageable Stone named him "Bucephalus" [after Alexander the Great's obstreperous mount], was eventually equipped with a Mexican saddle to help the new owner be secure in his seat. Stone wrote that Bucephalus "helped to get me into serious trouble." He described being captured as Areh's spy and held by the chief's enemy, the Ibadans, a direct result of being identified via Bucephalus. Stone's adventure is cited in studies by scholars of African history, including Samuel Johnson's *History of the Yorubas* and Ade Ajayi and Robert Smith's *Yoruba Warfare in the Nineteenth Century*.

In fact, Stone's memoir of his time in Africa is valuable to scholars in part due to his descriptions of Yoruba battles at Ijaye. In a letter dated August 28, 1860, Stone wrote: "[T]here is a terrible beauty about a battle in Africa which fascinates the eye. As the mellow light of the declining sun falls upon the wide-spreading, intensely verdant, and palm-dotted plain, which surrounds Ijaye, its beauty is indescribable. Imagine you have a far-extending view of this plain on a clear evening; hear incessant peals of rattling thunder echoing over its hills and through its vales; see silvery clouds floating in the bright light of a tropical sun, above the dark hosts engaged in combat, and you have in your mind what, alas, is too often realized by us."

Stone's correspondence, a personal account of his time in Africa, served as a report to his administrators of the missionary work he was doing; yet, his letters, journal, and book reveal a people, a language, a culture, and a personality of the Yoruba benefitting, as Falola says, the "local production of knowledge."[19] Stone created a vigorous history that contributes significantly in providing researchers with important historical information. Stone's documents also serve to cultivate a conscious, active, and purposeful engagement with that world and ours.

NOTES

1. Toyin Falola and G. O. Oguntomisin, *Yoruba Warlords of the Nineteenth Century* (Trenton, NJ: Africa World Press, Inc, 2001), 58, 186.

2. *Virginia Herald/Baptist* (reprinted in the *South Western Baptist*), July 23, 1863:1, Column.

3. Ibid.

4. *Christian Index* (Duluth, GA, September 18, 1863).

5. *Historic Culpeper* (Culpeper Historical Society, Inc., Culpeper, VA, 1974).

6. *The Annual of the Baptist General Association of Virginia* (Richmond, Va. 1915), 125–126.

7. *Christian Index* (Duluth, GA, July 1866).

8. Eugene Scheel. *Culpeper: A Virginia County's History Through 1920* (Culpeper, VA: Culpeper Historical Society, 1921), 259.

9. Ibid.

10. Richard Henry Stone (Missionary Papers, Virginia Baptist Historical Society, University of Richmond, Richmond, VA).

11. *Culpeper Deed Book*, February 1839, no. 4:361.

12. John Stone Household, *1850 U.S. Census Population Schedule* (Culpeper County, VA), 252.

13. John Stone to Mary Conway Stone Finklea, Private Collection E. Finklea Florey (Tuscaloosa, AL, 1944).

14. Mungo Park. *Travels in the Interior Districts of Africa, Performed in the Years 1795, 1796, & 1797. With an Account of a Subsequent Mission to That Country* (London: George Newnes, Ltd., 1906), 203.

15. Samuel Johnson. *The History of the Yorubas: From the Earliest Times*

to the Beginning of the British Protectorate. Ed. O. Johnson (Lagos, Nigeria: C.M.S. Bookshops, 1921), 330.

16. Toyin Falola, *The History of Nigeria* (Westport, CT: Greenwood Press 1999), 42.

17. Ibid., 40.

18. Achebe, *Chinua Achebe's 70th Birthday Celebration,* VHS (Bard College: C-SPAN archives, 2000).

19. Toyin Falola, *Yoruba Gurus: Indigenous Production of Knowledge in Africa* (Trenton, NJ: Africa World Press, Inc., 1999), 299.

ESSENTIAL READINGS

1. J. F. Ade Ajayi and Robert Smith. *Yoruba Warfare in the Nineteenth Century* (Cambridge, England: Cambridge University Press, 1964), 141. Ajayi uses oral sources to compile a history of Yoruba history especially focusing on Christian religious influences.

2. T. J. Bowen. *Central Africa: Adventures and Missionary Labors in Several Countries in the Interior of Africa, from 1849 to 1856* (1857). Bowen compiles maps of the slavery coast, travel descriptions and Christian missions in the Sudan and Yoruba territories.

3. Toyin Falola. *Yoruba Gurus: Indigenous Production of Knowledge in Africa* (Trenton, NJ: Africa World Press, Inc., 1999), 299. Falola discusses the value of local histories on the African continent.

4. Toyin Falola. *The History of Nigeria* (Westport, CT: Greenwood Press 1999), 42. Falola provides a time line of the success of Christianity and Islam as they rise to dominance in and around Nigeria.

5. Toyin Falola and G. O. Oguntomisin. *Yoruba Warlords of the Nineteenth Century* (Trenton, NJ: Africa World Press, Inc., 2001). Falola and Oguntomisin focus on the individual military generals and the overall battles and warfare of the Yoruba.

6. Samuel Johnson. *The History of the Yorubas: From the Earliest Times to the Beginning of the British Protectorate.* Ed. O. Johnson (Lagos, Nigeria: C.M.S. Bookshops, 1921). This is an inclusive history of the Yoruba including language, religion, government, war, manners, and customs. He refers to Stone and his capture by the Ibadans.

7. Mungo Park. *Travels in the Interior Districts of Africa, Performed in the Years 1795, 1796, & 1797, With an Account of a Subsequent Mission to That Country* (London: George Newnes, Ltd., 1906). A young doctor, Park traveled the Niger, endured captivity of a Moorish chief, and writes with sympathy for the African people of the turn of the century.

In Africa's Forest and Jungle

1

Along the Coast

For four eventful years, far from civilization, my young wife and I lived among the barbarous people inhabiting that part of Western Central Africa lying between the Bight of Benin and the Niger river and between parallels five and seven, north latitude. In this section of the continent about four millions of people speak a language known as "Yoruban." The natives, however, recognize a number of entirely separate principalities. The most important are Egbar or Abeokuta, Ejayboo, Yoruba, Illorin, Ejesha and Benin. In color, these tribes range from black through brown to copper. They are reasonable, brave and patriotic, and are capable of a very high degree of intellectual culture.

The contest for the African Empire between England and France has recently brought these people prominently to the notice of the whole civilized world, and I have thought some account of my long residence among them would not be wholly uninteresting.

Some years have elapsed since, just twenty-one years old, I entered the country. The striking incidents of my life made a vivid and lasting impression on my memory and the reader may be assured that this book is a narration of facts only: it does not contain a single line of fiction.

After a somewhat eventful voyage of thirty-three days from the time that Cape Henry faded from our view, the joyful cry, "Land O!" sounded from the masthead. Oh, the excitement, the joy, the curiosity! But it was not until next day that we entered the beautiful harbor of Freetown, Sierra Leone.

Of the origin and wonderful history of this place, so much has been written that it will be a needless repetition for me to add anything. I had intended to take the West African mail steamer here for Lagos, Bight of Benin, but our captain refused to pay port dues and was compelled to discharge his cargo outside. This stubbornness on his part compelled me to remain on our vessel until she arrived at Cape Palmas, two months later. When I saw the beautiful mail steamer come in and then go out without me, I realized then, if I had never done so before, that patience is a great virtue and withal a difficult.

One week of the time we were beating along the Liberian coast, was passed at Cape Mount and three weeks at Monrovia, the capital.

The surf at Cape Mount is very bad and the excitement of landing in it, helped to make the week's delay less tedious. After waiting until a certain number of rollers had passed, the half-naked Grebo canoemen would rush the canoe in on top of a big roller and beach it. So soon as the prow struck the sand, they would leap into the water and, snatching up all the whites, bear them safely out of the way of the pursuing, roaring breakers. The ladies of our party stood the ordeal very well, but this rude method of landing had led to the death of one young woman previous to our arrival. Not being properly instructed, she thought the native who caught her up so suddenly was going to kidnap her. She was so frightened that she never recovered from the shock.

Our stay at Cape Mount was also enlivened by some good fishing in which we caught a large, white shark and some very large and quite savory fish called "Red Horse." During our three weeks' stay at Monrovia, we went ashore almost every day and were most hospitably entertained by the celebrities of Liberia, from president down. Because of this and because a Liberian gave his life for mine before I left Africa, I shall always have a warm place in my heart for this heroic little colony. With the thrilling experiences of its early settlers, I suppose my readers are familiar. One of the most remarkable special providences of which I ever heard was the dream of the Liberian woman which caused her to fire the only cannon in the fort and thus saved the last remnant of the colony from entire destruction. This incident seems to predict that the Lord has yet a great work for the Liberians to do.

At Palmas, we were most charmingly entertained by Rev. Mr. Hoffman and his wife at the Episcopal Orphanage. I here had the pleasure of meeting a near kinsman in the person of Bishop Payne the head of the Episcopal Mission to the Grebos or Kroos. These Kroos are one of the most remarkable peoples on the globe. They are distinguished from other natives by a broad, blue streak extending from the top of the forehead to the end of the nose. I was informed that this mark is put there by the mother and is intended to be a pledge that they will die before they will submit to slavery. During my residence in Africa, I failed to meet any one who had ever seen a Kroo slave. For a living, they follow the sea only; and from their very infancy, they are as much at home in the ocean as if it were their native element. I have seen ebony tots form a line along the beach and plunge head foremost beneath a great roller. They would then appear like black specks on the foaming water until it scattered them, squirming and yelling, along the sandy beach. After they are older they will dive beneath a shark and stab it to death. They are among the most skillful boatmen in Africa. Few ships trading along the coast, can afford to do without them, and there are few places of importance on the west coast where some of them are not temporarily settled, though all return to Palmas periodically.

The Kroos live almost entirely on rice, and the quantity they can eat at a single sitting, is quite incredible. I once saw a party take breakfast, and I shall never forget the incident. Several Kroos formed a circle around a vessel full of steaming hot rice. The leader put in his hand, took a quantity, tossed it over and over until it assumed the form of a ball about the size of a baseball and then pitched it into his widely distended mouth. As he was swallowing the mass, he gave his body a snake-like squirm so as to leave as much space as possible for more to follow. All the others of the party followed the example of their leader, going round and round with clock-like regularity until the rice was all gone. By this time their stomachs were distended like those of cattle in early summer. I met among the Kroos the only leper I ever saw, and before I knew that he was a victim of this dread disease, I shook hands with him. Several of his toes and fingers had already dropped off. My feelings until I was assured that the disease was not contagious, may be imagined.

Ten days after going aboard the mail steamer at Palmas we cast anchor before Lagos, and from our position saw, about a mile away across a terrible bar, the thatched roofs of the town sweltering in a broiling tropical sun. In a few moments, immense red sharks, with backs as broad as those of horses, began to appear around our ship, and I was informed that the breakers on the bar which we were about to cross in a small boat, swarmed with these monsters and instantly devoured all who fell into the water. I could not help thinking of this while crossing the bar a few hours later, even though the boat was most skillfully handled by the inevitable Kroo boys. It is quite impossible for boatmen to show more dexterity than these half-naked natives did on this occasion. There were ten in all. One steered and another sat in the prow to direct the rowers by gestures. In the midst of the seething, hissing breakers, the rowers frequently sat perfectly still with their eyes fixed on the man in the prow. Then, at his signal, they would dash forward again. If it had not been the "dry season," we would have had a much more dangerous time crossing this bar and possibly, like hundreds before and since, may have found a grave in the sharks. Even now, it was very startling to see the great breakers suddenly start up before us and then, arching their necks, come roaring at us like great monsters.

2

Up the Ogun

Lagos is situated on an island of sandy formation, its shores washed by the Ogun river, the ocean, and a beautiful lagoon. This town, under the dominion of a king named Kosoko, who was supported by the Portuguese, was at one time a stronghold of the slave trade; but it is now a flourishing English colony. It is a tradition among the natives of Lagos that when the English conquered Kosoko, shells were seen darting about the streets everywhere and hideously shrieking, "Kos-so-ko! Kos-so-ko!" If Kosoko believed this, it is not surprising that he gave up the fight. For some years, Kosoko was very active in his efforts to stir up some of the native tribes to help him regain his throne and revive the slave trade, and in one of the revolutions caused by his intrigues I came near losing my life. But I will say more of this later.

Our destination was the city of Ejahyay situated on the direct route to Rabba on the Niger. The first part of the way we could go either by land or by the river Ogun. We decided on the latter course, and hired a native canoe with two canoemen and a young man to act as both interpreter and messenger. The canoe had been dug and burned out of a tree of immense size and length and the middle part of it was wide enough to receive our mattress spread out. Over this we built a tent of mats made of strong sea grass. (At this time strangers could travel from the coast to the Niger with as much security as they could in civilized lands. Slave wars had ceased and the wild beasts of the country were not feared on the roadways in the daytime.)

Early one morning, about a week after landing in Lagos, we placed all our earthly possessions in our canoe and, bidding adieu to the last vestige of civilization, crossed the beautiful lagoon and began our journey up the Ogun river. For some time our daily experiences were much alike. When night overtook us, we fastened our canoe to the bank in some open place and then waited until daylight returned before proceeding on our way. On account of the heat, the mosquitoes and the novelty of our position, we did not sleep very well. Furthermore, we were serenaded by weird sounds coming from the dense forests on the bank to which our canoe was tied, although we heard nothing which made us think we were in danger. At one place the canoemen recognized the track of an elephant in the mud on the bank, but we neither saw nor heard anything that made us fear an attack from one of these dangerous animals. The trees were immense but the undergrowth and vines were so rank that they often presented the appearance of a solid wall of green. The fauna as well as the flora of the country furnished us much diversion. During the day the little monkeys would peep at us from behind the leaves of overhanging limbs, and in the evening they would assemble in hundreds on the branches of some large dead tree to pass the night. They are a favorite prey of boa-constrictors, leopards, tiger cats and other animals, and they choose a dead tree that they may see the approach of any enemy in the night. It was really pitiful to hear them chattering while they were arranging themselves in little groups like timid children. Birds, large and small, including flocks of parrots, were constantly flying over us.

In the rainy season, the Ogun is a deep, wide stream with a strong current, but it was now the dry season and our canoe had to be dragged over shallows in several places. Although this caused some delay, it gave us a pleasant change, for we were much cramped in the canoe. We passed several villages on the river, and native etiquette required that I should stop and salute the "head-man" and make him a small present, and this afforded us another opportunity for recreation. My interpreter spoke "Pigeon English" and when he wished to know if I understood him, he would stop and say, "You sabby?" But he seemed to understand all that I said, although I did not always understand him. There is an abundance of fine fish in the river. Instead of using seines, the natives catch the fish in baskets or snares attached to ropes extending entirely across the river. These ropes are made of a native vine and often upset canoes, but, fortunately, our canoe escaped collision with any of them.

We came in sight of the mud walls of Abeokuta late in the afternoon of the fifth day after leaving Lagos, and landed at a small village about a mile from the south gate of the city. For the accommodation of myself and my wife, the missionary of the American Baptist Mission, Mr. Priest, had kindly provided two horses of pure African breed. Mine was so small that my feet nearly touched the ground, and it was with great difficulty, when I went down a steep place, that I could keep from falling over his head on to mine. But this equine pigmy carried me seven miles with so much ease that at times he was even unruly. His strength and endurance were truly wonderful. We tarried in Abeokuta about a week and were most hospitably and comfortably entertained by Mr. Priest and his excellent wife.

One bright morning, I ascended a lofty granite boulder in the heart of the populous part of the town and got a good view of the surrounding country. What I saw disabused my mind of many errors in regard to this part of Africa. The city extends along the bank of the Ogun for nearly six miles and has a population approximating 200,000 thousand souls. The view of the surrounding country is very extended, and it is both picturesque and beautiful, especially when covered by dewdrops sparkling in the rising sun. Spread out before the delighted eye as on a great natural canvas, is everything needed to complete a landscape. Here are the homestead, the winding river, the browsing cattle, azure hills, lofty trees and green, far-extending plains.

The outward condition of the people, who were swarming in myriads below me, was as great a revelation to me as the appearance of the country. Instead of being lazy naked savages living on the spontaneous productions of the earth, they were (excepting the little children) dressed with comparative decency and were industrious enough to provide everything that their physical comfort required. The men are builders, blacksmiths, iron-smelters, carpenters, calabash-carvers, weavers, basket-makers, hat-makers, mat-makers, traders, barbers, tanners, tailors, farmers and workers in leather and morocco, the last named making saddles, shoes, sword and knife scabbards, quivers, pouches, satchels, and bags of many sorts and sizes. The smelters reduce the iron ore and from it obtain a steel of good quality. They make this into razors, swords, knives, hoes, bill-hooks, axes, arrow-heads, stirrups, tools for the carpenter and blacksmith, and other things needed in ordinary business. The barber keeps a fine edge on his razors by whetting them on his brawny arm.

The farmers constitute the most numerous and important class. The "farms" of Abeokuta extend about fifteen miles around and beyond the city walls. They are merely small clearings in the tall grass and scrub growth of the country. Every one can cultivate as much land as he pleases and hold it as long as he cultivates it. Among the things grown are Indian corn, Guinea corn, West India yams, two kinds of sweet potatoes, cassada, rice, onions, beans, arrowroot, ochre, peppers, ginger, peanuts, sugar cane, tobacco, cotton, calabashes and many things peculiar to the country. They have nearly every tropical fruit found anywhere in the world, besides some that are native. Among these are oranges, limes, bananas, plantains, soursops, pawpaws, pineapples, guavas, mangoes, tamarinds, coconuts, and bread-fruit. The Badagary orange is probably the best in the world. The pineapples are very large, fragrant and juicy. But among all the fruits, my favorite was the delicious soursop.

The domestic animals are horses, cows, sheep, goats, hogs and dogs. Donkeys, mules and camels are found nearer the Niger. The African elephant is never domesticated. A large number of ducks, chickens, pigeons and guineas are raised. This is the native country of the guinea fowl and they are sometimes domesticated by the people in such large numbers that the united flock of a farm village have been known to cover an acre of ground. Turkeys are rarely found. The sheep are like those in the Temperate Zone excepting that wool is replaced by hair. They are very gentle and trot along with the dogs at the heels of their master as he goes out every morning to the farm. Each one has a name but does not respond except when the name is called by its owner.

One of the most remarkable farm products is a species of large calabash. These grow so large that they are used as ferry boats in all the country beyond Abeokuta. One never sees a canoe after passing that town, going into the interior. When the streams are made impassable by the rains, travellers are carried over them in these large calabashes, the passenger taking his seat in one while the ferryman swims behind and pushes him across. These calabash men affect to despise canoemen and the name "agayen" (canoeman) is used as a term of reproach among them. So easy is it to have fictitious standards of honor!

The women are even more industrious than the men. They have to support themselves and their children and they most diligently follow the pursuits which custom has allotted to them. They spin, weave, trade, cook, and dye cotton fabrics. They also make soap, dyes, palm-oil, nut-oil, all the native earthenware and many other things used in the country. They can be found spinning by the light of their little bowl-lamps until late at night and before day in the morning. They are indefatigable workers.

Rubber, ivory and cotton are important articles of export. The last is perennial and has pods in all stages of development during the growing season and the fibre is of a very fine quality. Elephants abound and are killed in large numbers by professional hunters. But the great staple of the country is palm-oil. Crests of palm trees dot the country as far as the eye can see. Men only can scale the lofty stems and gather the bunches of beautiful nuts, but the oil is extracted by women. One set of women separates the nuts from their integuments, another boils them in large earthen pots and still another crushes off the fibre from the kernel nut in large mortars. The crushed fibre is then placed in large clay vats filled with water and the oil is pressed out by trampling and rises to the surface. It is then gathered and boiled to free it from any water which may have adhered to it. No part of the palm-nut is wasted. Lamp oil and soap grease are made from the kernel of the nut and blacksmith's coal from the hull. The crushed fibre is used for kindling.

3

In Native Homes

Unless we except the broad ways that lead from the gates to the market places, there is neither in Abeokuta nor in other native cities in this part of Africa, anything that can be called a street. By Europeans, the dwellings are called "compounds." These are scattered about without reference to any particular plan and the lanes between them are always crooked and generally narrow. A "compound" is an enclosed space (generally in the form of a square) bounded by a mud wall about seven feet high. There is but one entrance to this enclosed space. At night or in times of danger, this is closed by strong double doors well barred. Inside, against this wall, the rooms of the house are built. These rooms are square and are covered by a thatched roof, which rests on the wall on the outside and on posts on the inside so as to give a covering for a piazza extending all around the enclosed space on the inside. In this piazza the inmates mostly live, the rooms being chiefly used for dormitories or for storage. Underneath the roof and on top of the ceiling they store such products of the farm as need curing before using. This ceiling is made of palm poles covered with grass mats which in turn are covered with a thick coating of earth. For this reason a fire often sweeps away the roofs of the dwellings of the people without destroying their homes. After a big fire the people go out to the farms, get a supply of poles, grass, reeds and vines, and in a few days everything is as before. They frequently lose what was stored on the ceilings under the roofs. When the only entrance to the compound is closed, there is no way of entering it except over the roof, and the court of the compound or the enclosed central space is therefore very secure against thieves and beasts of prey prowling about at night. It is for this reason little better than a barnyard. A pigeon cote frequently stands in the centre, while sheep, goats, chickens, pigs and dogs run about everywhere, trying the patience of the women who are cooking and attending to other household duties. The horses are tied to posts placed in convenient places. Cows have a compound for their special use and are never found inside of the ordinary human dwelling.

The average compound contains several dwellings occupied by as many separate families, but everybody in it is subject to the authority of one man who is called the *bale* (pronounced "barley"). This man is held responsible under native law for the conduct of every inmate of his compound and his authority is commensurate with this responsibility. Native etiquette requires that any one on entering a compound shall first salute the *bale* and make known to him alone the object of his visit. The *bale* is willing to bear all this responsibility for the sake of the honor, though men holding this position sometimes lose their heads for not keeping those under their authority in order.

The compounds of the chiefs are very large, sometimes covering several acres of ground. In such cases they are a perfect labyrinth of dwellings. If a stranger were put down in the centre of one of this kind, he would probably wander about for hours through little courts and passages before finding his way out. Away back in these recesses, surrounded by the most trusty of their wives and retainers, the chiefs pass their leisure hours; but they will always come out to see any important visitor, especially an "oyinbo" or white man. For some reason they greatly fear assassination and by sleeping in a different place every night in the midst of the intricacies of their dwellings, they make it impossible for any one but those they can trust to know where they may be found during the night.

The walls of the compounds are built of a kind of solid *adobe* and, when securely thatched, will endure indefinitely. The mission house was built of this material. Each layer of stiff clay is allowed to harden in the sun before another is placed upon it. If it is desired, the walls may in this way be carried up two stories. In the mission-house the walls had been made very smooth on the inside and then plastered with a kind of fine, blue clay. This had been so skillfully whitewashed with lime made from oyster shells brought up from the coast, that a stranger would never suspect the coarse material underneath. The doors, window-frames and sashes, ceilings, flooring and some of the furniture of this house, had been made of a beautiful wood called "roko," very hard and capable of a high polish. It was sawn in "pits" in the forest by the Liberian and Sierra Leone carpenters with the assistance of the natives.

Though the central court of an average compound is used as a kind of barnyard, it is kept in a comparatively decent condition. The poultry destroy what they can eat, the sheep and goats assist them as scavengers as far as they can, and the pigs and the dogs finish up most that is left. In front of the piazza, also, all around the court, the ground is frequently swept by those who live in that part of the house. The natives are very far from being untidy either in personal habits or in dress. They bathe once and sometimes twice a day, and their clothes are reasonably clean.

The main articles of dress worn by the males are a kind of loose trousers called *shocoto*, a cloth worn like a Highlander's plaid and a brimless cloth cap. Ordinarily they are barefooted, but when walking on journeys they wear sandals, and when riding they protect their feet with a loose morocco shoe or with European boots. When not engaged in manual labor, the men also wear a sleeveless vest under their shoulder-cloth. The *shocoto* is girt about the waist and extends to the knees and sometimes to the ankles. In the place of this, young men sometimes wear a garment exactly like a Highlander's kilt. Mussulmans always wear a turban. Among the prosperous a *tobe*, a loose robe, generally of white material, takes the place of the shoulder-cloth. This garment is gracefully worn and is often very beautifully embroidered. Cotton is the material out of which the clothing of the masses is made; but on state occasions, the rulers and rich men appear in garments of silk and silk-velvet. Through foreign merchants, these men obtain from Europe whatever they fancy, especially costly cloths and choice liquors.

Woolly heads are never seen among the men, who shave not only the face, but also the head and even the eyebrows and nostrils. Some leave a strip of hair from the forehead over the head to the back of the neck. Others leave little patches as marks of devotion to some particular deity, but such patches are concealed by the tight-fitting cloth cap or the turban. After a man has made a visit to a barber shop, his head and his face shine alike and, if he should have on a spotless tobe and turban, he makes quite a presentable appearance. Their tribal and family marks, however, often are so deep and numerous that they greatly disfigure faces that would have been otherwise good looking. These tell-tale marks on the face make it quite impossible for strangers to conceal their identity, and slaves rarely escape to the interior on that account. The fugitive is compelled to follow the roads leading through the towns and the gate keepers recognize them by their face marks and their scanty outfit, and they are captured and returned to their masters. For this reason also fugitives from justice rarely escape. Gate keepers are thoroughly posted in this kind of lore, and they know the nationality of every one passing through their gates.

The female toilet is better suited to convenience than to display. It consists of one or more cloths fastened around the waist, one thrown over the shoulders, and a turban, all of the same material, generally cotton cloth. Except in cold weather, the shoulder cloth is passed around the body just under the armpits and securely tucked on one side or the other. The cloths around the waist extend to the knee on one side and to the ankle on the other and are skillfully tucked over the hip. One of the cloths around the waist is used for the baby's hammock or basket, and here it laughs, coos and sleeps as happy as can be, suspended from its mother's back or riding on her hip with her loving arm for a support.

Both sexes blacken the margin of the eyelids with pulverized sulphuret of antimony, and the women dye their finger nails, their feet and the palms of their hands with pulverized camwood. When about to take part in some sacrifice, they frequently give the entire person a pinkish tinge. Beads, nose-jewels, and bracelets of gold, silver, brass and carved ivory are the principal jewels of the women. The rings are often worn on the ankles as well as the arms. Men also wear necklaces of coral and bracelets of metal. Tattooing in blue is practiced to a limited extent and is so well done that it resembles a covering of figured cloth.

The limbs of the young of both sexes are well proportioned and the hands and feet of the young girls are often perfect models. Their step also is so easy and graceful that they walk along chatting merrily with each other without once touching the jars of water that they carry on their heads. All take excellent care of their teeth, using the chewed end of certain roots for cleansing them. This is done every morning before breakfast.

One staple article of food is *ekkaw*, a preparation of Indian corn or maize. After the grain has been macerated until it ferments, it is crushed between two stones and then washed to separate the husks. The milky liquid is then boiled in large pots until it becomes a little thicker than rich cream. In this form a large spoonful is wrapped in a portion of a banana leaf and when it cools, it becomes a jelly-like substance having a slightly acid taste much liked by the people of the country and by everybody else who remains in the country for several years. From four to six of these are taken at each meal with a few spoonfuls of a sauce to be hereafter described. When travelling or engaged in manual labor, the natives make a hasty and refreshing luncheon of this cold *ekkaw* by breaking it up in cold water. *Ekkaw* is cooked under the shade of the trees in the streets and the market-places as well as in the houses, in the early morning and late in the afternoon; and before it is put into leaves, much of it is sold to people passing as a hot, refreshing drink. A small quantity is mixed with hot water in a calabash and in this form it is a kind of sour gruel and very anti-febrile and wholesome. I was exceedingly fond of it, especially when I was feverish and thirsty. At such times my appetite much preferred it to acid fruits such as oranges and limes. The same was true of my wife.

Another staple article of diet is the West India yam. Only one grows from each vine (which greatly resembles a bramble briar) but the farmers raise great numbers of them, from one to two feet long each. It is cooked by steam and is very white, sweet and mealy. In cooking it, a number of yams are cut up and placed in a very large earthen pot containing a small quantity of water and another pot of the same size is inverted and placed on top of the first and the joint is sealed with clay. The water is then converted into steam, and this cooks the yams. The native women seem to know by intuition exactly when to take off the upper vessel and let the yams dry off. Old, well-cured yams are a very delicious and nourishing article of food, whether eaten cold or hot. It is more expensive than *ekkaw*, especially in the form of *eyan*. This is made by pounding the yam in a mortar with a large, heavy pestle until, by adding a little water occasionally, it is converted into a stiff, puffy paste. In this form it is always eaten with the native sauce. In its simple form it is eaten in any manner. It is an excellent substitute for bread, and for this reason is an indispensable dish at a foreigner's table. A piece of sweet, mealy yam eaten cold is also a most palatable luncheon when one is on the road.

Dried cassada made into flour and then cooked until it becomes a stiff paste, is another favorite accompaniment of the inevitable native sauce. This sauce is a concoction of palm-oil, flesh of some kind, ochre, esculent herbs and the ground seed of a native melon. "Palaver sauce" is the name by which it is known among the Sierra Leone people and other foreigners because it is generally eaten in token of friendship after the natives have settled any difficulty; but the natives call it *orbeh*. It is made in both cheap and expensive forms. Poor people have no flesh and very little palm-oil in theirs. An ingredient called *ogere*, which has the disgusting odor of tainted meat, is frequently added by epicures.

Two very agreeable dishes are balls of cornmeal dough, seasoned with peppers and fried in palm-oil, and beans stewed in this oil and highly seasoned in the same way. These peppers are very small and are anti-febrile. The juice which flows from incisions made in the palm tree is very extensively used as a beverage. It resembles cider in flavor and is not intoxicating until several days old. They also brew a weak beer from Indian and Guinea corn. Wild bees' honey and a kind of taffy made from the juice of the sugar cane, are the only native sweets exposed in the markets. The children like to chew the cane and suck the juice, and they evidently enjoy this as much as children in more favored lands enjoy the choicest confections. Excepting very small children, everybody, both male and female, carries a small quantity of snuff made from the black Brazilian roll tobacco; but they put this snuff on their tongues, instead of using it in the ordinary way. It is ground with a small quantity of benin-seed and with *lubi*, an impure carbonate of soda found in the country.

4

The Story of Crowther

While these people are not in need of our sympathy on account of their physical condition, the miseries which are the natural fruit of gross spiritual darkness poison all their temporal blessings; and their wretchedness should excite in the heart of every true Christian, feelings of the liveliest compassion. They are the tortured slaves of superstitions which destroy everything like peace of mind, and they know nothing of that happiness that is found in every place worthy of the name of a Christian home. In this life they are in constant dread of the unseen power of malignant spirits; and in death, not a single ray of hope disperses the gloom of the grave: they seem to pass away in sullen, speechless despair. In religious things, their minds are a desert, a wilderness. But of this I shall say more in another part of my story.

A number of missionaries, both English and American had labored for years in Abeokuta before I saw the place and their faithful efforts to lift up the people had been crowned with reasonable success. The history of the city of Abeokuta and the way in which this missionary work was begun, is quite wonderful. This town belongs to the Egbar tribe. Some refugees of the slave wars who belonged to this tribe sought shelter and safety under the large rock which I have already mentioned as standing in the centre of the city. Hence the city was named Abeokuta (under a rock). Other similar unfortunates continued to be added until they represented the remnants of 110 large towns of the Egbar tribe. The city continued to grow so rapidly that the outer walls at the time of my visit, were thirty miles in length and it had become the greatest political and military power in that part of Africa.

Among those who had been captured and sold to the Portuguese by the slave-hunters was a certain little boy. On the night that he was taken prisoner, his father was killed and he had seized his bow and quiver and fought in his place until overpowered. When taken on board a Portuguese slave-ship with other captives of his people, they were told by the captain that the English had ships out looking for black people to eat, and that whenever a ship was in sight, they must run below. The little fellow believed all this and one day when he and those of his companions who were allowed to stay on deck saw a ship coming in sight, they ran below, frightened nearly out of their wits. This ship proved to be an English man-of-war, and when the captain of it came aboard the slaver and carried away everybody to his own ship, this little boy gave himself up for lost. When he saw large pieces of meat hanging from the yard-arms of the Englishman's ship and piles of cannon balls on the deck, his terror knew no bounds; for he thought that the balls were the heads of little darkeys like himself, and that their meat had been hung up to cool before being eaten. After his mind was disabused of this frightful impression and he found out that he was among friends instead of white cannibals, he is said to have cut some rare "capers." As he was a wild, little heathen, this was not surprising. One day he saw the captain of the Portuguese slaver sitting on deck. Slipping up slyly behind him, he gave the unsuspecting pirate a sharp rap on his cheek with the palm of his open hand. We may imagine the rage of the man at such an insult from such a source, but before he could resent it, his little monkey-like tormentor had disappeared below deck.

Soon this little African pagan was taken to Sierra Leone, named Samuel Crowther, and was educated first in the government schools at Sierra Leone. After visiting England, he became not only a well educated but a pious man. On account of his piety, ability and missionary zeal he rose to be a missionary bishop of the Church of England, and he had so many stations under his care that a steamer was placed at his disposal to facilitate his work. Before leaving Africa, I became well acquainted with him and learned to love and venerate him very sincerely; for he was gentle, humble and sympathetic, and was a great comfort to me in a time of deep distress.

The story of the wonderful rise of Abeokuta, fired his young heart to carry the gospel back to his people; for he was an Egbar and the whole tribe then dwelt within its walls. Accompanied by several others, after many difficulties and perils, he succeeded in reaching Abeokuta. Among the first fruits of his missionary labors in this town was the conversion of his mother and sister. After laboring here several years, during which time he translated most of the Bible, he was allowed to extend his labors along the coast and far up the Niger Valley. His translations of Scriptures have been of inestimable value to missionaries in this part of Africa, and all of them esteemed it a privilege to make his acquaintance. Notwithstanding the great change in his circumstances, he was not ashamed of his jet black face nor the tribal marks there which showed his pagan origin. He once laughingly told of an adventure he had in England when dining with some dignitary.

Feeling something soft touch his hand, he turned to find a little girl trying to rub off the *smut*.

Before leaving Abeokuta, I had the pleasure of meeting Rev. Mr. King, a Sierra Leone missionary and a colaborer with Bishop Crowther in the work of preaching and translating. He was a very humble and devout man and well worthy to be named in connection with Crowther.

But not all the Sierra Leone emigrants were desirable citizens. Some of them had evidently left their country for their country's good. One of the latter class it was my misfortune to secure as an interpreter, after sending back the one who came up the river with me. He was so dishonest and untruthful that I had to dismiss him after one month's trial. His successor, another Sierra Leone man, proved to be very trustworthy and remained with me as long as I needed his services.

In Abeokuta, I had to provide myself with native currency. This is a small shell (*cyproea moneta*) called *cowry* by the Sierra Leone people. Its divisions were cowries, strings, heads, and bags. Forty cowries make a string, fifty strings make a head and twenty heads a bag. A bag or twenty thousand cowries cost me five dollars in American money. This was a bushel of native money for five dollars in American money. Near the coast, as at Abeokuta, the silver coin was used to purchase foreign goods; but in the interior it was used in the manufacture of jewelry. The purchasing power of the cowries increases as the distance from the coast increases, for they are introduced at seaport towns. A ship would bring in a cargo of the shells from some coast on which they abounded and exchange them for native produce for the foreign market. It required a large room to hold the money needed to build a house and while building, it took almost the entire time of one person to count out the money every day and have it ready to pay the workman when night came. The cowries paid to an able-bodied man for a day's work, cost about five cents in American currency. The only thing that can be said in favor of such a medium of exchange is that it cannot be counterfeited.

All these things about the people and their circumstances I have mentioned here because the knowledge of them will be needed in order to understand other parts of my story.

5

In a Native Caravan

To prepare for the journey to Ejahyay, where I was to be stationed, it was necessary to obtain carriers for our luggage, a hammock and carriers for my wife, and a horse for myself. My kind host lent me a horse and his wife lent my wife her hammock, so there was nothing for me to do but to get the necessary carriers. Of these, I needed one for every sixty or seventy pounds of baggage, and four for my wife, the couples relieving each other every eight or ten miles.

Securing carriers is one of the disagreeable things connected with travelling in this part of Africa. They always begin by asking much more than they are willing to take and, if one is not well acquainted with the customary charge, he will be swindled at every point. Fortunately for me, Rev. A. D. Phillips, at whose mission-house I had arranged to stay while I was stopping in Ejahyay, was then in Abeokuta, and was going back to his home with us. Being familiar with the customs of the people, he consented to engage the carriers for me. All I had to do was to observe and learn. The interpreter was sent out to the principal market-place to notify professional carriers that I wanted to go to Ejahyay. The next day many people, both men and women, came to see about it. Those needed for the hammock were soon engaged, but when it came to the loads, the trouble began. Provisions, bedding, clothing, cooking utensils, household articles and such things, had been carefully divided up into packages of the usual weight; but when those who had come to offer their services lifted the packages they put them down with looks of affected dissatisfaction and, declaring that they were too heavy for the ordinary charge, demanded about double that sum. This being refused, they all left. In a short time the exact number we needed returned and through their spokesman or "head carrier," abated their demands a little. This being refused, they again left in a body. This time, however, they had hardly gotten out of sight before they returned and, finding that they were dealing with an *agbalagba* (man of experience), they came to terms.

Everything being settled, the carriers quickly and easily swung the loads to little cushions on their heads and trotted off in single file at a kind of shuffling "double quick," the head carrier bringing up the rear of his company. I next started the carriers with my wife's hammock and then followed on my pony. For several miles the carriers continued their trot and I found it difficult to keep up with them; but when the sun began to get hot they quieted down. We rested several hours during the hottest part of each day and made up the time by travelling early in the morning and late in the afternoon. So soon as we could see well, we started and then stopped for breakfast about eight o'clock. We then resumed our journey until noon. Resting until three o'clock we travelled until darkness made it unsafe. In this way we managed to endure the intolerable rays of the tropical sun, which seemed to pierce the thick covering of our white umbrellas like points of steel.

We passed the nights in the thatched mud huts of wayside villages temporarily established for purposes of trade with passing caravans. We met several of these caravans composed of hundreds of carriers of both sexes hurrying on to the coast. Palm-oil in larger carboy-like calabashes, and elephants' tusks, seemed to constitute the chief articles of export from the interior. The traders who were transporting these things, could be distinguished from their carriers by their turbans, their flowing tobes and by their long brass-handled swords in morocco scabbards suspended from their left shoulders by a large crimson cord with tasselled ends. While we were resting at one of the stopping places, a caravan going from the coast to the interior overtook and passed us. Their loads consisted largely of kegs of powder, boxes of trade muskets, salt, cloths of different kinds, copper rods, and still more largely of green boxes containing cheap rum. The trade muskets had flint-locks and some were the guns thrown away by European governments when adopting superior weapons. The copper rods were to be made into bullets so that wounded men might die of poison if they were not killed by the bullet itself.

It was then January, the dryest and hottest part of the year, and we suffered much from heat and thirst between the stopping places. Most of the way led through high grass and bushes of scrubby growth, but we were five hours passing through one of the forests. The path was just wide enough to allow my pony to pass between the walls of dense, impenetrable undergrowth on both sides. Sometimes he would get his feet entangled in a vine and nearly fall. We heard few sounds except the braying of immense toucans and the hoarse barking of large monkeys. But it would have been dangerous to pass through this forest in the night, for it contained elephants, leopards, wild boars and other dangerous animals. Lions are further north. We passed through the ruins of several large towns. These had been destroyed during the slave wars. In a distance of seventy miles in one part of this journey from the coast to the interior, we passed through the ruins of eighteen large towns destroyed in slave hunting.

About ten miles from Ejahyay, which we reached about noon of the third day after leaving Abeokuta, the carriers, instigated by their headman, put down their loads and declared that they were too heavy to be carried so far for the pay agreed upon in Abeokuta and that they would not carry them another step without additional pay. Mr. Phillips understood their language perfectly, and he pretended to argue with them for a while; then affecting great anger, he hurriedly mounted his horse and proceeded on the way telling us to follow him. I did so, wondering what was to become of all my worldly goods. At last I asked him to tell me. He laughed and said that the carriers would be along presently and get to Ejahyay before we did. Sure enough, they presently came up with us and passed us with a rush. He then explained that they were all Ejahyay people who had taken loads to Abeokuta. They were all mortally afraid of Kumee their ruler and he had told them that their conduct would be reported to Kumee so soon as he reached the city. He knew that this would frighten them and that they would not let him get to the city first. When we arrived at the missionary's home we found them awaiting us in the best of humors. We parted good friends and Kumee never heard of their conduct. Their danger arose from the fact that their ruler had notified the people of Ejahyay that the white man was under his special protection and that they must treat him kindly. Just outside the gate we had to cross a creek that is always past fording in the rainy season; but as it was the dry season, my wife did not have to cross in the calabash ferry.

There is nothing like a census among these people, but judging from the number of males in the city who were capable of bearing arms, the population of Ejahyay at that time must have been fully one hundred thousand. It was strongly fortified not only by a ditch and *adobe* wall, but by a belt of forest entirely encircling the place. To get through this forest, one would have had to cut his way foot by foot through large interlacing vines and creepers. Since this forest greatly added to the defences of the city, it was a capital crime for any one to disturb it in any way. Narrow ways led through it to the gates, so that the houses were invisible to any one approaching except from some high position on the outside.

One of the most notable things about this town, was its only market-place. It was situated in the centre of the town, was pleasantly shaded by large, low, spreading trees, and included at least twenty acres of ground. Here caravans from the interior met those from the coast. The former brought swords, sandal-wood, red fez caps, silk yarn, otto of roses, paper, beads and other things from interior and northern Africa. Caravans from the coast brought clothes of many kinds, cutlery, tin and earthen-wares, guns, gun-powder, rum, tobacco, salt and other things of foreign import. Here was found also, every kind of native produce. A particular place was appropriated for each class of goods so that those who came to purchase anything knew exactly where to look for it. Perfect order was preserved by the governor of the market who was appointed by Kumee and represented his authority. Three times a week, about twenty thousand or more people assembled in this market-place to buy and sell, or to have a good time generally. Fast young men with a company of admiring followers were displaying their fine new clothes by going from place to place amidst the noisy throng, and others were drinking and dancing and firing guns. Under the shade of the trees many others, generally the older men and strangers sat and gossiped while they contemplated the stirring scene around them. When night came, thousands of little lamps twinkled in rows over the whole market. The number of articles of native product may be imagined by what I have already said about their farming and manufacturing. Besides live poultry and the flesh of domestic animals, the meat market contained the flesh of many wild animals. In other parts could be found the pelts of leopards, antelopes and monkeys. Compared with people of colder climates, the Africans eat little flesh in their ordinary diet. Though they have every other kind that could be desired, they are especially fond of the flesh of a fat dog. When cooked in their "palaver sauce" it is in great demand.

The traders from the interior were generally Mussulmans, and they were so intolerant that nothing but the fear of Kumee prevented them from attacking missionaries while preaching in the market-place. On one occasion, a Mussulman even drew his sword to cut a missionary. Some of these traders had been as far as Stamboul, Cairo and Bagdad and had caught the intolerant spirit of the Turks. Converts to this faith were quite numerous in this part of Africa and they were rapidly increasing. I met with one of their missionaries who was a Persian. He had not seen his home since he was a young man, although he was then old enough to have a married son.

6

An African Despot

The character and history of Kumee, chief of Ejahyay, were singularly remarkable. He had been honored by the king of Yoruba with the title *Areh,* and by this name only was he known among his people, and by this name alone I shall call him in future. He was haughty, despotic, ambitious and cruel, yet he was just such a ruler as these people needed to keep them in order; for he was also firm, just and reasonable on most occasions. I never saw better order anywhere than I saw in Ejahyay while Areh was its ruler. But he was a bloody usurper. When he was a young man, he was a notorious free-booter and slave hunter. With a number of followers, who had attached themselves to his fortunes, he would go out from Ejahyay into some distant province on predatory excursions. By kidnapping in the farms and by plundering caravans he became rich and powerful and the leader of a party which favored his ambition to become the ruler of the city. So one night, with a number of his most daring and reckless adherents, he entered the chief's compound, slew him and all who attempted to defend him, seized everything that was his, and then proclaimed himself the ruler of Ejahyay. Through the terror of his name, all submitted to him, but many continued to hate him in their hearts while pretending to be very loyal. Sometimes, however, this dislike would show itself very unexpectedly. One day, I expressed concern on hearing that Areh was very sick and asked my informant if he would not be sorry if the chief should die. With a sly, side glance at me, he placed the back of one hand into the palm of the other and said in a low, significant tone, *"Be kawlaw bah koo, adieh ko sookoon."* (If the fox dies, the chickens will not cry.) I found that I was talking to one of Areh's secret enemies and immediately dropped a subject so dangerous.

The government of the kingdom of Yoruba, of which Ejahyay formed a part, resembled that prevailing in feudal times. The different towns were allowed to do about as they pleased so long as they acknowledged the suzerainty of the king and rendered him military service when he was attacked from without. The king of Yoruba, therefore, thought it best to accept Areh as chief of Ejahyay and he invited him to come with the other governors when they came to pay the annual tribute and render homage to their suzerain. In this way Areh was established in his usurpation. He also grew rapidly in wealth and power through the favorable situation of Ejahyay for commerce. There were two routes from the interior to the coast, one through Ebaddan, a large city twenty miles to the south and another through Ejahyay. In both of these towns caravans from the coast met caravans from the interior and as each caravan paid revenue at the gate which it entered, there was double the revenue which would have come from caravans passing through only. By placing bands of armed men at different points, Areh compelled all the caravans to come to Ejahyay. In this way he obtained an immense annual income. But he drew upon himself the hatred of the Ebaddan people and of other rival towns, and he would have been crushed, if it had not been for a very remarkable intervention of divine providence. The ruler of Ebaddan had grown so rich through the slave trade that his house was covered with cowries; and he hired many adventurers to join him in an attempt to destroy Ejahyay. He so completely cut off all communication with the outside world that Areh and his men were made desperate by starvation. So, one night, they decided to attack the Ebaddan camp and, if they could not break it up, die fighting, as they preferred death in battle to starvation. When they came to the camp of the enemy, it was not only deserted but it had been abandoned in such haste that it was full of provisions. These they seized and hurried back into the walls of Ejahyay, thinking that an ambush had been laid for them. When day came, it was found that the enemy had gone home for good and the starving Ejahyay people were abundantly supplied with provisions until they got more. Why the Ebaddans fled, I have never heard; but I have always supposed that they came to capture slaves rather than to fight, and when they found that they would have to face men made desperate by hunger, and that too in the darkness of the night, they decided that discretion was the better part of valor.

The king favored Ejahyay in this war, and at its close bestowed upon its determined ruler the title *Areh*. But Areh's increasing power alarmed even the king himself and he entered into a conspiracy to assassinate him when he came up to the capital to pay his annual visit. The plot failed however through Areh's vigilance and daring. Having left his horse at the gate of the king's house and approaching the king without any suspicion of treachery, he was attacked from behind and found himself surrounded by men with drawn swords. Drawing his own sword or wresting one from the hand of one of the assassins, he literally cut his way to his horse and escaped. From that time to the time of my arrival in Ejahyay, there was bitter enmity between the two, and both were making all possible preparations for any emergency.

As a ruler, Areh would endure no opposition to his will. As a concession to the established ideas of the people, he pretended to consult twenty-four elders, but no one was ever known to oppose him in a conference, and no one ever lived to disobey him thrice. Ordinarily, executions were performed by a special officer, but sometimes he would be in such a rage with the offender that he would rise from the judgment seat and strike off the head of the prostrate wretch with his own hand. Much of this ferocity was probably due to the fact that he was compelled to rule by force, as the people naturally did not venerate him as they would have done a legitimate ruler. Areh was not incapable however of appreciating and rewarding excellencies of character and nobility of conduct. On one occasion while I was in Ejahyay, a young man had been condemned to die for treason. When the executioner advanced to strike off the head of the criminal, his mother prostrated herself at the feet of Areh and pleaded that he would kill her and spare her boy. The tyrant was so much moved that he lifted her up and said with real feeling, "The son of such a mother will certainly make a true man. I will not only pardon him but he shall be, from this time, one of my most trusted servants." This young man was then assigned to some position in Areh's household, and remained loyal as long as his master lived.

Areh had a summary way of dealing with everybody. Possibly because he thought it would promote trade, he greatly desired that white men would live in his town. The missionary who preceded the one with whom I was staying, had been halted (as were all caravans on their way to Ebaddan) and compelled to come to Ejahyay instead of going on farther into the interior as he had intended; but while acting in this arbitrary manner Areh had guaranteed personal protection to the missionary and to any white men who might follow him. He would not, however, guarantee protection from persecution to native converts to the Christian faith. One of the female converts would not eat meat sacrificed to idols nor let her little son do so, and she was severely beaten by her husband for such sacrilege. When the missionary appealed to Areh to protect her for the sake of common justice, he simply asked, "Is she not the man's wife?" and then refused to give the subject further attention. As he viewed the matter, to interfere in such a case would be an unlawful meddling with the husband's conjugal rights. Again, when the family of an influential man complained that their relative had given his son to the missionary to be educated in the Christian faith, Areh replied, "Is the boy not the man's son?" His ideas of justice thus worked both ways. Though he gave the missionaries permission to preach the gospel to the Yoruban people, he would not listen to it himself.

Areh was a strange compound of childish superstitions and practical good sense. Very fine fish were sometimes caught in the brook flowing by the town gate, and when a man was accidentally drowned in it, Areh declared that the brook was angry because of the murder of its children, and he threatened death to any one who caught another out of it. That this superstition was peculiar to himself was proved by the fact that the gate keeper who was one of Areh's slaves, afterward took a fish from this brook and was not betrayed by those who saw him do so. When the missionary requested permission to fish in this same brook, Areh replied that as long as the natives did not fish in the brook, it could have no controversy with him; and if the white man wished to fish in the brook, he could do so, but when he got himself into trouble with the angry water, he must not call on him (Areh) for help.

Among the first things a foreigner is expected to do on arriving at a town in this part of Africa is to pay his respects to the chief ruler, and make him a present as a token of friendship. We paid our respects to Areh the third day after our arrival in his domains; but before telling about this visit, it might be well to give the reader some idea of his wealth and domestic surroundings. His "compound" was really a fortress and covered about eleven acres of ground. He had 300 wives and 1,000 slaves. His steward or manager of his domestic affairs was a slave only in name, for he himself owned 300 slaves and had a large domestic establishment of his own. Within the vast labyrinth enclosed by the outer walls of his compound, were stored away an untold amount of treasures of many kinds, such as guns, gunpowder, cowries, rich cloths, valuable presents from foreigners and all sorts of provisions. Much of the last was obtained from his own farm worked by his own slaves, but the most part came as a tax on farm produce. About daybreak every morning the people began to pour by myriads through the gates on their way to the farms, and when they returned in the afternoon during the gathering season, they carried baskets on their heads filled with farm produce. Two of Areh's officers stood on either side of each gate and extracted a yam, an ear of corn, a sweet potato or a small quantity of whatever the basket contained. It took a large number of slaves each day to transport what was obtained in this way to Areh's storehouses.

The place for the reception of visitors to Areh was a large space enclosed by a high wall which was also used as a place of public assembly and for the public trial and execution of criminals. Our company consisted of Mr. Phillips, my wife and myself with our necessary attendants in the way of hostlers and interpreters. We arrived at the gate of the court in a satisfactory degree of state, but just here, while the people standing there were gazing curiously at us, the condition of things was suddenly much modified. Mr. Phillips' horse, a tricky little fellow, unexpectedly took it into his head to "cut up." His reason for such conduct was known only to himself. During this very inopportune performance the saddle girth broke and the rider and his saddle both fell to the ground in a pile. Some little girls standing near immediately joined hands and commenced dancing, keeping step to a song which humorously but not insultingly described the scene. The manner in which they threw the description into impromptu measure and then adapted it to a favorite tune was really wonderful.

At last, we entered the gate and the rattle of a drum on our left announced our arrival to Areh. Through the sound of this drum the chief was always informed of what was going on in the front court of his rambling palace. These drummers are trained to make their instruments talk, and when we entered the drum said quite distinctly, "Areh, oyinbo day," (Areh, the white man has come). The piazza was about one hundred yards from the gate, and before we had reached it Areh, dressed rather plainly for a chief, came through a low door and took his seat at the usual place. A number of venerable men were already there sitting on his left. We advanced, saluted him through our interpreters, and took our stations on his right. The chief was in an excellent humor and chatted and joked with us during the whole interview. Noticing that I was holding my wife by the hand, he laughingly exclaimed, "Why are you holding your wife's hand? I am not going to take her away from you. Put her hand down." A general laugh followed this sally and I blushingly released my spouse's hand. We brought him a handsome saddle but he took little notice of it in our presence. Mr. Phillips said that this was his usual manner on receiving presents, but that he afterward inspected them in private with much interest. After receiving a present from him, we again saluted by saying, *"Aku! Aku!"* and then withdrew much entertained by our visit. We did not shake hands with him as we did with all other rulers we met, as, because of some superstition, he never shook hands with anybody.

7

Our First Dwelling

I suppose the reader would like to know something about our dwelling-house in Ejahyay, which we shared with the missionary already there. The walls were of solid *adobe* and were in the form of an oblong square divided into four compartments. One of these compartments made the sitting and reception-room and the others, the storeroom and two bedrooms. The ceilings of these rooms were of dressed boards of yellow *roko* wood. The whole was covered by a roof of poles and reeds so bound together by strong vines as to form a network for the thatching of long, dried grass. All around the house, the roof rested on posts so as to form a wide piazza and let the air circulate freely between the lofty roof and the body of the house, which was about eighty feet long, twenty feet wide and ten feet high. In this way there was a cushion of air above and all around which kept out the external heat. The piazza had large wooden shutters extending horizontally and resting on an *adobe* wall three feet high built between the posts all around the house. When these shutters were closed at night the piazza was as secure as the interior of the house, and we could leave the windows of our sleeping apartments open without fear and get the benefit of the air circulating in the piazza and over the body of the house. It was impossible for man or for any dangerous beast to enter the house without first forcing one of these shutters.

The house was furnished with everything necessary to simple housekeeping and to reasonable comfort. The bedsteads were of iron and had high posts from which mosquito curtains were suspended. Strong cloth fastened to the top ends of the posts made a flat roof or tester to the whole bed, thus protecting the sleeper from anything falling from the ceiling at night. At each end of the house were some small rooms as wide as the piazza, used for a dispensatory; a sleeping-room for our servant; a study, and a room in which we kept our drinking water. This last had the ground for a floor and contained several large water pots buried in the floor up to their rim to keep the water cool. We did not drink any water when travelling until it had been standing in these pots several days, because it took that time for the vegetable matter to sink to the bottom. We further purified and cooled it by first passing it through a filter and then putting it into a Brazilian cooler. The natives of this part of the continent are often afflicted with the dreaded "Guinea worm," and as they insisted it enters the system with the drinking water we concluded we could not be too careful.

The house was situated in a square of about an acre of ground, enclosed by a wall seven feet high. Two other walls connected the surrounding wall with either end of the house and divided the whole enclosure into two parts, a front and a rear. The latter was about half of the first and contained our kitchen garden and our fruit trees. Tomatoes and arrowroot were the principal things grown in the garden except that a pineapple hedge extended partly around it. The tomatoes grew so rapidly that the vines often measured fifteen or twenty feet, and would even climb trees. Besides pineapples, the fruits were oranges, limes, guavas, mangoes, soursops and pawpaws. The last was the West India species (*Carica Papaya*) and not only resembled a muskmelon but was a very good substitute for it. The fruits were all of a very superior quality, especially the oranges.

The front yard was well sodded with Bermuda grass, and was shaded by fig-nut trees. When any one wants shade and grass here, it is necessary only to scrape off the wild growth and then place a small patch of the grass every ten feet square and stick a limb of a fig-nut tree into the ground at the desired distance. In one "rainy season," there will be a good sod and a very good shade. The fig-nut makes a most excellent shade as it always puts on an entirely new coat at the beginning of the hot "dry season."

It was arranged that my wife and self should occupy one of the bedrooms, and that my wife was to superintend the housekeeping whenever she was well enough. In regard to board, all I had to do was to put two bags of cowries into the box every time Mr. Phillips put one. We had brought with us two barrels of Baltimore flour in hermetically-sealed tin boxes of twenty pounds each. By this arrangement we could use up what was open before it had time to ferment. Our flour cost us in Ejahyay twenty dollars per barrel; but it was of excellent quality, and we had the best "salt-rising" bread that I ever ate anywhere. We had also brought along with us plenty of sugar, tea, coffee and some other luxuries; and as the market here afforded everything else, we never suffered for anything. We had a handmill which made excellent meal, and as we had plenty of buttermilk, eggs and lard, we had excellent "eggbread." All kinds of flesh were very cheap. Fifteen cents worth of cowries would buy a leg of mutton and five cents worth, a fat fowl. We did not eat pork often, but sometimes fattened a hog for its lard. When I was well in time of peace, we did not have occasion to buy much meat, for pheasants and guinea fowls abounded in the farms. The flesh of the wild guinea fowl is the most savory I ever ate, not even excepting the pheasant.

8

Some Beasts and Insects

In one respect our compound was unfortunately situated. The belt of dense forest that surrounded the town was the home of many wild animals including leopards, hyenas and tiger cats. The house was located near a crumbling portion of the town wall and these animals would enter the town at night and prowl about our premises making it impossible for us to keep any domestic animals excepting horses. It was even dangerous for any one to walk about the yard of a dark night after the people had left the streets. In one corner of our front yard, we had a small compound for the use of such natives as were connected with the mission domestic establishment,— and for a Liberian who was allowed to have a sleeping place in our yard. Whenever I had occasion to go out to this compound, I thought it prudent to take some kind of weapon in my hand. During our stay in Ejahyay, the visits of these animals led to some exciting incidents, but none were really serious.

Although my wife knew that they could not get into the house, it was a long time before she could listen with composure to the unearthly howls of the large, "laughing" hyenas. To be suddenly awakened by one of those long-drawn demoniacal yells right under your window, is enough to chill the blood of the stoutest-hearted. But when we learned that they were the scavengers of the town and that their visits were acceptable to the people, we did not molest them. The dead bodies of bankrupts, mendicants, and babes in this country are not buried, but are thrown out into the "bush" along the town walls or into places reserved for refuse matter. Such places would soon breed pestilence if it were not for these noisy prowlers of the night. They had been so accustomed to roam with impunity that they sometimes came moaning up to our front gate before it was dark, but I did not dare to shoot them lest it might offend the superstitious. I was informed that the most savage among them never attacked in the daytime, and that those which wandered about the streets were not especially dangerous at any time. But I doubt this, for at night the people were always secure in their compounds and had no way of knowing what they would do. Yet some of the "old stagers" did seem to be partially domesticated. One evening about dark, I saw a young native man connected with the mission station run toward one of these old hyenas that was coming up a path leading from the wall to the yard gate. Instead of showing fight, the beast turned and shuffled back to the bushes along the wall of the town. When I remonstrated with him on account of such recklessness, he laughingly replied, "He is an old coward. He can't even run. He goes just so," imitating the awkward gait of the hyena. After they have been tamed by familiarity with the sight of man, as in this case, I suspect that the worst part of them is their prolonged howl.

The leopard is strong, agile, stealthy and ferocious, and the natives are much afraid of it. One night my hostler rushed into the house and told me that a leopard had just sprung over the wall, seized a kid near him, and then sprung back again. He appeared to be frightened nearly out of his wits. Another night one of the interpreters fired on a leopard as he was carrying away a goat, but the beast refused to give up his prey and replied with an angry roar. My own nerves were a little shaken up on one occasion. I was sitting at the table in the reception-room writing. Mr. Phillips had gone to a neighboring town, my wife had retired for the night, and everything about the house was so still that the slightest sound was audible, when I distinctly heard the rattling of claws on the floor of the back piazza. But the window shutter, as well as the door, was closed, and the animal could not get into the room. Presently the door was shaken with considerable violence. I sprang forward and held it until all was quiet again, and then slightly opened it to see what the creature was. The strong odor told me and I instantly closed and locked it. I tapped the alarm bell and called in my interpreter from the other side. He opened the door while I stood ready with my gun; but though we searched the entire back yard, we did not see our visitor. He had thought best to retreat. I found that one of the shutters of the back piazza had been left open, and the beast had boldly entered in search of prey.

Some adventures with smaller animals led to much fun. About daybreak on one occasion, we were startled by the loud report of a gun on the premises. Mr. Phillips hastened out and found the Liberian greatly frightened. He declared that he had just seen the devil and, not knowing him at the time, had fired on him. He said that a long, black beast was up the tree where his chickens were roosting, and that he placed the muzzle of his gun within a few inches of its body and fired. Instead of falling dead, it hissed in a dreadful manner, then sprang over his head and disappeared in the air. He had given himself up for lost. When morning came, however, he was overjoyed to find that the entire charge had entered an intervening limb of the tree, and his joy was as childish as his fears had been.

Soon after this there was another adventure with a small animal in which I was the victim. When the weather was very hot we not only allowed the shutters of the reception-room to remain open but even let down several of the shutters of the piazza sufficiently to allow a circulation of air, but not enough to allow a leopard or hyena to enter. Our bedroom adjoined the reception-room, and one night I heard a noise as if some animal was in there. The next night, I set a steel trap and waited developments. About midnight there was the sound of some heavy animal entering, then the muffled click of the trap and both animal and trap fell from the dining table to the floor with a great clatter. This waked my wife and, thinking it was a leopard, she gave vent to her fears as her sex usually does. I gave vent to mine by furiously ringing the alarm bell. My interpreter and hostler quickly responded, fearing that something dreadful was the matter. I had closed the door leading to the reception-room, but I could hear the beast snorting, growling, and gnawing the trap. We were much in need of volunteers to go on a scouting expedition, but I didn't volunteer. I did not come to Africa to investigate mysterious specimens in natural history. After a council of war in which I acted as commander-in-chief, it was arranged that the interpreter should enter the room armed with a long club which he had brought with him, and that the hostler, who was a mere boy, should hold a lighted candle for him. Arrayed in my sleeping robe, I cautiously brought up the rear. The beast had become still, and we did not see him until, with a sniff and rush he made at us from beneath the table. The interpreter struck it down and fastened it to the floor with the club while it struggled to free itself, growling and snorting terribly. The hostler was seized with a panic and fled with the light and closed the door behind him. I felt it to be my duty to hurry up and bring him back (?) The interpreter in the meantime was yelling for the light and for help. My wife naturally supposed we were all in great peril and again screamed with terror. Assuring her that we would protect her, I rallied my demoralized forces (including my own nerves) and went to the rescue of the interpreter. A few blows on the head laid out our enemy and brought peace once more to our household. It proved to be an animal that science places in the family of porcupines. It was about the size of a large opossum but was more like a rat than anything I ever saw that was not a rat. The Sierra Leone people call it "ground pig." We roasted it whole and found it to be most excellent eating.

The most troublesome of all our nocturnal visitors were the "driver" or "soldier" ants. They are savage and bloodthirsty and their strong, sharp nippers enable them easily to tear the flesh of any object of attack. When they are on a foraging expedition, they place themselves along the outside of the living stream and rush fiercely at any living thing, however large, that molests the workers in their charge. When the line of march crosses a path, the soldiers lock their feet and nippers together and thus form a strong arch under which the other ants march without being seen. So long as they are not disturbed, one can examine them at his leisure; but if the soldier ants have reason to fear that the column is in danger of attack, with head erect and nippers wide open, they will rush at the supposed enemy with utter fearlessness. For anything that has nerves, retreat is then imperative.

Issuing from some den in the ground, these creatures move in countless myriads, the column being about an inch wide and seemingly endless. When they reach a place where there is plenty of prey, they break ranks and spread themselves thickly over the ground as far as their numbers will extend. Sometimes in "driving" they cover an acre of ground or the inner walls of a large house. They pursue their prey in darkness only and quickly form a line when surprised by a bright light. Their presence in a house may always be known by the squealing of rats and mice and the commotion among winged insects. The driver ants are carnivorous and will devour anything living that either cannot or will not flee from them. If their victims would flee they might save themselves, but they stop to fight and are lost. A rat will stop to bite or scratch them off and he kills a large number of them, but in another moment the silly creature resembles a black, quivering ball and surrenders to its fate. The large, red-headed lizard which abounds here, acts differently. It will flee in the night but in the daytime it will cautiously approach a line and rapidly gulp down several mouthfuls of the ants before the guards discover what is going on. When these rush at the robber, it will run away apparently in great fear and after getting at a safe distance, will stop and bob its head up and down.

These ants had a den in the bushes about a hundred yards from the mission house, and we had many visits from them until I covered it with grass and burned it out. We did not object to having our premises cleaned out occasionally, but it looked as if they were about to include us as part of their prey. One night just after dark, I heard a child connected with our native compound give a piercing scream, and I immediately snatched it up and brought it to the light. Its neck appeared to be encircled by a large black snake, but when I tried to tear it off, I found that the thing was a mass of "driver" ants. After rescuing the child, I had a lively time freeing myself. Another night I was waked by piercing screams from my wife. I lighted a candle instantly and found her sitting up in bed tearing her hair like a maniac. Her neck was covered with "drivers" and they had also gotten into her hair. We had always kept the feet of our iron bedstead surrounded by some sticky substance, and in this way had generally escaped them when they entered our room: but that night, a part of our mosquito curtain had fallen to the floor and they had run up on that. We looked carefully to our mosquito curtains after that, and whenever I heard the noises that attend their arrival, I merely lighted a candle. In a few moments the walls were streaked with lines of march as they hurried to get out of the light. I made no attempt to destroy them until I found them trying to get their "eyah" or "mother" under our house. They showed amazing strength and perseverance in guarding and transporting this singular object. It would have been taken for a large cigar only that it was covered all over with small, thin scales. It is needless to say they did not succeed in getting their "eyah" under our house. I kept this natural curiosity for sometime, but failed to bring it home with me.

In the large white ant of Africa, we had a more intolerable pest than in the driver ant. The Sierra Leone people call them "bugbugs." They devour anything except metal, stone and the hardest wood, and they do this in such an insidious manner that the mischief is not even suspected until the destruction of the object is accomplished. In the storeroom at Ejahyay there were some trunks containing valuable cloths and pelts. I frequently opened the door to see if they were intact and found everything in apparently good order. One day I opened one and found that it contained nothing but earth. All the others were in the same condition. They had devoured hundreds of dollars worth of stuff. They never come to the light but approach everything through secret passages covered with earth. The roof and woodwork of the first house occupied by Mr. Phillips were completely devoured by them before he ever suspected their presence. Having noticed some ridges of earth on the walls, he opened them and found that they were covered ways of the "bugbugs" leading from the ground to the woodwork above. An examination disclosed the fact that the timbers of the roof and the ceiling were mere shells full of earth. The first strong wind would have brought the whole fabric down on his head. Fortunately there is a wood, called *roko*, too hard for this voracious mite, and out of this the natives construct the woodwork of their houses. Missionaries learn to follow their example but not until they have paid dearly for the knowledge. Books, furniture and clothing were destroyed before their owners learned to place nothing which these ants can devour so that they can approach it under the canopy of earth. All wooden boxes were made of *roko*. Provisions were generally kept in tin.

9

Life and Language

After our visit to Areh, we settled down to the regular routine of domestic life. Ejahyay being only a few degrees north of the equator, the sun rises and sets about six o'clock all the year round. We generally retired about nine, rose about six and breakfasted about eight. When we were well, we would frequently take a ride or walk before breakfast, but before going out or taking any kind of exercise, we would drink a cup of coffee or cocoa or suck an orange. After we learned to like hot *ekkaw*, we would often drink a calabash of this instead of coffee. We rarely braved the vertical rays of the sun in the hot season. In the afternoon we would go out between four and seven. While out, if on horseback we rode about the town or took short trips outside the walls; if on foot, we went to the market, strolled about the streets, or visited the people in their houses. In these trips, we had many amusing adventures. Since Areh had given us such a cordial reception, we were safe anywhere as long as we behaved ourselves and we never felt afraid. Sometimes my wife would mount her pony and, attended by the horseboy alone, would ride about the town for an hour at a time and then return surrounded by a crowd of merry, rollicking children.

By showing the natives that we did not fear them, we won their confidence and I think we soon had some real friends among them. Among these was Orgeh, a trusted officer of Areh, who was famous both as a warrior and a hunter. He showed his confidence in us by giving his daughter to my wife to be instructed by her and to be her waiting maid. Areh's chief messenger, also, gave us a little son and a little daughter to be educated. To these Areh added one of his own children, a boy about eight or ten years old, requesting us at the time to instruct him as if he were the son of a white man. We did not try to understand the enigmatical conduct of these three men, but prayerfully tried to be faithful to the trust which God in His providence had committed to us. At night, we placed these children in the care of the wife of one of the interpreters. In the day, they went where they pleased inside of the mission walls. They were much entertainment for us, and Orgeh's daughter was exceedingly useful to my wife.

From these children we learned the language, for they spoke it more plainly than the older people did. In trying to learn their language and to teach them ours, we sometimes had quite a gay time. In the Yoruba language every word terminates with a vowel sound, as, Jamesee instead of James, Jacobu instead of Jacob, Jesu instead of Jesus, and so on. We, in turn, had much trouble in putting the accent on the right syllable. One morning at breakfast, the children were convulsed with laughter by my wife saying that there was a *horse* in her cup of coffee. The word for *horse* and the word for *fly* is the same, excepting that the accent is on the first syllable in one case, and on the second, in the other case. This made a visiting missionary tell of one incident in his experience. Soon after he commenced preaching without the aid of an interpreter, a number of the converts came to condole with him on account of his feeble health. After he had recovered from his surprise, he found out that instead of commencing his sermon with the words, "My dear friends," he had been saying every Sunday morning, "I am very tired." The two expressions are the same excepting the accent.

In reducing the Yoruban language to writing, Crowther greatly diminished the size of the words by modifying the Roman alphabet and also by giving the Roman rather than the English sound to some of the letters. For instance Ejahyay is written Ijaye; Awyaw, Oyo; Ogbomishaw, Ogbomiso; Ebaddan, Ibadan; Ejayboo, Ijabu; ekkaw, eko; and so on. The expression, "Be kawlaw bah koo, adieh ko sookoon" would be written "Bi kolo ba ku adie ko sukun." This was a wise expedient to reduce the size of the Bible.

The language is very rich in salutations, there being one for almost every conceivable occasion, special words being added to the common term *Aku*. As the language is made up largely of vowel sounds, these salutations, especially in the mouths of women and children, are very musical, for they often prolonged euphonious sounds in a way very pleasing to the ear.

This abundance of salutations in the language is only the enforced expression of their persistent adherence to all spoken forms of politeness. Even strangers rarely pass each other without exchanging salutations. When the rank of each is known, the superior usually salutes first, and when the disparity of the position is great, the inferior usually prostrates. When they are of the same rank they bow low and use the same salutation whatever that may be. Young people prostrate themselves to the aged and sons to their mothers and senior female relatives. Women kneel only, and it is done very gracefully. All forms of salutation are modified by rank. I have seen old women kneel to boys because the latter had royal blood in their veins. The aristocracy are very proud of their ancient lineage and keep the memory of it before the people by the use of *Agoons*. These are men fantastically dressed and entirely disguised who speak in gutteral tones as if they were visitors from the dead. These claim to be the departed ancestors of the man. No one can prove to the contrary for it is death for a native to touch one. One man in Ejahyay could send out fifteen *Agoons*.

At that time there was a singular character in Yoruba who was not required to prostrate to any one, not even the king. He was called the "Father of the king," because to him belonged the prerogative of appointing a successor to a deceased king. It was said, however, that he was too modest to avail himself of his special privileges, and that there was often an amusing contest between him and King Ardayloo as to which should secretly creep up and prostrate first.

10

Superstitions

The market of Ejahyay was an excellent place in which to observe the people in all their outer life, but one could get very little idea of the misery of their inner life by what he saw in the noisy and apparently happy throngs around him there. Hidden in the recesses of their secret life are many hideous spectres. Prominent among these is the *mental* unrest which constantly tortures those under the dominion of cruel superstitions. While acknowledging the existence of a Supreme Being under the name of "Orlorun" (Professor of Heaven), they declare that he does not concern himself about his creatures on earth, but has left everything in the hands of one whom they call "Orisha." But Orisha, they say, is not willing to be bothered by the trifling affairs of men, and so has appointed a number of inferior deities to whom men may come in times of emergency. They believe, also, that the spirits of the dead are present in the world, and that they have power to bring evil or good to people in this world. I have frequently seen the living praying to their dead friends and invoking their protection and blessing. If these friends have while living been eminent for any cause, sacrifices are also offered to them as well as prayers. Under the name of Ashu, they worship the devil. He is always represented by a hideous black image. In this case, however, they only deprecate, begging the fiend not to hurt them on a journey or in an enterprise. Near the landing at Abeokuta, a priestess of Ashu with a large image of him, sat to receive the offerings made by the canoemen as they were about to start down the river. As they think that death only intensifies the evil in human nature and increases the power of malignant spirits to work mischief, they live in constant dread of the malice of invisible enemies.

The most terrible of their inferior deities is Shango, god of thunder and fire. They say that he was once a man, but being too wicked to live he was taken up to heaven and made the god of fire. The special devotees of this god are known by a tuft of hair allowed to remain in the place of an Indian's scalp-lock. When lightning strikes a house, to them is granted the especial privilege of seizing any chicken, sheep, goat or hog that may be found in the street at the time. The people have learned to keep these animals shut up during a serious thunderstorm, for when thus taken, they are to be offered at once in sacrifice to Shango. In the dread of his attributes, the next in importance is Oro. During my two years residence in Abeokuta, the town was frequently given to Oro, and on these occasions malefactors were punished and political matters of importance were transacted. The voice of Oro was frequently heard in the streets after dark. It began in a low moan, then rose to a kind of scream and then sank into a moan. This noise was made by whirling a flat stick, but it was a capital crime for any one to intimate as much. It was a capital crime, also, for any woman to remain on the streets after the voice of Oro was heard at any time.

Another inferior deity is Efa. He is the god of secrets and is represented by a dove standing on a wooden plate on the margin of which is carved a single eye. All devotees of that god carry sixteen consecrated palm-nuts. The priest takes these nuts and puts them into a wooden urn. He then takes a number at random and scatters them at random on a board covered with wood dust and marked into small squares. From the position that the palm-nuts take on the board, the priest pretends to find out what kind of sacrifice Efa demands. This ceremony is repeated to find out if a chicken or something else must not be added to the first thing to be offered as a sacrifice. The priest in the meantime talks to the person consulting the oracle and finds out pretty well what kind of answer is desired. Sometimes the applicant wishes him to interpret a dream or to assist him in a business or a matrimonial enterprise. Priests of Efa are very numerous and they rob the people of much of their income.

Ogun, the god of war, is fitly represented by an iron bar. To him human sacrifices are sometimes offered. One of these dreadful scenes I was forced to witness, and a description of it is given in another place. There are also gods of the farms, of the house, of the family, of the city, and of many other things. They offer sacrifices to streams, to trees, to birds, to snakes, to rocks and to other objects, animate and inanimate. They claim that they are not rendering worship to these objects, but to the deity therein enshrined. By striking a hatchet into a tree near the walls of Abeokuta, I so excited the people that I found it difficult to appease them. The tree was an object of worship and at its foot was a rock used as an altar. On another occasion, the people prostrated themselves in worship before an immense python snake that appeared on the great central rock of the city. They believed that the tutelary deity of the city had assumed that form and taken up his abode under the rock, that he might look after their welfare. As showing how their dark imaginations multiply terrors for them, I mention that they believe a certain night bird which has a dismal croak to be an evil spirit who has chosen that form more effectively to approach them. Whenever they hear one of these birds near their houses at night, believing its presence betokens some approaching calamity, they are tortured by anxiety and fear until some new fear distracts their attention.

It is impossible for rest to find a home in minds so filled with spiritual darkness and nameless terrors. In attempting to break off the shackles of superstition from their benighted souls, I would often be amazed to find how completely idolatry had mastered their every idea. For instance, a young man expecting to go to war boasted that he wore over his vest a coat of mail that no bullet could penetrate. It was made of shells which were easily broken and some "medicine man" had swindled him into paying a large sum of money for it. After he had swaggered a while, I told him that I had a gun which could shoot through his "medicine." He defiantly challenged me to shoot at him at short range. After some argument, he was persuaded to take it off and let the interpreter shoot at that only. When the smoke of the gun cleared away, the shells were, of course, found to be completely shattered. He immediately fell at the feet of the interpreter and worshipped him, begging him at the same time to give him some of his "strong medicine." The expedient which was intended to convince him of his error seemed only to confirm him in it.

Their belief in the malice and power of Shango so dominates their thoughts, that the most thievish among them will not touch anything which is protected by the symbol of Shango's power. People on the farms often expose for sale by the highways fruits and vegetables while the owners are far away at work. The price of the articles is indicated by pebbles lying near, and over the whole is an erect stick with a bunch of dried grass tied to the end. The natives believe that if any one should dare to take anything which is thus protected, the angry god will immediately compel some one to burn his house or to inflict some worse injury on him. Shango does not put things off very long, and for this reason he is dreaded the more.

About six months after my arrival in Ejahyay, while I was standing at the gate of the mission premises, I saw a little boy, said to be possessed by the spirit of Shango, issue from a compound near the mission chapel. He was soon followed by a crowd of people, old and young, piteously beseeching him to spare them. As some of these people were frequent visitors at the mission house and attendants on the chapel services, I thought I ought to hasten and see what was the matter. Just as I came up, the boy, whose distorted and scowling countenance is still vividly impressed on my memory, lighted a torch of dried grass at a fire where a woman had been cooking and started back with the flaming grass toward the door of the compound from which he had come. The crowd followed and with extended hands implored him to have mercy on them and not burn their house.

"What will you give me? What will you give me?" shouted the little fiend.

"I'll give you something, you little imp of Satan," I yelled, as I darted at him and tried to seize him by his Shango tuft.

When he looked up and saw the white man glaring at him so ferociously, the demoniacal expression of his countenance immediately changed to one of abject terror. He threw down his torch and fled with all his might, hotly pursued by one greater than Shango; but he slipped through a hole in a wall and I failed to capture him. When I turned around expecting to hear expressions of gratitude from the people whose house I had saved, I found myself facing a dangerous and angry mob. They denounced me for such a sacrilegious act and hurled at me the most terrible curses known to them. My blood was now up, too, and lifting up my voice above the uproar I shouted,

"You are a lot of fools. If Shango is a god, he does not need you to fight for him. Let him fight for himself. I defy him."

I could now speak their language very well and they understood what I said. They continued to gesticulate and curse a little longer, and then dispersed without doing me any harm. A mutilated form of this story was afterward published in England in which it was stated that I dispossessed Shango with a rod. If this had been true, I should not have lived to write this true account of the affair.

The next day, I went to see the old *bale* of the threatened compound and talked to him about the folly of believing in such things. He seemed to be much depressed and frightened, and preserved a profound silence during my whole visit, only saluting when I came and when I went. A few days after this, both the *bale* and the little boy suddenly died, being evidently assassinated by poison. Why they were killed and by whom, I could never learn. I suspect, however, the little boy was murdered by the priests of Shango to avoid exposure, and that the old *bale* murdered to frighten the people away from the mission chapel.

Those who make and sell amulets claim that they are security against all kinds of evils. They are securely protected in morocco cords and bags, and are worn around the waist and arms or suspended from the neck. The amulets sometimes seen on the persons of chiefs and rich men often represent a large sum in native currency. Many lose their lives by trusting too implicitly in these "refuges of lies."

Among the wicked occult arts is the preparation of poisons to be used in assassinating, and those who engage in this business have many customers. Some of these poisons kill slowly, but so surely that the victims cannot prove who poisoned them, nor when, nor how. They murder by poison because in this way they can more easily escape detection. To draw even a little blood in times of peace is a capital crime. There is much quarrelling and even fighting among the women, but they rap each other over the shoulders with the palms of their hands in such a way as to hurt without drawing blood. When fighting, young men frequently tap each other over the head with short sticks upon which little iron rings have been strung. In this way they can knock each other down without breaking the scalp and drawing blood. One morning about light, I heard some people shouting, *"ehjeh! ehjeh!"* (blood, blood) as if a murder had been committed, but on investigating, found that a woman had drawn a little blood by scratching the face of a man. If the matter had not been hushed up before it got to the ears of Areh, the offender might have suffered decapitation.

I do not remember a single instance in which a poisoner was detected and punished by the authorities. People might be suspected, and the fear of poisoning would sometimes scatter the people of a compound, but legal proof was generally wanting. Loud lamentation once caused me to stop at the house of an acquaintance. I found the *bale* and those around him in deep distress. Two of his sons had just died suddenly and he was in dread of the same fate. Though he probably suspected the murderer, he dared not express his opinion in the matter. There were several dwellings in this compound, but in a few days I found it deserted and as silent as the grave. Each family was afraid of the others and had sought homes in other compounds.

Another thing that adds much to the mental disquietude of the people is a firm belief in the "evil eye." For this reason they often avert their eyes when a stranger looks at them. When they fear that some one has smitten them with an "evil eye," the rich often spend large sums of money in buying "medicine" to wash their eyes. I once knew a powerful chief to start up from his seat and flee to the remotest recesses of his vast compound because his eyes had accidentally met the black, angry eyes of a missionary whom he had wronged. For days, he washed his eyes with the most powerful "medicine" to break the wicked spell.

By a thoughtless prank, soon after coming to Ejahyay I became an object of suspicion to the natives as a person having an "evil eye." Desirous of making some nocturnal observations, I concealed a lighted "bull's-eye" lantern under my rain coat and went out into the town one very dark night. I went some distance before I was discovered by the passing people. I then began to return. Sounds behind me showed that I was being followed by a large crowd and when I was near enough to the mission house to feel safe, I drew the lantern from my bosom and flashed the focused rays around me. They all fell back as if shocked and then the still night air was filled with the sound of running feet. The next morning some old men, looking very grave, called to see Mr. Phillips on special business. While waiting for him to come in, one of them said to another in a low voice, "Ojoo boobooroo." This means "wicked eye" and is their expression for "evil eye." When Mr. Phillips entered, they informed him that the night before I had taken fire out of my breast and thrown it at the people. I was somewhat disturbed at this serious turn of affairs and at once brought out the lantern and showed them how I used it. They were greatly surprised and seemed satisfied, but it was sometime before the people stopped averting their eyes whenever I looked at them.

11

Polygamy

Another skeleton in the Yoruban closet is polygamy. This is universal and so is the treachery, strife and domestic disorder which always accompanies it. Yorubans know little of that happiness that is found in every place worthy of the name of home. A girl has to take the husband selected for her by her legal guardian, however disagreeable the union may be to her. Betrothals in infancy are common, but the usual age of betrothal is five or six years. It is regarded as very disgraceful for a girl to speak to her betrothed husband until the day of marriage. There is, therefore, no room for courtship or for "love's young dream." I knew, however, of several instances of elopement. The bride had formed a romantic attachment for a young man, and had fled the country with him just before the day of marriage with her betrothed husband.

There is much closer intimacy between a husband and the wife of his youth than any contracted with those who follow her. All the other wives approach her with reverence and respectfully address her as *"Eyah"* (mother or superior). As long as she lives, she alone prepares food for her lord and manages all his domestic affairs. The Yorubans are not insensible to the evils of polygamy and recognize the wisdom of having only one wife.

Along the wall in our reception-room were benches for the accommodation of visitors, and it was seldom some of these were not occupied during the day. Among the callers one day was a young man unusually dignified and quiet. His countenance was much cast down. My wife was not very well and was reclining on a lounge while I was holding her hand. The young man sadly regarded us for a while and then said with much emphasis:

"White man, you are right."

"How?" said I.

"In having only one wife," said he.

"What makes you think so?"

"Well," said he, "one year ago, I took a bride and I was happy with her; but two months ago, like a fool, I took another wife, and I have had no peace since."

It was with some difficulty I could suppress a smile while I condoled with him on his sad fate. But a man's position and importance here are estimated by the number of his wives and the men seem willing to make almost any sacrifice for a little fictitious notoriety. This young man's unhappiness was not caused by strife between himself and his wives, but by the strife between his wives on account of jealousy.

Troubles about their children and their earthly possessions are also sources of misunderstanding. In passing a compound, I would sometimes hear quarrelling among the women, then the voice of an angry man, then something like blows with a rod. Everybody from the *bale* down would put on "company manners" as soon as I entered and I could not tell what had taken place; but my interpreter would afterward explain that some husband had given his wives a whipping to stop a childish and silly brawl over some trifle. They are very much like children and do not bear malice as a general thing when they have been punished by their lords for bad behavior. But the husband cannot always trust them, especially when they are of other nationalities than his own.

The poisoning of the husband by the wife for some cause is not infrequent. One of my acquaintances, an old man, bought a young wife in the market. Now this captive maiden had a lover in her own country who followed her to Ejahyay, hoping to be able to redeem her, and the two met in the market-place after the girl had become the wife of the old man. It was quickly arranged that the girl should poison her husband, the young man providing the material. But not being an adept, the girl stirred the poison into the old man's dish of "palaver sauce" with her finger and in this way was herself fatally poisoned. The old man recovered sufficiently to come to see me and get relief. I went to see him once, but he died in about a year, his death being evidently hastened by this attempt on his life. The girl got more of the poison than he did and lived only a few hours, making a full confession of her guilt. Her partner in guilt escaped in some way to his own country. The old man never mentioned the name of either without a dreadful imprecation.

But I would not leave the impression that there are no cheerful scenes in a compound. Where there are so many children, there must be fun and merriment. The women also are vivacious, sensitive, and sympathetic.

For the purpose of getting acquainted with the people, of winning their confidence, and of instructing them in the truths of Christianity, I visited them in their homes whenever I was well enough to do so. Generally my reception was polite, but sometimes I would get into a house where the people did not conceal their dislike for the innovations of civilization and of Christianity. The reader may imagine me surrounded by a crowd of men, women and children, sitting on a grass mat in a low piazza of a native compound. Sheep, goats, chickens, pigs and dogs are running around everywhere. After calling for the *bale* and exchanging the ordinary salutations with him, I request permission to *"sawraw Orloroon,"* that is, "talk the word of God." This being permitted, for courtesy's sake I address myself to the *bale*, though it is understood that I am talking to all within the sound of my voice. The greater number pretend to listen, but I am frequently interrupted by the children who, while pressing around to hear and to see, manage to get up a dispute among themselves. Then about half of the grown people reprove the little offenders while the remainder try to explain the cause of the trouble. Things being quiet, I get along very well for five minutes or less, when I am stopped by the yell of a woman who has detected a thievish goat, sheep or dog taking something from her market calabash. The rogue having received a sound thrashing and a noisy berating, order is again restored. Other similar disturbances may occur but the people are so accustomed to this state of things that any attention which they may be giving to the speaker, is not long distracted. Sometimes after I have finished talking, one of them in compliment to me, tries to explain my teaching to the rest of the company. These pretend to be much pleased. One says, "It is good"; another, "It is true"; and still another, "We will believe."

When I leave, the *bale* had some of the women and all of the children, accompany me to the door and there take leave of me with many kind wishes, and the children shout their adieus as long as I am in sight. Often in my walks and visits, the children would meet me with shouts of childish glee, and seizing my hands or clinging around my knees, would give expression to the innocent confidence peculiar to their tender age. Sometimes when my wife's duties would permit her to walk out into the town with me, little children would cling to her skirts until we entered our house, and then they would tease her with questions and entertain her with their prattle until it was time for them to go home.

When the *bale* or some other "headman" was absent from the compound the women frequently declined to hear me, but generally they would consent to quit work a little while and listen to me. When, however, I would begin to talk, they, too, would begin. After a few minutes one of them would try to explain to the other what I was saying, and they would all chatter together like a flock of magpies. At first, I did not know what to do, but after I understood their habits better I would quietly but firmly tell them that if they wished me to talk they must be silent. After this they would interrupt me now and then with exclamations only.

Their priests take tribute from all of them, and until they understood that we would not accept a present, they always offered one when I visited them. This was often some cola-nuts, presented in their best dish with much ceremony. These are so highly esteemed among them that they have a proverb which says, "Anger draws arrows from the quiver; good words draw cola-nuts from the bag."

Polygamy not only destroys that unity which is essential to a home, but also undermines all domestic affection. When my wife was very ill on one occasion, a visitor expressed great surprise because I was so much concerned about the matter, and asked if that one was the only wife I had. The natural love which God has put into the heart of the mother for her offspring, seems to be about the only silver lining to this dense cloud. The memory of this awakes chords in their souls that nothing else can. One night I heard a little orphan boy telling of a dream to a playmate. He said that he saw heaven open and his mother looking down at him from above. She told him that she was watching over him every day and then she let down something for him to eat. Then the heavens closed again and he awakened, crying for her to come back to him. It was plain that this touching dream had voiced the memory of a mother's love.

The gospel of Jesus Christ is the only cure for the ills which afflict the victims of such spiritual darkness. While I was in Africa many illustrations of this truth came under my observation. Two cases in Ejahyay are worthy of special notice. Among the converts here were two women of exalted Christian character, named Ofeekee and Osoontala. Because the latter was so much like Mary of Bethany in character, her name had been changed to that of the gentle sister of Lazarus. There is no reason to think that, before their conversion, they were different from the average heathen women around them; but when I arrived in Ejahyay, they were already distinguished for every Christian virtue. They often endured the most bitter persecution without a murmur, supporting themselves by their implicit faith in the promises of God. This was all to which we could point them, for Areh, as I have before said, declined to interfere. They came at stated times and, repeating the words after some one, would commit whole chapters of the Bible to memory. When discouraged, they would strengthen their faith by repeating passages of Holy Scripture to themselves. I asked Mary if she did not feel afraid that the people in her house would poison her.

"The Lord is my helper: I will not fear what man can do unto me," she replied.

When Ofeekee would not eat sacrifice at the family festivals nor permit her little son to partake, her husband would often flog her most cruelly. One Lord's day we noticed an expression of pain on her countenance and enquired what was the matter. She said nothing, but merely lifted her shoulder cloth and exhibited the lacerated flesh. Her husband had just beaten her.

Mary's husband simply ignored her, and let others persecute and annoy her without noticing them. When he was killed during the bloody siege of Ejahyay (of which I shall tell farther on) Mary had an opportunity to show the difference between a Christian and a heathen. She obtained permission to live with her little son in the native compound connected with the mission premises. After she had been there several months, she learned that a young man who had been a ringleader in everything devised for her annoyance, was lying, desperately wounded and entirely deserted, in the compound of which she had been an inmate. Getting permission from Mr. Phillips she had her enemy brought to that part of our compound in which she was living and nursed him back to life as if here were her own son. If I had not already become a Christian, the wonderful change in the character of these two converts from paganism, would have led me to become a disciple.

12

Some African Maladies

About one month after arriving in the country I had my first ague. There is a great shaking accompanied by severe pains in back and limbs; this is followed by a burning fever and a headache so severe sometimes as to make the patient delirious—during the following night. If, by a free use of proper remedies, the return of the ague can be prevented on the third day, the patient is safe and with the exercise of proper precaution, will be up in a week. If the chill is not broken, the case becomes more and more serious. The ague will recur earlier every time it is repeated, and when only six hours intervene the case is well-nigh hopeless. Some attacks are so violent that the patient becomes unconscious at once and dies in a few hours. In this way Mrs. Phillips had died, except that she was delirious only.

My wife and I got on very well for the first seven months. We were generally up three weeks out of the four and we fortunately had our agues in separate weeks so that one of us was always well when the other needed a nurse. In the eighth month my chills could not be broken and I was brought to the door of the grave. From four o'clock one afternoon until light next morning I was unconscious, with my life hanging by a thread. In Africa, excitement often made my wife very ill and, when my condition became so serious, she had to be removed to another room, and was soon as ill as I. We both extracted from Mr. Phillips a promise that if either was found to be dying, we should be allowed to see each other at once. One day, my interpreter ran into my room and attempted to take me into his arms. I knew what this meant and, to my great surprise, I rose from my bed and tottered into the room where my wife was. I found her just recovering from unconsciousness. The sight of my face soon revived her and we were able to converse for a while. The excitement of meeting under the circumstances seemed to revive us both, and we commenced improving from that day.

Such is the strange character of this disease that often a change of scene, the sight of a new face, or the meeting of some loved one from whom we have been long parted, will do more good than medicine. When very sick, even to death, my wife was greatly benefited by a visit from a German missionary and his wife. I believe the visit saved her life. Mrs. Townsend, the wife of the celebrated missionary of that name, seemed to be hopelessly ill, but was taken at her request to a grass-thatched hut in the Abeokuta farms—and began to recover from the first day. In a few weeks she was as well as usual. On one occasion, I had no energy or appetite, and joined an English missionary in the same condition, in a picnicking excursion. We took along what we supposed would be an ample supply of provisions for a week. We were driven home by hunger at the end of three days.

All white people who go to this part of Africa should expect to be sick. If they escape malarial fever they will meet chronic dysentery and the last is worse than the first.

When visiting among the people, I frequently found myself near some one broken out with smallpox, but as the natives showed no fear of the disease, I thought I ought not. Here the patient lies in the open air, in the piazza on hard mats. They eat sparingly, drink warm water, and never touch any preparation of chicken. The disease is allowed to run its course, the patient enduring the itching as best he can and breaking the pustules by rolling about on the hard grass mat. Air, a hard bed, light clothing and a simple diet generally prevent this dreaded disease from assuming a very virulent form among the natives. In our own home only did I see it in its worst form. Our cook, a Liberian woman, was taken down with it and was extremely ill for many days. When she recovered her face was like a piece of perforated paper. Mr. Phillips was then taken down but he had been vaccinated in his youth and his case was not quite so severe. I followed next but escaped with my life because I had been vaccinated. My wife nursed every case, but escaped entirely though she remained with me day and night. But it fell to her lot to have the "Guinea worm," a disease she dreaded as much as she did the smallpox. The natives, however, did not abhor it as they did smallpox for one of their curses was "May the smallpox catch you."

None of us escaped the boils and the dreadful ulcers, which sometimes follow attacks of malarial fever. Once forty boils, painful in the extreme, bloomed on my breast at one and the same time. The ulcers are large and deep, but not so painful. They often leave deep scars.

My wife continued to have attacks of fever as long as she remained in the country, but I seemed to be very well acclimated after the first year. But I enjoyed advantages in the way of recreation that my wife did not. One of these was hunting. This leads me to say something of the *fauna* of this part of Africa.

13

Hunting

In the scattered, cultivated spots, five miles beyond Ejahyay, there was plenty of game of many kinds, but my favorites were a species of pheasant about the size of a small hen, called *arkparro* by the natives, and the guinea fowl. In its wild state, the guinea is much larger, especially in the breast, than when domesticated. It is also more palatable. Antelopes of all sizes abound. They range from the size of a hare to that of an ox. Eagles, immense toucans, hornbills, touracos, cranes and other large birds fly about within gunshot all the time. I generally found the *arkparrows* and guineas in large flocks feeding in the farms. Here also the antelopes were found, but their flesh tainted so quickly that I gave them little attention.

Leopards, wild boars and hyenas are hid about in the grass, and elephants are sometimes found in these clearings. I was very careful not to enter any place where I had reason to fear a "rogue" elephant might be hid, for they are the most dangerous animals now in the world. I had no desire whatever to see one. Large python snakes have their homes in the rocks and make paths through the grass leading to these dens. The natives declare that there is a very large bird like an ostrich inhabiting the "bush" here. I failed to meet with a specimen, but from the description they gave it must be a species of cassowary. Buffalo abound but they prefer the larger plains near the Niger. They seem to be nothing but wild cattle.

The African wolf, a species of hyena, going in large droves, are known here. The natives dread them very much. Ejahyay received one visit from them in its early history. When the howling was heard in the distance, the gates of the houses were closed and the people did not go into the streets again until all the wolves had passed through. Some of the beasts are said to have climbed over the roofs of the houses and jumped down into the compounds, so ravenous were they. Among the smaller animals, I met with some surprises. Of these, one was a grey squirrel exactly like the small mountain squirrels found on top of the Blue Ridge mountains of Virginia.

Though birds of all sizes are so numerous, one hears little "music in the air." Some scream, some chatter, some croak, and some bray like donkeys. Only a few modestly attired little ones really sing. There was one sound, however, that always had music for my ear. That was the familiar cry of the guinea fowls from the tops of the palm trees as I galloped home in the gloaming. As a magic wand, the sound would often call up memories of childhood's home.

The gorgeousness of the plumage of many of the larger birds, especially of the cranes and touracos, is indescribable. One who has seen a touraco darting up and down the limbs of a tree, will not soon forget the beautiful vision. Once, there appeared over me two cranes clothed in all the colors of the rainbow, and I brought them down with a single shot. They were about five feet tall, had gold-colored crests, and much resembled the Balearic species, only they were more gorgeous in plumage.

Some species of the guinea fowl were also very beautiful. One of these has a large black plume and another has a spray of gold running from the root of the bill back over the middle of the head to the neck. These last are blue-black and live only in the forest. The former are of the color of the ordinary guinea, but they are much larger. The little parroquets were also very beautiful. We had some of these for pets once, but the "drivers" killed them all in one night.

I shot but one monkey. This was a large black one which acted in such a way that I thought it safest to fire on it; but when my wife saw it, she begged me not to shoot another. While its head was hanging down over the back of a native boy, it looked for all the world like a human baby. They are all so troublesome, however, that I came very near shooting another soon after. I noticed that a large animal of tawny color was stealthily following me through the grass and I took a position and prepared to shoot it when it showed itself. As my gun was charged with ball, I did not feel alarmed. When it did appear it was a large monkey following me through curiosity. I raised my gun to fire but it appeared to be so harmless that I could not pull the trigger. After regarding me with averted face for a while, it slunk away without the slightest show of hostility.

I really had no hunting adventures that could be called dangerous. Once when creeping through the high grass I came suddenly upon a large python. I retired. I returned to the spot after getting sufficiently composed to shoot with good aim, but it was gone. The sudden apparition of one of these great constrictors is a very disconcerting thing. It might not have hurt me, but I learned not to put too much confidence in anything here in its native wilds. There is no telling what humor may have possession of it when we happen to meet.

For ordinary shooting in this part of Africa, one need not be a walking arsenal. My gun was of laminated steel and was made to carry either shot or ball. I used the best rifle powder and often brought down game with heavy shot at most astonishing distances. This gun was of English manufacture and cost about sixty dollars in London. It would shoot a ball with wonderful accuracy and force, and I believe it would have killed an elephant at short range, but I am thankful to say that I was never called upon to test the matter. The way in which the professional native hunters kill the elephant does not require a specially good gun. They approach them stealthily by paths known only to their fraternity and shoot them with guns charged with poisoned darts or bolts. This poison coagulates the blood without injuring the flesh. After making many struggling efforts to retain its feet (in which it is assisted by its friends in the herd), the wounded elephant at last succumbs and is abandoned by the rest. The hunter escapes by a secret path and when the noise ceases, he returns with some of his companions and joyfully takes possession of his gigantic game. For him, its tusks, its hide and its flesh constitute a small fortune.

In hunting the leopard, they tie a kid where its pitiful, baby-like cries may be heard by the prowling beast. This sometimes requires quick work, for the cunning creature will often take the kid at a single bound and disappear like a flash. Wild boars and some other animals of chase, are hunted by means of dogs as they are elsewhere. The most remarkable way of taking game was that practiced by Abodere, a son of Areh, and a reckless young man. With a number of his boon companions, he would go to a den of pythons. He would then place his young men in two rows facing each other on each side of the mouth of the den. Tying a strong cord to both his feet and leaving instructions to one of his followers to pull him out when he gave the signal by shaking his foot, he would crawl into the den of pythons and seize the tail of one in both hands. At his signal both were drawn out together and the snake was despatched with clubs. The natives declared that the flesh of this snake is white, juicy and sweet, and for this reason Abodere ran so much risk to capture them. His love of adventure, however, was the real cause.

It was natural that we should try to enliven our solitude a little by having some animal pets, but the "drivers" made it impossible for us to have any that had to be confined in cages. In a parrot and a monkey which had the freedom of the premises, we found some pleasant diversion. The aptness of the African grey parrot for quickly learning to imitate any sound, greatly surprised us. My baby parrot which rejoiced in the name of Aryaykotor (the world is all wrong) learned to imitate the singing of a hen and the cries of a distressed puppy in a few days. The counterfeit was so complete that I once ran to the rescue of the supposed puppy and never doubted but that our old hen was enjoying herself until I caught Polly performing the hen act. But in the midst of her useful life she fell among thieves and we never saw her again.

Older parrots would learn to repeat short sentences with equal facility. To one of these its owner said one day, "Why don't you pray, you rascal?" A few mornings after this while its owner was praying at family worship, the parrot suddenly screamed, "Why don't you pray, you rascal?" After this, the owner was more careful in speaking to his pet.

Monkeys were not only amusing but often useful in keeping the premises clear of those pests of the African house—the goats. The monkey would leap on the back of the goat and ride it, wildly bleating and frantic with terror, until it escaped from the yard. If the goat happened to run into the house, then "confusion was worse confounded." Little whiskered fellows about the size of a squirrel which could be carried about on the shoulder and which would take refuge in a side pocket when frightened were the favorite of some, but the ordinary pet monkey was about the size of a rabbit. The chimpanzee is a too hideous caricature of a human being to be a pleasant pet. Their actions as well as their appearance are almost human. I have seen them amuse themselves by playing with native children just as an old man would.

On account of birds of prey, we obtained little profit from our poultry yard. Buzzards waddled about the kitchen door and acted as useful scavengers, but they sometimes devoured young ducks and chickens. Hawks swarmed over the city all day, darting down and catching up anything they could seize, even from the calabashes of the market women. I could not frighten them away with my gun. After I had driven them away by shooting a few, they would return in full force in an hour or two.

A species of crow having a white breast were as numerous as the hawks but not so troublesome. They roosted in the trees of the town and passed the day in the farms. Their cawing in the early morning was always a signal that day was breaking and that the people were leaving for the farms. The natives seemed to have a superstitious affection for them and the crows, in turn, seemed to have as little fear of man as do domestic fowls.

14

Mental Solitude

During our first year in Ejahyay, things were very quiet, excepting when a sudden conflagration swept over the city, often greatly endangering our house. But while we were reasonably comfortable physically, the lack of social privileges made us feel very lonely. This sense of solitude was relieved somewhat every two weeks by the arrival of letters from home. We kept a messenger on the road all the time. The mail reached Lagos every two weeks and it took our messenger a week to go and a week to return. He always received an ovation when he entered the mission yard on his return. I took my wife to Abeokuta once, but I found that on account of the heat and fatigue, she received more harm than good.

At no time while we were in Africa did we miss the comforts of material civilization as much as we did the intellectual privileges enjoyed in more elevated conditions of society. The customs and ideas of the people around us were either too cruel or too novel to admit of any intellectual congeniality between us. Mentally we were thousands of years apart, and this sense of loneliness was like being thirsty in the midst of a briny deep. I have no doubt this sense of desolation in the midst of teeming thousands, has overwhelmed many missionaries in the midst of careers of much usefulness. It is a cross that crushes mortality to the earth.

Once after I had formed a kind of intimacy with a man who seemed to be reasonably kindhearted, some of his ideas so shocked me that I was always afraid of him afterward. It is a custom with these people to make the *bale* of any compound in which an insolvent debtor dies pay the debts of the deceased. When any insolvent debtor, therefore, is found to be very ill he is taken out and thrown into the bushes to miserably perish. They know that this is very cruel for the worst curse used among them is, "May you die in the bushes." (Okoogbeh.) On one occasion a man who was a renegade convert, was brought in a dying condition into our mission yard. He was an insolvent debtor and the *bale* was about to have him thrown out, when he begged to be brought to us. We received him of course. This act of humanity greatly disgusted my native friend.

"Why don't you throw him into the bushes and let the hyenas eat him?" said he, his eye gleaming with suppressed ferocity.

"I am not strong enough to carry the man," said I, jokingly.

"Then burn him with hot irons and make him walk," replied he.

But the difference in our habits of thought was not always so painful. The appearance of my wife on the street was always the signal for the assembling of a crowd of children who followed us commenting all the time on something about our dress or manners. One exclaimed, "Look at the cloth! Look at the cloth!" Another (in a sort of undertone) "What a fool the white man is. He cuts his clothes all up into little pieces and then sews them up again." And so on.

Their dress and many of their customs showed their ancient and Eastern origin, and what I saw and heard around me frequently reminded me of scenes and incidents described in the Bible. This novelty was by no means displeasing, but rather added to the interest I felt in these people. Among our children was a bright little lass of copper color. She had a copper bracelet on her wrist but would not tell us what it meant. One day, a man of some prominence entered the gate of the compound while I was standing in the door of the mission house. So soon as this little girl saw him, she fled like a frightened fawn and I was nearly overturned in her effort to rush into the house. When I enquired with some heat why he had frightened the child, he laughingly replied, "That is my little wife, white man." I then learned that girls were betrothed at a very tender age and that, from the day of the betrothal, they were regarded as married, the fact of the betrothal being indicated by a bracelet on the wrist. This girl's apparent fright was caused by the fact that it is regarded very indelicate for a girl to speak to her betrothed husband before they are married. Sometimes, in passing about the streets, I would see a little girl dart suddenly away as if greatly frightened, and I knew that it was because she had seen her future husband approaching. It was quite amusing to see the "mannish" dignity that boys sometimes manifested when they saw their future wives flee from their august presence.

When the day of the marriage arrives, the bride, closely veiled, is taken to the house of her husband. She comes without resistance because she knows that if she does not do so, she will be brought by force. If she comes with honor, adorned with jewels and with handsome cloths, she marches several days after the wedding day through the streets. Her approach is heralded by music, she is escorted by a large number of maidens and receives congratulations and presents from her friends. In this way she is treated with much honor. If she is unworthy, the parents are required to refund the whole sum advanced in betrothing her, and the partner of her infidelity, if he is discovered, is prosecuted for adultery.

A messenger always carries some kind of staff as his credentials. The credentials of Areh's messenger was a crook of brass. Mr. Phillips and myself used our walking-sticks when we sent a messenger to Areh. Whenever Enigbio, Areh's messenger, came in to see us without his crook, he was no more than any other respectable man; but when he came in and placed Areh's staff into the hand of one of us, it was Areh that was speaking, and to disobey was banishment or death.

When carrying a message, Enigbio never saluted any one, however superior in rank. This was to remind the people of the authority of his master and show the importance of his message. It was said that if Enigbio had spoken to any one while the brass crook was in his hand, he would have lost his head. I did not believe this story until I happened to see Areh in a rage. Accompanied by my interpreter alone, I called to pay my respects. When he appeared, his countenance was darkened by a scowl that completely transformed it. As he did not seem disposed to converse, I thought it safest to retire. On turning to go, I saw crowds entering the gate and prostrating themselves as if in humble supplication. At the gate I met a man whose head was covered with ashes and whose face displayed the most abject terror. I did not learn what his fate was, but after seeing Areh's face that day, I knew he was capable of any ferocious deed to sustain his authority.

Richard Henry Stone 1837–1915

Susan Broadus Stone 1834–1903

Native ruler giving a reception

A native prince and attendants

Section of market

Wives supporting children and themselves at market

15

Waylaid and Captured

I must now take the reader under a cloud, but before I do so, I will explain what led to such an unhappy change in the state of the country.

Though the rulers of Abeokuta had taken sides with the English in their war with Kosoko and his Portuguese allies, many of the other rulers of the country had not. They earnestly desired the restoration of the slave trade, and they hated the missionaries and those friendly to them, because they rightly supposed that the missionaries were opposed to the slave trade. Therefore, these rulers were desirous of driving them from the country. Among these rulers was Ogumulla, the military leader of Ebaddan, the friend of the king of Yoruba, and the deadly enemy of Areh.

The death of the king of Awyaw about the middle of our first year, seems to have given rise to a very ambitious scheme in the mind of Ogumulla, who seems to have been a sort of African Orgetorix. This was to form an alliance offensive and defensive with Benin on the east, with Dahomy on the west, and with Kosoko's party on the coast, and then drive out of the country all foreigners opposed to the slave trade. The destruction of Ejahyay and Abeokuta, and the recapture of Lagos, was included in this scheme. Ebekoonleh, the civil governor of Ebaddan, was a friend of Areh and was opposed to all this, and he not only kept Areh secretly posted as to the conspiracy, but he did all he could to thwart Ogumulla's plans. But the latter succeeded in forming a powerful war party not only in Ebaddan but in all the kingdom of Yoruba, and Ebekoonleh was compelled to fall in with the movement. Of volunteers from the towns of Yoruba and from Benin, Nufe and other slave-hunting nations near the Niger, Ogumulla gathered a large army to attack Ejahyay. In the meantime the Dahomians were to prevent any assistance by destroying Abeokuta.

Of all these things, we knew nothing until a desperate adventure into which I was precipitated by circumstances beyond my control, brought them unpleasantly to our knowledge. Among the members of the mission church were two Liberian carpenters, named Vaughn and Russell, who had lived in the country so long that they were natives in all respects except in dress and in religion. The first of these had established a farm camp about twenty miles from Ejahyay on the road to Abeokuta. The other had been living for some years in Ogbomishaw in Awyaw, the capital, towns that were friendly to Ebaddan. Both of these men were nearly white and they were also men of excellent character.

Before Mr. Phillips had entirely recovered from the smallpox, Enigbio hurriedly entered the house one day and brought a message from Areh saying that our friend Vaughn was in great danger, and that we should warn him to come into Ejahyay immediately. We had heard that Areh might have some trouble with Ebaddan because he had refused to acknowledge allegiance to the successor of his old enemy, but we could not see how that could affect the safety of a foreigner who was entirely neutral in the matter.

The night before I started on the journey suggested by Areh, Russell arrived from Awyaw, and to this providential fact I doubtless owe my life. I had naturally thought of buckling on a seven-shooter but my wife dissuaded me from this and persuaded Russell to accompany me. We decided to take no arms, but in case of real danger to make use only of the mettle and the bottom of our horses.

I was most unfortunately mounted for this particular occasion. The oracle of Efa having counselled Areh to ride only a white horse, he purchased a beautiful Arabian of that color. Not being willing for any of his own people to ride his old war horse, he persuaded me to buy it. It was the largest horse in all that country and, for that reason, was known everywhere as "Areh's war horse." He was so savage and unmanageable that I named him "Bucephalus." To be more secure in my seat and to be able to subdue him, I ordered a Mexican saddle and spurs, and these with a pair of boots arrived just in time to be used on this journey. This outfit, in connection with Areh's famous horse, helped to get me into serious trouble.

We set out on the morning of the first anniversary of my arrival in Ejahyay. We found the farms and wayside villages entirely deserted. By this we knew that we might meet enemies at any moment and proceeded with increasing caution as we got farther from home. But I was too young and too thoughtless to take in the seriousness of the situation, notwithstanding the fact that my companion had become both watchful and silent. I could not realize that a Yoruban might harm me, and I tried to enjoy the ride as if all was peace. On the other hand, my companion had been a soldier in the Liberian army and he knew what war in Africa meant.

In about six hours, one of which was occupied in passing through a dense forest, we came to the farm shanty of our friend and found that it was in Ebaddan territory. About one mile farther on was a collection of huts used as a stopping place for caravans on their way to and from Abeokuta. From this place a road branched off to Ebaddan which was about twenty miles distant. Pigeons were flying around the shanty and a bunch of bananas was hanging at the door, but we could get no answer to our calls, and my companion rode on to the wayside village to look for Vaughn.

After waiting sometime and hearing something like the sound of an uproar in the distance, I rode on to join Russell. But soon everything was silent again. Just before reaching the village clearing, I was met and quickly surrounded by a body of men armed with guns and cimeters. At first I did not feel much alarm. It was plain that some of them were not Yorubans and, from the way in which they looked at me, I knew that they had never seen a white man before. They seemed to be under the control of an officer or leader, but I did not at all like their countenances. The eyes of some of them were greyish and had the cold, merciless gleam of the steel in their hands. They stared up into my face and pressed closer and closer to me like beasts of prey ready to spring upon their victim.

"Whence do you come?" demanded the leader.

"From Ejahyay," responded I.

As quick as a flash, they sprang forward and attempted to unhorse me. But I touched my powerful horse with the spur and he broke loose from them with me still in the saddle. But they got my broad-brimmed grey felt hat, my umbrella, my lunch satchel, and also tore my coat skirt to tatters. The strong leather strap of the satchel broke before they got me out of the saddle. In their ferocity they jerked it too hard. Their leader was evidently a Yoruban and when he gave me a signal to surrender, I thought it was an invitation to flee and escape. I wheeled my horse and endeavored to do so, but they closed up in front and after a desperate struggle in which I came near being shot, I was unhorsed and thrown to the ground with great violence.

But their leader pressed them back with his drawn cimeter and thus gave me an opportunity to spring to my feet. In the Yoruban language, I rebuked them sharply for thus wanting to kill an unarmed man and the officer appeared to approve what I said. But they stood looking at me in profound silence. Not a single word had been spoken by one of them during this whole time. That dreadful silence was their sentence of death. But the officer firmly cleared the way to my horse and commanded me to mount. On hearing this command, the cutthroats seemed to fear that they were about to be cheated of their lawful prey and the uproar that followed was more appalling even than their strange silence had been.

At this juncture, my companion was brought up, still mounted, but a prisoner. The sight of his face confirmed me in my belief that I was to be killed. He was from a friendly town, but his face plainly showed that he was expecting to be murdered. He understood their language perfectly, and knew what they were saying in all this din. I saw and heard enough to chill my blood. One man yelled, "We can't sell them. If we take them to Ebekoonleh, we will not get anything. Let us kill them now." For several moments we waited in sickening suspense the decision of the commander-in-chief as to our fate. Then a young man, with the bearing of one high in authority, suddenly broke through the noisy throng and, taking my horse by the bridle, led him down by a very narrow path into a dense and dark forest. My companion came along behind, while a soldier with a gun brought up the rear. We thought we were being led to death.

When we came to a little opening, the young man in front called a halt and seemed to be waiting for some one. Presently I heard a sound that made my blood freeze in my veins. It was the rattling of war accoutrements of soldiers approaching us rapidly from behind. With deep emotion, my companion called to me and said, "They are certainly going to kill us now, sir." I looked back and saw those same wolfish eyes glaring at me through the foliage. My guard now halted, took his cimeter from his shoulder and came up to the side of my horse. Pointing to the men who had just come up, he said with much authority and dignity, "Oto geh!" (It is enough.) The last word was pronounced with great emphasis and prolonged into a deep growl.

It seemed certain now that, helpless and defenceless, we were about to be butchered in that lonely spot and our bodies given to the wild beasts of the forest. Language cannot picture my feelings at that moment. I have been several times called to look death in the face since that time, but never in a form so indescribably hideous. But the young man, instead of being our executioner, was our guard. After uttering the words mentioned above, he sternly commanded our pursuers to return and to take the places assigned to them and to fight like men, for Areh's army was coming to attack them. They faced the young leader in silence for a while and then, to my inexpressible relief, reluctantly and slowly retired.

Then with long but not ungraceful strides, my guard plunged deeper and deeper into the forest. This was a very merciful providence to me, for I was entirely bareheaded. When we came again into the burning tropical sun, my Liberian companion placed his own hat on my head and made a turban for himself out of his handkerchief. My neck was already blistered and this thoughtfulness of his probably saved me from a deadly sunstroke. We had no idea what our captors intended to do with us, but escape was impossible and there was nothing for us to do but to trust in God alone and to resign ourselves as much as possible to His will. Yet it was with a sinking heart that I came in sight of Ebaddan and saw its brown thatched roofs extending many miles over hill and dale, for I had reason to fear that it was to be my prison until it became my grave.

We entered the city about sundown and were taken at once to the judgment place of the governor, Ebekoonleh. This was a counterpart of that of Areh. At the gate or door of the court, the young man ordered us to dismount and, placing me under guard of the soldier, entered alone to report to the governor. After a little delay, I was taken in under guard. I have a very vivid recollection of something that happened just here for which I cannot certainly account unless I had now become partially crazed by heat and thirst, combined with excitement. When I saw the majestic and ponderous form of Ebekoonleh on the judgment-seat, and a great crowd of people standing on the left, a sudden feeling of indignation seized me, and by the side of the soldier I stalked defiantly up to the governor, looking him squarely in the eye all the time. But he did not seem to notice my disrespectful bearing, and with quiet dignity ordered me to take my position on his right. He was a remarkably handsome man, and before the trial ended, proved to be a wise and just judge.

The soldier then prostrated and preferred his charge. He declared that I was an officer of high rank in Areh's army, that I was riding Areh's war horse, that I had come with an army to attack the Ebaddans at Edo, and that I had been captured after a desperate fight. He cunningly left the governor to infer how great a slaughter I had made. Knowing that every officer taken prisoner in this country is put to death, I suddenly awoke to the fact that I was charged with a capital crime, and that if I could not disprove the lying accusation of the soldier, there were but a few moments more between me and a bloody death. Speaking respectfully but earnestly and using my companion as an interpreter, I explained everything fully. The governor replied to this by saying that a white man had been brought to Ebaddan badly wounded and that he was then with some friends in an adjoining house, and he supposed that this was the man we had come to warn of his danger. He then demanded my gun and my sword, but when these could not be produced, he gave a grunt of displeasure. He seemed to think that the soldier or the person whose agent he was, had trifled with him. Still he did not seem satisfied and he hesitated as to his decision.

After a short pause, he took from some one behind him, a very long and heavy sword, and handed it to a man of a very stern and repulsive countenance who stood on the left. When the scowling brute ordered me to follow him, a desperate plan of escape flashed like lightning through my excited imagination. I determined to wrest the sword from the hand of the executioner, fight my way to my horse and escape by any way that might be open. I am more than six feet tall and have a large frame, but fortunately for me, my companion was as cautious as I was hasty. With a loud exclamation, in the Yoruban language, I sprang at once to my feet, but Russell quickly intervened and hastily explained that the governor was only going to send me to prison. There was much confusion at first, but after order had been restored, speaking through my companion, I sincerely apologized for my unseemly and hasty conduct.

But I could not suppress fears of treachery, for the countenance of the man with the sword as well as other things, showed that he was the regular executioner, and as I passed on to the gate the people averted their faces and eyes. After going some distance, we saw the lights of a missionary's house. It was a vision of paradise, for it meant rest, sympathy, and congenial society. But when we came almost to the gate, I was ordered to follow the man with the sword down into a dark gorge. My suspicions being confirmed, I refused to obey; but my companion again exhorted me not to resist yet, but to obey until I knew positively what they were going to do. As I turned away from that vision of a Christian home, to go down into that dark valley, it was like a lost spirit turning away from a vision of heaven to go down to hell. My young heart with all its cherished hopes still clung to life, and I felt determined to make all reasonable effort to escape when any seeming opportunity presented itself.

After going some distance in the hollow, we entered a large compound and we were placed formally in charge of the *bale*. Our new guard, after conferring a while with the governor's messenger, took us back the same way we had come to the missionary's house, with the warning that if we left there without the permission of the governor, we would be killed by Ogumulla's men. The missionary, Mr. Hinderer and his wife, were absent in Abeokuta, and we were placed in charge of the assistant of Mr. Hinderer. He received me with such tender sympathy that I sat down and gave vent to my feelings in a flood of tears. Thank God for tears! After that, I felt more like a Christian man ought to feel under the circumstances. I have no doubt that I would feel very differently now, if I should be placed in similar circumstances, but I must tell things as they happened. Yet I sincerely thanked God that my hands were still unstained with blood.

The next day Mr. Hinderer and his wife arrived from Abeokuta, and told us that Dahomians were rapidly approaching that place in accordance with the agreement with Ogumulla. He then informed me of other things in connection with this man's schemes, some of which I have already mentioned. I found out that while Ogumulla had not yet invaded Ejahyay territory, he had cut off all communication with that town by the regular ways, and that he had gotten together in several camps on the roads leading to Ejahyay, an army numbering about 100,000 men. These soldiers were not only from Yoruban towns favorable to the war, but many thousands of them were from Nufe, Benin, and other warlike and marauding nations nearer the Niger. I was told that the men who captured me were Tarkpar and Foolah adventurers under the command of Ebaddan officers, and that to save me from them, the son of the governor himself had brought me to Ebaddan and delivered me to his father that I might have a fair trial before being delivered up into Ogumulla's power. As powerful as he was, the latter dared not assume to be superior to Ebekoonleh in authority. The reverence these people have for their legitimate rulers is one of the most remarkable things about them, and according to venerated custom Ogumulla was only Ebekoonleh's lieutenant, and could command no forward movement until he received orders or at least permission from his superior.

During the five days that I was prisoner in Ebaddan, the two chiefs were said to have had a stormy conference every day, Ogumulla demanding an immediate attack on Ejahyay and other things, and Ebekoonleh refusing to order what he demanded. Ogumulla also demanded that I should be put to death and that Areh's horse should be given to him. I found out that the reason I was allowed to retain my horse was because the governor was not willing that his ambitious subordinate should have the horse I had ridden. I was not allowed to lay my case before the governor, but Mrs. Hinderer made many very touching appeals for my release, telling of my wife and of the sick missionary in Ejahyay. The governor's reply was that it was needless to go back to Ejahyay, for that would soon be destroyed; and that, if Ogumulla's men did not kill me before I got there, they would do so afterward. When Mrs. Hinderer asked the messenger what would become of my wife, he seemed disgusted and asked, "Is that the only wife he has? Why can't he get another?"

I now saw that the only way to get away from Ebaddan was to leave secretly without the knowledge or consent of the governor.

At first, I thought of escaping in the night and trying to get around the Ebaddan camp into Ejahyay before morning. But Mrs. Hinderer suggested that I try to get to Awyaw and lay my case before the king. This I finally decided to do. Mr. Hinderer had been too sick to render me any assistance since his arrival, but his energetic and tactful spouse provided me with a guide, some "cowries" and some presents to help me on the way to Awyaw. The route for two days was at right angles to the one to Ejahyay and was nearly *one hundred miles* farther; but I was willing to endure any fatigue and to run any risk to get home alive.

16

Flight from Ebaddan

On the afternoon of the fifth day of my capture, accompanied by my Liberian friend and by my guide, I quietly left Ebaddan by the Awyaw route. We reached Lahlookpon, twenty miles distant by dark. This is a wayside village protected by a stockade and placed in the midst of a dense forest. There is no way of entering or departing except by the way which passes through it—and it is just the place for dark, treacherous and bloody deeds. Here I passed a night, every incident of which will remain vividly impressed on my memory as long as reason remains. About dark, just before we came to the gate of the stockade, my companion suddenly exclaimed, "They are following us, sir." I turned back quickly and saw a man dodge into the bushes on the side of the path. I jumped to the conclusion at once that Ogumulla's men were following us. If they were not enemies, why should they hide from us? But we were allowed to pass the gate and I received permission from the *bale* of the town to pass the night in his house. To make him as friendly as possible, I gave him a handsome razor. While I was sitting and sadly meditating on my situation, the gatekeeper entered and prostrating to the *bale*, warned him to be careful about what he was doing, for I was riding Areh's horse and I was the white man Ogumulla had captured. He did not know that we heard. I now remembered Ebekoonleh's warning and I believed Ogumulla's men were following either to murder me that night or to carry me back with my horse to Ebaddan. I supposed that they hoped the *bale* would not allow me to stay inside the stockade and I would be in their power. What it all meant, I never knew. The *bale* had a conference with somebody, and I was not disturbed. But I thought that there was a plan on foot to murder me that night and this supposed discovery, led to a most painful mental conflict. I had a cutlass at my service, but I knew that resistance would be in vain even if it might be right.

When I realized that there was no possible way of escape, my heart fainted and I sank into a state from which I could not arouse myself, not being able either to speak or to move. By shaking me, calling me by name and shouting in my ear, "Don't do that way, sir," my faithful friend succeeded in arousing me so that I could speak, but I found it quite impossible to partake of any nourishment. During this physical prostration, my mind was abnormally active. I seemed to see many of the scenes of my boyhood days. I also saw my wife wandering weeping about our home in Ejahyay. I tried to find some rest on the ground with my saddle for a pillow, but I passed a night full of horror. So soon as I would begin to doze, some suspicious sound would make me start up to listen. It was too dark to see anything, but my hearing was intensely acute and exaggerated every sound. I was also in most intense physical pain, having had a very severe ague in the first of the night.

About midnight there was a great alarm. The stillness of the hour was suddenly broken by a piercing shriek. Lights flashed about and I saw men taking down their guns and powder gourds. Then there was a cry of, "Fire! Fire!" I thought the Ebaddans had fired the house to drive me out, but I awaited developments before taking action. After some suspense, I learned through my companion that a child named Ena (fire) was thought to be dying, and all this noise was the result of the efforts of the people in the house to drive away the evil spirit that was dragging away the little soul. The woman who screamed was its mother. She first discovered the desperate illness of the child and gave the alarm. The men ran for their "medicine" gourds and rattled them over the child to drive away the evil spirit. For some minutes the frantic mother continued to call its name while she forced apart its eyelid and breathed into its nostrils. Then it revived and all was as quiet again as if nothing had happened.

So soon as we could see, we resumed our journey. Knowing that the gatekeeper was our enemy for some cause, and that he had had plenty of time to communicate with Ebaddan, I rode for an hour or more in constant dread of an ambush, but we met no one who seemed to be hostile. We met soldiers hurrying on to join Ogumulla's army, but they passed us without even saluting or noticing us in any way. Our path led through a very dense forest of lofty trees. About noon we came to the Orbar river where we had to pay a kind of internal revenue tax. Just before reaching this place, I heard a man yell, "Allah Mohammedu!" When I came up to the place, I found him crouching in the vines by the path as if very much afraid of me. When he saw my big horse and Mexican saddle, and the cadaverous face of the rider, he doubtless thought I was an apparition from the unseen world.

The tax collectors at the river were all Moslems. Their turbans and tobes were spotless, and their vests and trousers were of the finest velvet. Just a little beyond the river was the town Ewo, one of the oldest and best fortified in the whole country. This town was in the league against Ejahyay and I entered it with some misgivings, not knowing what instructions the governor might have received from Ogumulla during the past night. Often these rulers have secret communication with each other during the darkness of the night and plot any amount of mischief before daylight. Professional hunters become spies and scouts in war and are very efficient instruments for such secret conferences. I found the chief sitting in state surrounded by the twenty-four elders of the town, all dressed in turbans and tobes and evidently discussing something very serious. I saluted him respectfully and asked permission to go through his town to visit the king. He replied very pleasantly, granting the permission and then dismissed us with the usual polite expressions.

Through our guide we got some information that made me determine to change our proposed route. We had intended to turn to the left here and go straight to Awyaw, but we learned that Ogumulla's men had been seen on the road between Ewo and Awyaw and that the only way to escape them would be by going on to Ogbomishaw, a neutral town, sixty miles further in the interior on the border of Western Soudan. I was much distressed at the necessity for this change, for it would add an additional hundred *miles* to my journey. But I was willing to do anything to keep out of the way of Ogumulla's people, and determined to hide in Ewo until the next morning and make an early start for Ogbomishaw.

Our guide conducted us to the house of a man who, he said, had once been a member of the mission church of Ebaddan and who was a friend of the white man, and could be trusted. When night came, I was almost as much depressed as I had been at Lahlookpon. I was now going away from Ejahyay and things began to look as if I would never see that town again. I could not endure the thought of my wife falling into the power of those ruffians from whom I had just been delivered. But I was not yet free myself, and was in as much dread of being intercepted on my way to Awyaw, as I was when riding out of the Ebaddan gate. The route from Ewo to Ogbomishaw leads sixty miles through a very wild country, and I contemplated it with much anxiety. An almost unbroken wilderness lies between Ogbomishaw and Awyaw, and at that time one could travel the whole of the last named distance without meeting anybody but people engaged in the chase or in war.

I was now quite ill with African fever. When a heavy rain came up and beat in on me where I was lying in the piazza, a woman in the compound kindly offered to vacate her sleeping apartment for my relief. But soon a greater surprise than this awaited me. As I was lying on a grass mat in the little room, by the light of a little native lamp I saw the mat which hung over the door pushed aside. Then a hand holding a book was thrust within and that book was an old English Bible. Our host could not speak English, and why he had the Bible, I can't imagine. But the sight of it brought indescribable joy to my heart. I arose from the mat and opened it at random. The first thing my eye fell upon was the twenty-seventh psalm, and as I read it aloud, it seemed to be the very voice of God speaking from heaven. After the reading, we both kneeled together and I prayed aloud. While I was praying the burden of my heart seemed to melt away, and I became conscious of a very strong assurance that I would soon be delivered out of my distressed condition. The feeling was so strong that it greatly strengthened my body by refreshing my spirit. My body was racked with the pains of the African fever but my heart was sweetly at rest in God; and the night I passed in Ewo is vividly contrasted in my memory with my hideous experience at Lahlookpon.

A broiled piece of porcupine meat tempted me to take a little nourishment—the first I had tasted since leaving Ebaddan. During the night we heard a mother silence her child with the warning, "Kumee will catch you." We gathered from this that we were not yet among the friends of our chief, and that it would be advisable to leave the town as soon as practicable. We had left our horses outside the gate of the town in charge of our guide and so soon as the gate was open we mounted and set out for Ogbomishaw. When leaving, I told my companion of the change in my feelings.

"That is just the way I felt, too, sir," said he with a brightened countenance; for up to this time his face had worn an exceedingly sad expression.

But he had always been cool, sympathetic and brave in all this great trouble.

The enlivening of my spirit showed itself that day in a most astounding physical endurance. Though so weak that I mounted my horse with difficulty, I rode sixty miles that day, keeping the saddle until late at night and allowing the guide only time to rest. My stomach would not retain food and my back and limbs ached dreadfully, but I did not allow these things to delay me a moment. My mind had been lifted up from the darkness of despair to the light of hope. The intellectual and spiritual were masters for the time of the physical and animal. My experience that day seemed to me to be a philosophical hint of the fact that while the body is essential to a complete humanity in any case, there may be an intermediate state in which the soul has conscious life and vigorous activity without the aid of matter.

We found that the first stopping place for caravans was in the heart of a forest and, as it was still early in the afternoon, I persuaded the guide to go on, feeling that it would be better to camp in the jungle among the leopards than in another Lahlookpon; and among the leopards, we came near having to camp, sure enough. The sun went down as we emerged from the forest, and darkness overtook us many miles from Ogbomishaw in a jungle swarming with leopards noted in the country for their boldness and ferocity.

The air was filled with doleful sounds, the wild animals began to move about, and once the guide became alarmed, but we had no adventure with any kind of wild beast. I do not positively know that I even saw any. I was more concerned at that time about ferocious bipeds than about quadrupeds. Yet we had reason to be thankful we were not molested, for I was told, after reaching the town, that leopards had even been known to tear down the farm huts and devour the inmates, and that one had attacked a woman inside the walls in broad day.

After some anxiety, we saw in the distance a speck of light which proved to be a lamp at the gate of Ogbomishaw. This town being neutral, I was secure as long as I was inside its walls. The house of the American Baptist Mission was then temporarily occupied by two travellers with abundant supplies, and here for two nights and a day, I found food, shelter and rest. The missionary was absent in America, but the house was in charge of his interpreter, and everything was exactly as he left it.

Before parting with the travellers, I exchanged horses with one of them, telling him honestly why I did so. I never saw Bucephalus again. I heard that the traveller sold him to a Sierra Leone merchant who killed him in trying to subdue him, having galloped him twenty-one miles in a single heat. He was as fiery as ever at the end of that time, but the next morning he was stretched out dead—unconquerable to the last. I never saw his like before and I hope I will never see it again. To better fit him for war, he had been trained to bite people and to strike at them with his forefeet. He would spring at the hostler and make his teeth crack together like a lion's. Even after I had galloped him long and furiously, his fierce snort and wild neigh would make children flee as if a lion were coming.

17

Home Again

Forty miles from Ogbomishaw on the road to the Niger is Illorin, the most interesting of all the towns in which the Yoruban language is spoken. Its population consists of two distinct races, the Foolahs and Yorubans, living in separate districts of the city which is a kingdom or principality in itself. The chief ruler is called "Emir" and was chosen from the Foolahs only. While he ruled the Yorubans with moderation, he treated them as a conquered race and gave them no share in the government. The Emir at this time was not only a Foolah but, like most of his race, a bigoted Mussulman, and would not suffer any Christian missionary to settle in the town. No stranger could enter the city without special permission from the Emir and was in the hands of an officer as guide and keeper until he departed. At that time, the officer who performed this duty was named Nasamo and was quite famous on account of his intelligence, courtesy and dignity. But the most remarkable thing about him was that he had never had but one wife, and was then a widower with two daughters who looked after his household. As he was a very old man, it is doubtful whether he ever married again.

The Emir was a member of the Masonic fraternity and would grant special privileges to any stranger who furnished proof that he belonged to that order. Ordinarily his person was screened while giving an audience to Nazarenes and other foreigners, but when he discovered that his visitor was a Mason, he pulled the curtain aside and embraced him with many manifestations of joy and affection. He was a white Foolah and like all other rulers of his race, preyed on the Pagan towns near him. Illorin boasted the largest slave market in that part of Africa. The Yorubans who lived in the town as subjects of the Emir were mostly pagans and had little social intercourse with their haughty masters, and they were secretly cherishing at that time a burning desire to free themselves from the Foolah yoke.

I will add here as a sort of note that this desire has recently been gratified. In a battle fought between the English and the forces of Emir in the beginning of the year 1897, the Yorubans turned against the Foolahs and placed themselves under the protection of the English. The Emir was defeated and fled to Ogbomishaw. Illorin was captured and the Yorubans are now freed from the oppressions of their Mussulman masters. With Illorin also fell Bida, Socotoo and other Foolah towns, and slave hunting, with all its diabolical cruelties and unspeakable horrors, has been broken up in that part of Africa for all time. This should open a way for missionaries, but the Niger company is more interested in trade than in missions, and will do little to curb Mussulman bigotry unless there is a change in its policy. The Emir still refuses to allow Christian missionaries to preach in Illorin and the farthest they can go in that direction is Ogbomishaw. Here Rev. C. E. Smith of the Southern Baptist Convention, is at the head of a most interesting and successful mission.

Illorin being in alliance with Abeokuta and Ejahyay, it seemed wisest at first for me to go to Illorin and thence to Abeokuta and Ejahyay; but being informed by traders that the road to Awyaw from Ogbomishaw was certainly open, I finally determined to go directly to the capital and to place myself under the protection of Ardayloo, king of Yoruba. I knew that my wife was in great trouble and that it was a matter of much importance that I should inform her of my safety as soon as possible and, if Ardayloo was favorable, I would be in Ejahyay in a few hours after leaving Awyaw. I also felt happy at the thought that my face would now be turned toward Ejahyay. A number of men who were going to Awyaw desired permission to make a part of my company and in this way our party was augmented to a considerable band.

We were delayed in the beginning of our journey by a very sad event. Just after we had left the gate of the town, my Liberian companion reeled in his saddle and fell from his horse. As this town had been his home for many years, he had many friends here, and I left him in their care and resumed my journey, though distressed to part with him under such circumstances. I never saw him again, but that sad face shaded by long raven locks, will always remain in my memory as vivid and real as life. If he had not gone with me, I would not have survived this adventure. His life was given in exchange for mine. Not once did he express any regret that he had gone with me. He recovered sufficiently to get to Abeokuta by a circuitous route and he was there at the station of the American Baptist Mission when he died a short time afterward. Mr. Phillips informed me that his nervous system was so completely shattered by this unfortunate adventure, that he talked of little else, often shuddering and praying while recounting the incidents of our capture, trial and flight. I am thankful to believe that he at last found rest in the peace of a Christian's hope, and that at some future time, we will meet where "the wicked cease from troubling and the weary are at rest."

On our journey to Awyaw, we met no one except some hunters in a little grassy opening in the forest. These came toward us running, shouting and leaping high over the bushes and grass, and as they had guns in their hands and had the accoutrements of soldiers, we at first thought they were Ogumulla's men coming to intercept me. It is needless to say that I was greatly relieved when I found that they were not. The object of their pursuit ran just in front of my horse and was supposed to be a wild boar.

At noon we rested on the bank of the Orbar river under the great trees of an open grove. Such a natural phenomenon is so rare in Africa that I was tempted to wander some distance up the river under its refreshing shade. This pleasant recreation was brought to a sudden conclusion by a loud roar in the still forest. If my Ejahyay gun loaded with ball had been in my hand, I would have investigated before retiring; but under the circumstances, I thought it best to leave and not be too slow about it, either. The country north of this is infested with lions, but the natives call a lion *kinneu*, and a monkey or anything of that tribe, *aryar*; and they said that the sound had been produced by an *aryar* and not a *kinneu*. As I had just seen a large number of big, black monkeys in the trees a little back in the forest, I had to abandon my lion story.

As these are not allowed in any other than the royal city, one can always know when he is approaching Awyaw by a sight of the *arkarbee* or towers on the king's house. It was with a strange mingling of dread and joy that I caught a distant view of these peculiar structures in the last rays of the setting sun. In the mysterious providence of God, the petty African despot who sat under these towers had become the arbiter of my fate; and I fervently prayed again, as I had done before, that God would put it into his heart to grant my petition.

While in Ejahyay, I had made the acquaintance of Rev. T. A. Reid, the missionary of the American Baptist Mission in Awyaw, and to his house I proceeded as soon as we entered the town. He gave me a joyful welcome. He had heard of my disappearance and had just returned from a hazardous trip in search of me. Supposing that I had fallen into the hands of Ogumulla's men, he started for Ebaddan under the protection of a royal messenger. At Ewo, he learned that a silent white man, who was riding a very big horse and looked sick, had passed through there on his way to the interior. He was so well satisfied it was I that, most fortunately for me, he returned at once to Awyaw without proceeding to Ebaddan. He had just dismounted when I rode up. He sadly told me that the same messenger who had informed him of my disappearance had also told him that my wife, supposing that I had been murdered, had been prostrated by her grief and was not expected to live.

Mr. Reid sent to salute the king and to inform him of my safe arrival, but that I was too much fatigued to appear before him in person. The king sent a messenger at once congratulating Mr. Reid on account of my safety and giving me permission to proceed at once to Ejahyay without appearing before him. I will say here, by way of parenthesis, that I was very fortunate in this matter; for Ardayloo was very much under the influence of Ogumulla, and was, also, a man of uncertain humors. A short time after he treated me so kindly, he threatened to behead two missionaries who came to Awyaw from Abeokuta to get permission to visit Ebaddan. It was only through the intercession of Mr. Reid, who seemed to have much influence over him, that they were even permitted to return to Abeokuta. Their lives were spared upon condition that they would be a certain distance from the city in one hour after they had been warned.

Mr. Reid accompanied me to the outposts of the Awyaw army, and then bade me an affectionate adieu. I did not see him again until we met in America.

As the pickets had been instructed to let me pass in safety, I soon found myself on Ejahyay territory. In coming suddenly out of a belt of forest, I came upon a number of Ejahyay soldiers plundering the Awyaw farms, and it was very amusing to see how the fellows stuck to their baskets of yams while they scampered away supposing that the horsemen of the enemy were coming. A little farther on I came to the outpost of the Ejahyay army. The commander received me kindly and wanted to detain me to give some account of what I had learned of the Ebaddan army, but I was too much excited to be willing to stop.

The forest which belted Ejahyay was now in sight. All suspense was now over. I was safe. I was free. Oh, the happiness of that moment! My heart was ready to burst with tumultuous joy and, for a moment, I forgot what might be before me. With an exultant shout I put spurs to my horse and went in a sweeping gallop across the plain. Dashing through the intervening forest and the city gate, I came in another moment to the mission compound. But nobody greeted me. No one was in sight, and the silence of the grave reigned throughout the place. My heart sank within me. I leaned over the wall and saw my interpreter within a few feet of me reclining on a mat in the piazza of his house. His countenance was much dejected, and when I saw how really distressed he was, I was much moved by this evidence of his sincere affection. In a low tone, I spoke his name, and when he looked up, I made a gesture for silence. But there was no restraining him. At first his eyes dilated as if he had seen a ghostly apparition, then he sprang to his feet with a loud cry of joy, and started for the gate with his arms held aloft as if about to fly. As I rode into the gate he threw his arms around me and dragged me from my horse. Soon all the children of the mission compound were clinging to my hands and my knees, frantic with delight. Freeing myself from these I rushed into the house and met my wife, pale and tottering, at the door of her room, and all our troubles were over for one while, anyhow.

In a short time all the converts and many of the neighbors crowded in to hear the story of my deliverance, and the joy they manifested was very gratifying. In a few days both my wife and myself felt almost as well as usual, so much has the mental to do with the physical, especially in this strange climate.

From the time of leaving Ebaddan until reaching Ejahyay, my head had been protected from the sun by nothing but a brimless cloth cap and my neck and face were badly blistered, but I did not receive any enduring injury from this dangerous exposure. It is possible that starvation and excitement may have been used as instruments by a merciful Providence to save me from fatal sunstroke. During the ten days of my adventure, I did not eat as much as I ordinarily ate in a single day.

In relating her experience during this trying time, my wife told me that she was much disturbed when I did not return the first night, but hoped that I had been detained to help Vaughn get his property home. When I did not appear at noon the next day, she persuaded two other Liberians named Barbour and Smith that were in the country and happened to be at that time temporarily sojourning in town, to go in search of me. These men were full-blooded Africans who had fallen from a state of civilization to the level of the heathen; but, while they were desperadoes, they still possessed many excellent traits of character. From pure sympathy, they agreed to go in search of me, notwithstanding their knowledge of the people made them realize what extreme peril would attend the undertaking. Fully armed, they set out about noon to go to the shanty of Vaughn. Impatient from suspense, my wife attended by her native maid, followed the road some distance from the town, still hoping to meet me, until the setting sun compelled her to return to her darkened home.

About midnight, she heard the men talking in a low tone in the piazza and knew by this that they were hesitating from sympathy to tell her what they had learned. She then swooned and remained very ill until Sunday, believing all this time that I had been murdered by the Ebaddans and my body given to the wild beasts. It is needless to describe her anguish of mind during this time. One vision that specially tortured her was that in which her delirious imagination pictured the hyenas devouring my body.

On Sunday, the sixth day after my disappearance, after Mr. Phillips had given up all hope of her recovery and, possibly, just in time to save her life, Areh hurriedly sent a messenger to say that I was alive and in Ebaddan. He also said that Ebekoonleh had sent word to Areh that Ogumulla wanted to kill me but that he did not intend to give me up. This was all. There was no assurance that I would be allowed to return to Ejahyay, but she felt certain that my life would be spared and that we would meet again in this world in some place if not in Ejahyay. Good news in Africa is better than medicine and she began to convalesce at once and when I arrived unexpectedly three days afterward, she was able to rise from her bed to meet me.

The manner in which Areh got his information concerning my safety showed that he still held communication with the governor of Ebaddan. The man who acted as spy on this occasion told us that he climbed the city wall and then went into Ebekoonleh's compound by a secret door in the rear.

In relating this story, I have described what I felt, not what I ought to have felt; what I did, and not what I ought to have done. Possibly if I had been older, I would have acted differently. But the discipline was not altogether thrown away on me, for it proved to be a good preparation for the trials that were just before me.

18

Opening Battles Around Ejahyay

When Areh heard that I had arrived, he sent to say that he would not eat until he had seen me. This was equivalent to an order. I was secretly conducted by many little doors, courts and passages to the centre of his vast compound. I found him lying on a mat under the shade of a tree attended by one trusty servant only. He questioned me very closely in regard to what I had learned of Ogumulla's intentions and about his army. Not wishing to be a partisan in the matter and desirous of illustrating a Christian spirit before him, I respectfully asked him to excuse me from giving him any information of a military character. He then tried to make me say that Ogumulla was a very bad man, but I replied that we were all wicked in the sight of God. He seemed to be entirely nonplussed, and after expressing his surprise at my way of putting things, he dismissed me without a present. This showed that he was not at all pleased. But I did not feel afraid that he would do me any harm. He did not look at any time as he did on the day that I saw him so angry and when he probably executed a man with his own hand. Yet I felt relieved when I got safe and sound out of his den, for I was still weak and nervous.

A few days after this, we noticed that the gates of the town were closed and guarded, and that everything was strangely quiet. We kept within doors and awaited developments. The next day everything was reversed. The streets were filled with merry crowds, and sounds of boisterous revelry came from the houses. *Areh Argo* (the chief next to *Areh*), taking advantage of his master's precarious situation, conspired to wrest from him some of the power he had usurped. Argo's followers seized the gates and informed Areh that unless he made certain concessions and confirmed them by giving 200 bags of cowries and 300 slaves they would open the gates to Ogumulla. This was a dangerous thing to do to such a man and the masses were very uneasy until the thing was settled. Areh pretended to treat the whole thing as a good joke, told them that they did not ask enough,—and then gave them much more than they required. Then the people sent word to him that they would "fight the devil" for him. The money was spent in feasting and revelry. Thus did the poor people sell their homes and their lives for a mess of pottage.

About ten days after getting home, I witnessed for the first time a military demonstration in Central Africa. During the night Areh sent out all his horsemen supported by about 30,000 infantry, to attack, in the early morning, the Ebaddans who were plundering the Ejahyay farms. About ten o'clock, they returned through the gate near our house and filed past the yard gate. Some were armed with swords and shields, some with bows and arrows, others with great cross-bows, but the greater part had muskets. It was a barbaric host of very warlike men, but they did not look as merry as they did the day they sang in drunken glee, "We'll fight the devil for Areh." Areh Argo mounted on a beautiful Arabian pranced up and down, reviewing the line. A number of prisoners and of men carrying the heads of Ebaddans slain in the fight, preceded the flowing tide of warriors. Members of the same family were on different sides in this war, and when the women recognized some men connected with Ejahyay families among the prisoners, they began to dance and to sing, saying "Areh will make a pile of heads." A few days after this I passed through the gate leading to Ebaddan and just on the side of the way was a heap of human heads arranged like cannon balls. Areh had made a "pile of heads." Prisoners not natives of Ejahyay were sold or redeemed as slaves.

A vast, open, grassy plain lay on the Ebaddan side of the town, and just out of sight over a hillock, the Ebaddan host was permanently encamped. They were waiting the new moon to begin the attack. The first appearance of the slender silver crescent, was greeted by the roar of myriads of muskets, the fusilade continuing for many minutes. It could no longer be concealed from the people that some desperate fighting was before them. Five days were given by the enemy to feasting, then early one morning the sentinel's gun told us that the enemy were approaching. They filled the plain for many miles and were a terrible sight.

Ebekoonleh had been brought over to join in the war and commanded a strong force in the centre. Ogumulla held the right and another powerful subordinate chief, the left, with corps equally large. Though Ebekoonleh was nominally commander-in-chief, Ogumulla was the leading spirit. He could be easily distinguished from the Ejahyay lines by his scarlet robe and fine horse. A great war-horn was loudly praising him and breathing out threatenings for his enemies. Areh's drums bid him fierce defiance. Much of the day was given to manœuvering and getting the bushy, grassy plain in a condition for a fight.

In the stand-up contest which followed, lines of men several abreast, streamed to the front, fired, and then turned and flowed back to the rear. They thus formed an endless chain from one end of which there poured a constant stream of fire. For a while an incessant blaze issued from the front of both armies. Wherever the lines of battle were within a hundred yards of each other, the work was quite deadly, but outside of that distance the fire was not very effective. The roar of the muskets was deafening, and the ground often sensibly vibrated. Neither side had any artillery, but the sound of the battle was heard in Abeokuta, two days' journey away. A creek imbedded in high grass and bushes, lay between the opposing forces, and each commander tried to induce his opponent to cross first. At length Areh's officers lost control of the younger and more reckless, and they forced one of the fords and drove the Ebaddans back for nearly a mile. But they were dreadfully punished. That evening our mission yard was full of the wounded, all of them young men.

We had received an intimation as to what we might expect from a young man who was the first to come. He stepped quietly into our piazza without saying a word. This was so unusual that I desired to know what he wanted. He simply raised a cloth from his shoulders exposing a hole in the centre of his breast from which blood was trickling. Before we could give him any relief, the wounded began to come in such numbers that my wife had to become, for the time being, a hospital nurse.

We did all we could for them, sewing up cuts, and taking out bullets and broken bones. The bullets were of iron or copper. The copper bullets were made by cutting off about three-fourths of an inch of a copper rod one-half inch in diameter. These produced gangrene and were much dreaded by the soldiers.

Although the enemy were held in check, they were not discouraged, for they had just begun to fight. Areh did not praise his men that day, because they had run over their officers in the battle. The third day after that battle, the enemy reappeared in increased numbers, but received a signal repulse, the more remarkable because they were so overwhelmingly superior in numbers to the Ejahyay people. In the high grass on the enemy's right flank, Areh posted during the night about ten thousand men under the command of the brave and faithful Orgeh. By a pretended retreat next morning, he drew the enemy across the creek thus exposing their flank and rear to Orgeh's furious charge. The rout was complete and Areh galloped up and down his lines shouting, "Fight for your wives and your children, my people. It is hard to take a man in his own house."

One of the most famous warriors in the Ebaddan army was killed in this battle, and Areh had his heart taken out, broiled, cut into little pieces, and then distributed among his generals to be eaten by them to make them brave in battle. This was the only instance of cannibalism that I heard of during my sojourn in Africa. It is not impossible that there was cannibalism during the famine which at one time attended the siege of the town.

Three more pitched battles followed in quick succession, the Ebaddans pressing the Ejahyay people with all their might because they knew that an army from Abeokuta, and possibly one from Illorin, was coming to the assistance of the besieged. In comparison to the great host marshalled against them, the Ejahyay army looked like "a little flock of kids"; the Ejahyay people showed, however, no sign of fear, but rather exhibited wonderful courage and patriotism. The women assembled in the rear of the line of battle with water and provisions. If any part of the line gave away, the women jeered until the retreating warriors rallied. The men often displayed Spartan-like fortitude when wounded. While I was attending to one wounded man, another who had been shot in the eye and must have been suffering intense pain, gave several deep groans. Presently the other impatiently exclaimed, "Quit that. If you must die, die like a man." The poor sufferer writhed several times after this but did not groan again.

But nothing could have saved the city many days longer, when the scarlet cloaks of Abeokuta horsemen appeared on the hill just outside of the town. The intervening strip of forest being in a hollow, the opposite hill seen above it, seemed to be very close to us, and it was with much joy and thankfulness that we saw them file out of the bushes and begin to prepare camp for the coming army. Before night, the whole hillside was black with men working like bees, building a fortification around the camping ground, and little thatched huts for tents. About 20,000 arrived on the first day and all were under the command of the Bashorun, the military chief of Abeokuta and a man of royal birth.

So soon as he was comfortably settled in camp, he received a visit from Areh gorgeously arrayed in a scarlet robe of silk velvet. The Bashorun was dressed in flowered silk of the same color. Both wore red caps of velvet ornamented with gold lace. In the exuberance of his joy on account of the arrival of his supposed benefactor, Areh danced before him; but if he had suspected the motives which influenced the Bashorun in coming, he would not have been quite so hilarious. Than these two, it is hardly possible for two men to have been more unlike in character. Though implacable to his enemies, Areh was frank and generous to his friends. On the other hand the Bashorun was very scheming, covetous and deceitful, while he was not altogether free from the charge of cruelty.

The mounted scouts of the Ebaddans were bold riders and often performed feats of impudent daring. Just outside the gate leading to the battlefield was a large and lofty cottonwood tree used as an observatory by the sentinel. He would ascend to the top of this and on seeing the enemy coming in any dangerous numbers, would descend and fire off a great wall musket that made a report something like a small cannon. One day, a short time after the arrival of Areh's allies, while the sentinel was up the tree, a single horseman dashed up to the foot of it and, after enjoying the fright and surprise of his captive, coolly sent his compliments to Areh, congratulating him on account of his guests and saying that the Ebaddans would whip him and his visiting friends, too. He then dashed along in front of the Egba camp, yelling defiance at them. Notwithstanding he was so provoking, we could not help laughing at his humor.

After a few weeks' delay, the allied armies formed a junction and disappeared over the hill in search of the Ebaddan camp. Areh and his people had become impatient on account of the delay, but the Bashorun was very cautious and hesitating. He seemed to favor defensive rather than offensive tactics. But they disappeared over the hill in splendid order and I had no doubt but that the battle of that day would end the war. In a few hours, we heard that the enemy had abandoned their camp and fled to Ebaddan and other places, and we were beginning to think the war would end without another battle, when the eastern horizon was shaken by a tremendous peal of distant thunder which continued to reverberate for about thirty minutes. Then all was silence. I thought the enemy had been attacked in the rear and routed. Again the roar of battle shook the eastern horizon, but this time the sound was nearer. I had gone about a mile in the direction of the sound when I met a man greatly exhausted but still trying to run.

"What is the matter?" I enquired.

"Areh orders that the gates shall be shut," he pantingly replied.

I knew then that the allies had been defeated and were not only retreating but running. I kept up with the weary courier and got in before he shut the gate. When I reached the mission station, I found my wife alone and, not being willing to leave her, thus took her with me and started out in the town toward the gate of the city to learn what I could. We had gone only a short distance, when a great cry of lamentation through the whole city, showed that the people had given themselves up for lost. I then hurried back into our house. We had hardly gotten in before Mr. Phillips, all the inmates of the station, and many of the converts came running in. We all fell on our knees while Mr. Phillips briefly but fervently supplicated God's protection in this hour of peril.

Just then many of the panic-stricken Abeokutans, some of them desperately wounded, rushed into the mission yard. All that could fight, we succeeded in rallying and in persuading to take a stand at the city gate. But fortunately, the Ebaddans were so much encumbered with their prisoners that they did not press the siege that time, and when the sun went down not an enemy was in sight. By morning the defeated allies had somewhat recovered from their demoralized condition. Some, however, continued their flight to Abeokuta, and a few crazed by their experience that day, did not stop until they reached Lagos. It was, indeed, a very appalling disaster.

The Ebaddans, each one with a fillet of grass around his cap to distinguish him from his foes, had spread themselves out for several miles and hid in the tall grass or canebrake of a small stream. In some way they succeeded in lulling the suspicions of the allies and their charge took them entirely by surprise. They made a brave stand for a while and then broke. Areh succeeded in rallying some of them and in holding the enemy in check for a few minutes, but finally everything gave away and the whole plain from there to Ejahyay was covered with a confused mass of men fighting in all sorts of ways, even with sticks and rocks. Swords were used very freely. The flesh had been peeled off from one man's neck from his ear to his shoulder by a sword cut. We pasted it back with sticking plaster after sewing it a little, and he got well. I took a bone from the wrist of another where it had been nearly severed by a sword-cut. This man afterward rendered me an important service as a reward but of this I will speak later.

A man told me that after he had been taken prisoner, he threw his captor down and killed him by choking him and cramming earth down his throat. But the mêlée was not without its comic side. One of the men was heard begging, "Spare me! Spare me!" and when one of his companions ran to his assistance, he found that the humble suppliant was held, not by an Ebaddan, but by a bush.

The night after the defeat was one of great gloom. The whole city, including the mission station, was filled with mourning for the dead or the missing. Enigbio, the chief messenger, who had two little children with us, was shot dead on the field. It was very touching to see the little ones wipe the tears from each other's eyes as they wept. There was also great sorrow in the Egbar or Abeokuta camp, and trumpets were wailing all night calling the names of the missing in the hope that they might be hid in the "bush" and be directed by the sound to the camp. All the officers and chiefs who were taken alive, if recognized, had been immediately slain; but the other prisoners were either redeemed by their rich friends or sold as slaves.

19

Worshipping the Dead Prince

The conduct of the Bashorun on the battlefield had been so wanting in courage that the women of Ejahyay began to make songs about him. To prevent a breach between him and the Bashorun, Areh ordered these songs to cease.

After waiting long enough to dispose of their prisoners the enemy again appeared perceptibly increased in numbers, and advanced to attack the Egbar camp, but Areh frightened them by another flank movement and they fell back to the old battle ground. We were thus spared the sight of a battle right in front of our door. We could easily see the Egbars as they lay in the trenches of the camp waiting the approaching Ebaddans, and would have witnessed all the incidents connected with the assault.

For a week the two armies skirmished, each trying to induce the other to begin the attack; then Ogumulla, becoming impatient, took an oath that he would enter Ejahyay on a certain day. On the morning of that day he offered up a great sacrifice, the smoke of which ascended like a great, white pillar from the plain in the rear of the Ebaddan host. It took him until four o'clock, to get his unwieldy masses in fighting order, and then the charge was sounded all along the line. The lines of the allies were like a solid wall. They redeemed their prestige lost in the last defeat, displaying wonderful courage, for they were outnumbered at least three to one. For several hours it was like a volcano in eruption, and when night came on and the lurid flames of the blazing muskets lit up the mass of white sulphurous smoke that hung over the plain and city, the scene was truly appalling, made even more so by the fact that the combatants were yelling with all their might the whole time. The allies humiliated and incensed by their recent rout pressed closer and closer until in some places the bright threads of fire seemed to cross each other. At length the astonished Ebaddans, no longer able to stand before a fire so galling, broke and fled in dismay, pursued for a mile or more by the exultant allies, whose fire did not slacken to the last.

After this unexpected display of spirit on the part of the besieged, the enemy changed their tactics and tried to weaken them by cutting off their supplies of salt, for they knew that food was of no use in this climate without this indispensable ingredient. But the people of Ejahyay were now starving by hundreds. The supplies brought from Abeokuta by military caravans were used only for military purposes, and the poor who could not secretly escape from the town, were left to miserably perish. For some reason many preferred to die on the bank of the creek where it flowed through a grove near the gate in front of the station. Every day a number of living skeletons would totter and stagger along the way by our yard to reach this hallowed spot that they might lie down and die there. After death they would look like mummies, and the Egbar soldiers would throw their dry and wasted forms in heaps on each side of the path leading to their camp.

Than this famine, in all its circumstances, I never saw anything more pitiful. At first, I took a portion of the food I happened to have each day and standing by the side of the path, would try to induce the starving to eat a little, but they would look at me with a vacant stare showing that they were unconscious and too far gone to be benefited by human aid.

The famine and suffering among the people failed to enlist any sympathy from those in power, yet scenes would always occur at the gate when a military caravan was leaving for Abeokuta which ought to have moved to compassion the hardest heart. Large numbers of these poor people who knew what their fate would be if they did not get away, would gather at the gate and piteously beg to be allowed to go along with the others. Sometimes they would try to force their way through and be dreadfully beaten and even killed by the soldiers guarding the gate.

I was never able to wholly understand why they were detained, but thought at the time it was because if they let the poor and aged go away they would have to let many go away whom they intended to seize and sell on some pretext or other to obtain means to carry on the war. By being detained, also, multitudes of the people of Ejahyay were compelled to put their children in pawn to the Egbar warriors. These children were then sent to Abeokuta and kept in slavery until the redemption price was paid. In most cases it was never paid.

Many persons brought their children to us with the request that we would take care of them until the war was over. We were very glad to make this arrangement, for by it many children were brought from under the influence of paganism and put under the influence of the gospel at a very receptive age. As we would not be able to sustain so many children in this famine-stricken town, it was decided that Mr. Phillips should take most of the children and go to Abeokuta, while I would remain in charge at Ejahyay, retaining my wife's little waiting maid and some of the children whose parents were not willing for them to leave Ejahyay. Mr. Phillips succeeded in getting them all safe to Abeokuta, but some of them were laid up for some time from exhaustion, for the soldiers moved rapidly in these military caravans. Thus originated a native orphanage which afterward became an important centre of Christian influence among the people of Yoruba.

As the famine increased, many little homeless, starving wanderers came into the mission compound at Ejahyay. Some of them appeared to be demented by sickness and hunger, and when we were not watching, returned to the streets to perish. Those whom we could get to remain, we nursed into health and then sent them to Abeokuta in baskets on the heads of soldiers. In this way, I sent down about seventy more children to be placed at the orphanage. Of these, we will hear more later on, but starvation had so broken the health of some of them that they soon pined away and died. Only seventy remained when I reached Abeokuta about eight months later.

Under very trying circumstances, the care of an important mission station had suddenly and unexpectedly devolved upon me, but I had an excellent interpreter who was always faithful to me, and I could not speak the language very well for ordinary purposes myself. I instructed and encouraged the converts the best I could, and whenever her health or the condition of things would allow it, my wife continued to teach the children. Whoever had food in the town kept it concealed, but as long as there was any in town to spare, I was able to buy a little on the sly, the people who sold bringing it in the night. Once I was entirely out of cowries and had nothing that anybody in town wanted to buy. In special prayer, I laid the matter before the Lord, and that day a man came from the Egbar camp and offered to buy the colt of my wife's riding mare. The sum that this brought lasted us for some time. We had some rice and some arrowroot. We also had plenty of sugar, tomatoes and oranges. We preserved the tomatoes and ate them with the rice. We made some of the arrowroot into battercakes, but they were rather sticky and tough. Mr. Phillips was able to send us some flour once. I sent to Areh for help only once. He sent me a small quantity of worm-eaten corn with a message that showed he was not pleased with me about something.

But Areh's great power in Ejahyay was now broken, and he had practically become a subject of the scheming Bashorun, and I had unwittingly given assistance to the conspiracy through which this change had taken place. It was in this way. After Mr. Phillips left, the Bashorun made frequent calls at the mission house. On the first occasion, he was mounted on a large fiery horse and dressed in his most splendid habiliments of state. Black ostrich plumes waved from his shoes and his gold-laced cap. He was attended not only by officers of his household, but by a bodyguard of soldiers. I received him in all the state I could muster, and when he departed presented him with a dish large enough to hold a roasted wild boar. This visit was to break the ice. Of course, I had to return it. A few days after this, my wife and I arrayed in our best but rather time-worn clothes, paid our respects to his Highness in camp. He gave us a most condescending reception, and when we left, walked some distance by my side in the sight of the whole army, a courtesy he rarely extended to anybody. I was greatly puzzled to know what all this meant, for I could not imagine how I could be of service to him in any way which would lead to so much affability on his part at a time when he had me and everybody in Ejahyay from Areh down, so absolutely in his power.

A few nights after this, when I was about to retire, I heard a gentle knock at the door. I cautiously opened it and found the Bashorun dressed as a common soldier standing before me. He had only two attendants, and they were dressed like himself. After talking a while, he requested that I would allow my interpreter to act as his private secretary and write a letter for him. To this I readily consented, of course. He made several visits like this, each time calling for my interpreter to act as his amanuensis. I knew that the letters were addressed to the king of Abeokuta but, supposing that they had reference only to military arrangements, I did not inquire of my interpreter as to their contents. I do not know whether they were written in English or Yoruba, but that was immaterial for the king's private secretary was a Sierra Leone man and could read and write both languages. I found out, however, that one of the letters began, "There is a great cottonwood tree in our way, and we must cut it down," and my interpreter hinted that Areh was the cottonwood tree.

I had often wondered what the inducement was that led the Bashorun to come to the aid of Ejahyay, and I now understood the whole matter. All who witnessed the last battle knew that it was the steadiness of the Egbars that had saved the city, and that battle dated the beginning of the wily Bashorun's efforts to accomplish completely the mission upon which he had come—the absorption of Ejahyay and its dependencies as a part of his personal possessions. He was of royal descent, and he claimed with some show of plausibility that Ejahyay was a part of his ancestral inheritance.

After the king had agreed to everything, the Bashorun proceeded to cut the cottonwood tree down. He called a meeting of the Ogbonees, a powerful and secret society to which many of the most influential of the Ejahyay chiefs belonged, and obtained a decree conferring some high title of honor on one of Areh's generals. This was the first stroke of the axe. Areh scornfully refused to acknowledge any title not conferred by himself, and he practically executed his general for accepting it by exposing him to certain death in battle. All this worked exactly in the Bashorun's hands. One very dark night, all the Ogbonee elders, including many of the most powerful men of both armies, met under the cottonwood tree standing just outside the gate, and sent a preremptory order to Areh to appear immediately before them. As they evidently meant to put him to death, he refused to obey but at the same time showed a disposition to make every concession possible by sending 200 bags of cowries and 300 slaves. From that night, the Bashorun was the real ruler of Ejahyay; for Areh did not dare to disobey any decree of the Ogbonees, and they decreed in this particular matter whatever the Bashorun desired.

Whenever any one disobeys or offends the Ogbonees, the executioner of the lodge requires him to eat a poisoned cola-nut in the presence of the lodge. When this is done, he is told to go home and put his house in order by the time the Ogbonees come to seize his property. I have always believed that this was to have been done with Areh, but as they could not get him into their power without violence, I suspect they ordered him to commit suicide. In this way only can I account for his insane rashness on the battlefield soon after this event. The two armies were skirmishing very heavily when Areh with all his slaves charged suddenly right into the blazing muskets of Ogumulla's centre. Unsuspicious of anything of the kind, I happened to be looking at him at the time. Then followed one of the most exciting events I ever witnessed on a battlefield. A simultaneous yell went up from both armies, there was a wild rush of thousands of men to that point and a desperate hand-to-hand conflict, while the muskets crashed all along the line. The enemy were driven back, and Areh was brought out apparently unhurt, but his beautiful Arabian war horse was covered with blood. I do not think he ever again appeared on the battlefield.

Some months after this and after I had left for Abeokuta, he died either from the effects of wounds received on this occasion or from poison administered secretly by the orders of the Ogbonees. My interpreter told me that during the last week of his life Areh repeatedly sent for me and repeatedly enquired when I would return. What he wished, I could never learn, but I have sometimes thought it might have been a merciful providence that took me to Abeokuta before he died. In his last hours he possibly wished to wreak his vengeance on me for my supposed complicity in the conspiracy against him. But it may have been otherwise. He may have wished to tell me that he believed the gospel and had repented of his sins.

An event almost as strange as this would have been, did actually occur a short time before I left Ejahyay. A man named Ardayloo, an officer in the Egbar army, was taken very sick and sent for me. He informed me that he had been a neighbor of the missionary of the American Baptist Mission in Abeokuta, and that he was a frequent visitor at his house. He had learned to know, he said, that the white man was kind, and he had sent to me for medical assistance. Seeing that he was very ill, I persuaded his men to bring him to the mission compound, and I had him put in a room of the native department.

After a few days, it was evident that he would die. When he realized this, he sent for some of his men and confessed to them in my presence that he was a believer in "Yasu Christee" and that he had not personally sacrificed to his people's gods for several years. He requested them to give his body to me to be buried according to Christian rites and to surrender his personal effects to the Ogbonees that they might take what it pleased them to confiscate. The embarrassed but sardonic grin with which the leader of the men heard these words is still vividly pictured on my imagination.

After they had gone out, he made a full confession of his sin in hesitating to confess Christ before his family and his people, describing the great trouble in which such a course would have involved him with the Ogbonees and with his kindred. He then prayed that the Lord would forgive him for his timidity in neglecting to confess him before men until now and asked to see the book that told about "Yasu." One was placed in his hand. He looked at it for a while and then exclaimed in a kind of rapture, his countenance lighting up suddenly as if he saw something that greatly rejoiced him, "Yasu, ewaw ne Olugbalah me! ewaw ne Olugbalah me!" (Jesus, thou art my Saviour! Thou art my Saviour!) He continued to look at the book until it dropped from his hand and then his eyes closed as he faintly said, "Amee law elay" (I am going home). It was like a bright shining light from heaven in the midst of the dense spiritual darkness of paganism. If that missionary had done nothing more than lead this poor heathen into "the light of the knowledge of the glory of God in the face of Jesus Christ" he would have been amply compensated for all that he suffered while in Africa. He doubtless never knew anything about the conversion of this man until he met him in heaven. And many other missionaries may expect the same experience. They must work and wait. God will give the increase when it pleases Him, but it will certainly come sometime and that when it is best that it should come. If there are those who are skeptical on this subject, it is all the worse for them. We cannot but believe what we see and hear. I made his coffin with my own hands and buried him by the side of Mr. Phillips' wife. Not one of his people honored his memory with their presence on this occasion.

A few weeks after this, I witnessed another burial ceremony of a very different kind on the same spot. Bashorun's heir was desperately wounded and brought to me in the mission compound. Nothing could be done for him and he died as the heathen die—without a ray of light from the other world. His body was wrapped in costly silk and lay in state until night. Then the

Ogbonees came and carried it to a grave that had been dug for it near that of Ardayloo's. As a mark of respect to the Bashorun, I had followed, but when my presence was discovered, I was politely informed that the ceremonies which had now begun could not be witnessed by any but an Ogbonee and I was not favored with a view of the ceremony in full. In about thirty minutes, the "mysteries" were finished, and Prince and subject were sleeping side by side waiting the judgment day. Let us feel thankful that all judgment is in the hands of a merciful Creator, but what disciple of Jesus does not feel that everything possible should be done to scatter the darkness which hung over the grave of that heathen prince with the heavenly light that glorified the face of the dying Ardayloo.

The next morning the younger brother, attended by a bodyguard, came to the grave and prayed to the spirit of his dead brother, kneeling down and audibly asking for protection in battle and success in the affairs of life. After their young master had finished his supplications, the soldiers stood in a line and fired a volley over the grave.

20

Leaving the Doomed City

The scenes through which we had been passing for a year were beginning to tell seriously on my wife's health. Outside our faith, we had little to cheer us. Daylight brought battles, blood and suffering, night brought alarms. While awake, we were in a constant suspense which was very trying on a female constitution in this climate. The faith of the converts during all this ordeal was as simple as that of children, yet it made them giants in the strength of their characters. It was, indeed, an impressive object lesson.

We had to give up everything like domestic order. Except in the seclusion of our sleeping apartment, privacy was impossible. Visitors and wounded soldiers were always in and about the house, and we encouraged them to come. We wanted them to feel that we and everything we had were at their service, to see in us as much as possible the spirit and character of our divine Master.

For more than thirty days at a time of great fighting and tumult my wife was extremely ill. She was beginning to have chills every six hours when the disease yielded to remedies. Her recovery, under the circumstances, was almost miraculous; for she would often have to listen all day to the roar of battle, not knowing but that before night the Ebaddans would be in town, plundering, burning and murdering. One dark night, we had a most appalling alarm from which sleep kindly delivered her. Without the slightest premonition, the crash of hundreds of muskets simultaneously shook the air. The sound seemed to be just outside our yard. Immediately the whole town and camp were in an uproar, the men yelling and the women wailing. I learned afterward that it was a demonstration of the Ebaddans to find out whether the Egbars were in their camp or not. They had been informed that the Egbars had fled to Abeokuta.

When my wife had fully recovered, it seemed to be my duty to take her to Abeokuta as soon as possible. The Bashorun still continued to make us informal visits, more for the sweets we gave him than anything else, I suppose. It was my duty to present him with something, however small, whenever he came, and I finally satisfied him with some tomato preserves or "white man's honey" as he called them. He would eat so much of these that I would have to give him a dose of medicine almost large enough for a horse to cure him. I learned through him that he had established a strong force in a fortified camp halfway to Abeokuta and that in this way his caravans were so well protected travelling to Abeokuta in them was reasonably safe.

The camp was situated between two mountains where the Ogun river cuts its way through them. It is one of the wildest spots I ever saw. From this camp scouts went out and scoured the forests between that place and Ejahyay every day, and the Bashorun always knew when it was safe to start a caravan for supplies. I told him of my purpose to go to Abeokuta and requested him to let me know when it seemed to be safe for me to do so, and to furnish me with the needed carriers. This, after a little delay, he promised to do, and I began at once to prepare for the journey, the converts received permission to accompany me. I was not willing to go without them for I knew that the town would certainly be taken and there was no reason why they should remain unless they were capable of bearing arms. Those that now remained were either widows or children. The Bashorun, therefore, had no excuse for detaining either them or me.

The military caravans always started early in the morning with a great rush, and they travelled very rapidly in a kind of "quick-step" so as to reach Okee-Magee (two mountains), the fortified camp, before night. It was decided, therefore, that I should pass my last night in the Egbar camp, the Bashorun guaranteeing protection not only for my wife and self, but for the converts and children. We waited until dark and then swiftly and silently left the mission yard for the camp. It resembled a funeral, and before ordering the start, I went hastily back into my room and fell on my knees in the dark and fervently prayed in a few words for the doomed city. Poor Ejahyay! Before many months had passed there was nothing left of it but blackened ruins, the homes of the wild beasts of the forest. In this great solitude of forest and jungle myriads who rejected the gospel now sleep in death awaiting the resurrection of the judgment day. Then it may be found that there were some poor timid souls who lived and died in a faith which only Jesus saw. There must have been more than one Ardayloo in all Yoruba.

I felt quite secure in camp, but did not sleep much. During the night the younger warriors engaged in a war dance, moving in a circle and chanting a tune indescribably weird. In the dance they would strike each other with clubs smeared with the war "medicine" of each dancer. Whoever was least hurt by morning, was supposed to have the strongest "medicine." Some of them were badly hurt by the poison, but I do not think that any of them died from the effects of this hideous carousal. Because of the attention I had shown to her wounded son, the Bashorun's head wife did us the honor to come into our little room and personally see that we were as comfortable as the circumstances would admit. She conducted herself with much dignity, but appeared to be very sad.

During the night, some of the soldiers fired on a leopard which was prowling around the camp. On account of the number of the dead people, the hyenas had revelled every night, but the armies had either driven away or destroyed much of the prey of the leopards, and hunger was beginning to make them very bold both in the mission yard and in the camp. The Bashorun had had a rather startling adventure a few nights before. The old gentleman was very fond of chicken in his "palaver sauce" and so were all his "boys," especially in time of war when delicacies were scarce. He knew that while his life was safe in the hands of his "boys," the lives of his favorite birds were not. So he always slept near the door of his low tent with the basket of chickens hanging just within. Not finding any nobler game, a leopard crept up and had his neck stretched out over the ponderous form of the Bashorun, trying to get a mouthful of chickens, when he touched the sleeper and waked him. A loud yell from the Bashorun brought some soldiers to his assistance and saved the chickens and their owner. The disappointed beast retired to the wall and there howled or roared back angry defiance at his pursuers. Not until he had been struck by a ball would he take refuge in the bushes.

The Bashorun hurried us off next morning as soon as it was light enough to travel. A trusted officer, whom we knew, had been instructed to give special attention to the safety of my party; for the people of the caravan acted upon the principle "every man for himself," and there were some young people in my party who could not keep up through the whole day with the excited, hurrying throng.

A stubborn battle had been fought a few days before in which the allies had been pressed back slowly to the last line, showing that they were barely able to hold their own. We feared that, encouraged by this show of weakness, the enemy might send a large detachment of their vast horde to attack our caravan. About noon, we came to a place where a road from Ebaddan entered our way, and the officer warned us all not to speak while passing that place. For about thirty minutes, we hardly breathed. After going a mile or two farther, we met one of the scouts from the camp at Okee-Magee, who told us that the way was certainly safe to that place, but we were still in the enemy's country and I could not feel wholly out of danger.

Late in the afternoon, we came in sight of the camp of Okee-Magee. Wrapped in mantles of azure, with their faces illumined by the departing sun, the twin sisters seemed to greet us with a welcoming smile. I tasted again the cup of happiness of which I so freely drank when, after passing the outposts of Awyaw, I came in sight of Ejahyay. The mountains were still a long distance away, but our buoyant spirits annihilated space.

Just as the sun set and when we were still several miles away from the camp, I heard the rumbling of distant thunder. Yet I could see no cloud. The mountains had now taken on a very sombre hue and seemed to warn us of coming danger. Suddenly a great black cloud, made more appalling by the constant play of vivid lightning, issued from between them and came rushing and roaring straight at us. The violence of the shock so completely scattered my party that we did not get together again until next morning and one of the female converts was not found until the afternoon of the next day. In less time almost than it takes to tell it, the carriers, converts and children were thrown down by the force of the wind and lay wallowing and choking in water nearly knee deep. The carriers of my wife's hammock, being stalwart warriors, managed to keep their feet to the last. My wife lay, half-strangled in a pool of water, but I managed to keep at her side until the tempest had swept past. The rain was blown almost horizontally and in sheets instead of drops. It struck us like the current of a rushing river.

It was now quite dark and we had much difficulty in getting up the rocky defile into the camp. At last we entered amidst the deafening roar of guns as an expression of joy for the safe arrival of our caravan.

For about an hour, the condition of my wife and self was very forlorn. When I sent to the commander for a tent in which to pass the night, I received permission to occupy a little thatched arbor which was open on all sides. We were soaking wet and getting very cold in the fresh breeze that followed the storm. We sat here for a while in the darkness and were not only cold and wet but weary and hungry and there was no one to get anything for us. Our people had all disappeared in the storm and darkness excepting my faithful interpreter, who was now acting as my messenger. I found out that the commander was Ogubona, one of the most famous chiefs of the Egbars and known in England as the "friend of the white man." I sent another message to him reminding him of this and requesting him to give me a place in which we could be more comfortable. The chief's messenger then came and carried us to a small but very comfortable tent with clean floor, and after a short time food was brought to us by one of Ogubona's wives.

Though we slept on nothing but a grass mat, we passed a comfortable night and were much refreshed next morning. During the night I waked once and made the astounding discovery that we were sleeping in Ogubona's private tent and that he was lying not more than a few feet from me. However, this did not disturb me at all, for it was a guarantee of protection so far as his power and authority extended; but I never heard of the like the whole time I was in Africa. African generosity could hardly go farther than this.

I found him to be a very handsome man. He was said to be the handsomest man in all that part of Africa. I am sorry to say that I never had an opportunity to meet him again and to express my thanks to him in some tangible form. He died from the effects of exposure a short time after this event. He was highly esteemed by the English, who invariably spoke of him as "His Highness." In one room of his house he kept all the curious presents made to him by foreigners, and it was said to be like a small museum. One of his amusements was to try to make a number of clocks strike together.

About daybreak next morning, we heard a child calling outside the camp fortifications and found that it was one of our little boys who had been so blinded and exhausted by the storm that he had not been able to find his way to camp until then. I sent out a hunter for the lost female convert. She was found sitting at the foot of a tree utterly exhausted and ready to perish. Thus all were saved.

We resumed our journey with light and thankful hearts, and from Okee-Magee to Abeokuta it was like a picnic. We took up our abode in the house in which we had been the guests of the missionary when we first arrived at Abeokuta. Mr. Phillips gave us a kind reception and we made the same domestic arrangements that we had while in Ejahyay.

After becoming settled in our new home, having no further need of the services of my interpreter in Abeokuta, I sent him back to take care of the house in Ejahyay. The Bashorun promised that, in case the Egbars retreated, he would notify him in time to escape. On getting to Ejahyay, he found that some marauding soldiers had tried to drink the acids in the dispensatory under the impression that they were alcoholic liquors. Fragments of the broken bottles were lying about everywhere, and things were smashed up generally as if by some one enraged or in pain. The robbers must have been dreadfully punished, but I heard nothing more from it. So many people were dying from all sorts of causes and life was valued at so little, that it is probable if any were killed the tragedy attracted little or no attention.

A short time after settling in Abeokuta, I was greatly flattered by a delegation from the converts who came in to congratulate me on my attainments in their mother tongue. I dismissed them with many expressions of sincere thanks, for they were evidently very sincere in the compliment.

21

Partial Civilization

Our house in Abeokuta was differently situated from that in Ejahyay. The city had outgrown its original limits so much that quite a little town had sprung up outside the gate leading to Ejahyay. This town contained a small but comfortably shaded market-place. The mission compound was built on the outside of this collection of houses and stood just on the edge of a great plain which furnished pasture for the cattle of the town. This plain was made very picturesque in many places by lofty rocks or boulders, deep hollows, and wild gorges which would have been ideal abodes for Pan himself. But something more useful and substantial dwelt here in the form of *arparrows*, antelopes and other game, and I found much needed recreation wandering with all freedom through the high grass and bushes and exploring the mysterious recesses. But the vines and grass and many other sorts of growth were so thick that it was often difficult to find even large game after I had killed it. Once while I was pushing through a tangled growth higher than my head, an antelope as large as a cow, sprang up into full view about ten steps away. I discharged the entire load into its side and it seemed to be wounded, but I could not find my prey. It had slunk along underneath the vines and bushes and hid in some impenetrable recess.

These rocks are a favorite place of abode for pythons, and I did not care for this reason to pursue the search too far. One of the very largest specimens of these reptiles lived in a large cleft boulder just inside the walls near the mission house. The people of the city treated this as they did the one living in the great central rock and frequently left offerings to it as one of their tutelary deities. My curiosity got the better of me one day and, holding a strong, sharp knife in one hand, I passed through the central cleft looking into the hollows on each side, but I did not see his godship. I think now that my conduct on this occasion was rather foolhardy, but I did not think so at the time. In this connection, I will say that the greatest snake story I ever heard anywhere was told to me in Abeokuta by a native who seemed to be entirely in earnest, but I do not wish to be held responsible for the truth of his statements. The man declared that an acquaintance of his saw the head of a large python protruding from a hole in the bank of a rivulet. When he cautiously approached, it was withdrawn. The hunter then thrust his foot and leg into the hole and after an hour the monster had swallowed it up to his knee. The hunter then killed the snake by splitting it from his knee to his foot with a sharp knife.

The rocky nature of the soil made the mission yard at Abeokuta the favorite haunt of a reptile which we dreaded much more than we did the leopards of Ejahyay or the pythons of Abeokuta. This was the small white scorpion, about three inches long. There was another species about half of a foot in length and of a jet black color, but these were not so dangerous as the innocent looking white species. The latter generally came out after dark and it was at that time the children were most frequently stung. When I would see a girl or boy fall suddenly to the ground and writhe in speechless agony, I knew what was the matter. A missionary was stung one night about dark and he screamed and groaned until midnight. He said that the pain was indescribable. I had some very narrow escapes. Once the sting struck the skin without breaking it. Even then there was a sharp pain for a few moments, but the fright was worse than the hurt. Anointing with palm-oil is the favorite native remedy. To infants the sting of the smaller species is often fatal. We may well imagine, therefore, the terror of a missionary's wife when she lighted a candle one night and found six scorpions around her baby's crib.

The large snakes in this part of the interior, are dangerous only as constrictors; but we had snakes in Abeokuta that concealed themselves in the short Bermuda grass of the mission station, the bite of which is as deadly as the copperhead of America. We seldom saw one, but they gave us much concern on account of the barefooted native children connected with the orphanage.

In my rambles in the bush back of the mission premises, I met with several surprises in the *fauna* of the country. One was a large hare. Another was a chamelion. This strange animal furnished me much unique entertainment for sometime. I knew that its color would change according to the thing upon which it was placed, but I did not know before that it is a double animal, one half of it acting entirely independently of the other, but my observations on this occasion forced me to this conclusion. The two protruding eyes seldom looked in the same direction. One was horizontal while the other was up, down, backward, or forward. Then they would be in opposite directions for sometime, quickly changing. Occasionally there appeared to be a contest between the two sides as to which way the whole should move. It was really unpleasant to see the struggle, for the little creature seemed to be suffering pain until one side or the other surrendered and it could move without hindrance in one direction or the other. I also came across a species of armadillo, showing that the opinion that no species of this animal is found in Africa is incorrect.

Among the rare *flora* of the country I came upon some specimens of ebony and of rosewood as beautiful as can be found anywhere. I also found some wild tomatoes about the size of cherries and proved their excellent quality by eating heartily of them myself and bringing some to my wife.

We did not feel so lonely and homesick in Abeokuta as we did farther in the interior. In Ejahyay we saw only one white man and one white woman (and these only for a few moments) who were not of our household; but in Abeokuta there were three English missionaries with their wives. My wife especially, who had been cut off from congenial female society for two years, greatly enjoyed this pleasant change in our social privileges. The ladies would not only exchange calls but even make visits of days. One of them was the wife of a missionary physician and a daughter of Issac Taylor, one of England's most famous authors. Through her introduction, we afterward had the rare privilege of passing a week at the home of her distinguished father near London.

Just before we left Abeokuta, the very sudden death of one of the other ladies, a very attractive and cultured woman, cast a deep gloom over our little world.

The mission compound included an acre or more of ground and this space was divided into a front and back yard. Many native houses were in each. These were occupied by the children, their teachers, the necessary servants and inmates and many refugees from Ejahyay, including the converts. Only the children were dependent on us for support. Excepting that they attended chapel services several times a week and family worship every night, the others lived as they would in a native compound. According to native law, the man in charge of the mission station was the *bale* and was responsible to the authorities for the conduct of his people outside as well as inside the compound. His authority was, therefore, recognized as absolute inside the mission compound. The attendance varied a little, but the number of people generally present at night was over 100.

By far the most interesting and important appendage to this establishment was the orphanage. I call it by this name, because, while some of the children had been left temporarily in our care that they might escape starvation or slavery, most of them had lost one or both parents and had to be educated and started in life by the mission. The boys were placed in the back yard in charge of the Sierra Leone teacher and his wife; and the girls, in suitable houses in the front yard, in the care of some of the older female converts.

Some of the girls were of a very tender age. Each of these had one of the older girls for an *eyah* or mother whose business it was to look after the toilet of her little charge and to nurse her in case of serious sickness. They also bought the food of the little ones.

A trusty boy was appointed to count the cowries and each child received a certain number of cowries per day and they all bought their food in the little market near the house. Each had a little dish of native earthenware to hold the "palaver sauce" and that was the only thing needed in the way of table furniture. Their only bed was a grass mat. The dress of the boys consisted of a brimless cloth cap, shocoto, and a shirt of some cotton material reaching to the knee. Among the people this shirt was recognized as a badge of civilization. They also had the usual shoulder-cloth, but it was principally used as a covering at night. Besides one undergarment, the dress of the girls was a turban and a gown of some cotton material. Food was provided by an appropriation from the mission, but the material for the clothing was given by philanthropic people in England irrespective of religious denomination and was made up by the girls under the instruction of my wife assisted by the wife of the teacher.

As a contribution to the school and to relieve my wife, I sent for a sewing machine. It proved to be one with a "chain stitch." I had never seen one before but I entertained myself very pleasantly for a day or two sitting on the floor and studying it out. After I got it to working, it caused much astonishment among the children; first, by sewing so quickly, and second, by the speed and suddenness with which its work would unravel. The little monkeys, prompted by curiosity to see how the thing was done, would keep picking at the thread until they secured an end and then with loud exclamations of amusement would pull until their clothes dropped to pieces. They did not seem to have much opinion of the "chain stitch"; neither did I, after sewing the same garment several times. When their curiosity was entirely satisfied, we got along much better, and with little trouble were able to keep the orphans clothed.

The distress that had come upon them, led the Ejahyay refugees to think and feel more deeply in regard to the gospel and during the first year of my residence in Abeokuta, many of them made a profession of faith in Jesus Christ, so that the mission church was much enlarged from those who had persistently resisted the gospel in their own town and in happier days. Among these was my wife's little waiting-maid, the daughter of Orgeh of Ejahyay. When Mr. Phillips told her she might have to die for Christ and then asked her if she would be willing to do so, she wept aloud and said, "If it is the Lord's will, I will try to do so." She died early but she remained a consistent Christian to the last.

22

Love Letters

The health of Mr. Phillips so completely failed that he was compelled to leave the country for eight months. During this time all the cares of the mission station again devolved on me.

Among the first problems that faced me after I came to be *bale* was the dissatisfaction of the children, instigated by well-meaning native friends among the women, because they had not been betrothed. According to the usage of their country, most of them had already passed the age for this ceremony and they were becoming impatient. Some had even passed the marriageable age. One day a delegation of converts waited on me and suggested that the matter be attended to at once. Wishing to discourage such long betrothments and such early marriages, I argued them out of the idea and they cheerfully acquiesced. But the young people were not satisfied and proceeded to betroth themselves by a secret correspondence. At that time they could not write in their language, but by the use of cowries, beads, colored strings, pieces of cloth, feathers and other things arranged in certain ways and thrown over the dividing wall, they settled all their love matters to their satisfaction if not to mine. There seemed to be some very decided "cases" among them and I found out that love laughs at mud walls as well as at locksmiths.

The betrothals were consummated several years afterward, but not all the unions proved to be entirely happy. A few of the girls were not included in this affair, because they had been betrothed before coming to the mission, and their friends were not willing that the covenant should be broken. One of these was required to marry a man in Ebaddan. She was one of the brightest and best looking among them and her betrothed husband demanded either his wife or her dowry, and she was compelled to go to be the wife of a man whom she had never seen, and of whose character she knew nothing. She died early. Although deprived of Christian society, she was true to her faith to the last. Another of the girls unfortunately attracted the attention of the powerful Egbar chief, Ogoodookpeh, who took advantage of an anti-

English riot to violently transfer her to his harem. After a few years, she succeeded in escaping to Lagos, leaving a little son in care of its father.

Much interest was added to our daily family worship by the aptness of the children in learning to read in their mother tongue. All who could read gathered around the table in the central room and joined in reading the lesson for that night. Then followed a hymn and a prayer, both in the Yoruban tongue. They all had good voices, some very sweet, and I never think of the evening gathering around the table in the mission house at Abeokuta without a perceptible softening of the heart. Several of the boys are now zealous and effective ministers of the gospel among the people. All of them sooner or later made a profession of Christianity and most of them are useful Christians; but sometimes when I remember the pathetic history of some of them who are dead, there is a suspicion of tears in my eyes.

All of them had to go through many trials of their faith. After I had departed for America, the authorities of Abeokuta broke up the mission stations. Most of the converts and children fled to the coast, but they had been warned of such troubles when they made a profession of Christianity and were not wholly taken by surprise nor at all discouraged in their Christian life.

It was very interesting to watch the conflict between light and darkness in the minds of these Yoruban children, for they still believed in many of the superstitions of their parents long after these superstitions ceased to wield any evil power over them. One night, I heard the girls jeering at a "witch-bird" which was croaking near their dormitory and shouting to the innocent little offender, "Go along, you old witch-bird. We are not afraid of you now. We trust in the white man's God." It was plain that, while they were no longer afraid of it as they had been in the past, they still suspected that it was a real witch or evil spirit.

The smaller children were sometimes prone to pervert our teaching to suit their convenience. Two little boys found themselves greatly tempted to steal and eat a roasted chicken. One of them declared that it would be a sin to do so, but the other pleaded that the white man's God was very merciful and that they would eat the chicken and pray a great deal and God would forgive them. This argument prevailed and they ate the chicken. When it was traced to them, they made a "clean breast" of the whole matter.

The presence of so many children full of life and fun, generally made things about the mission compound quite cheerful. They quarrelled little and entered into their sports with great zest. In the schoolroom, the Sierra Leone teacher used the rod quite freely, but the little victims seemed to think this was the right way to do and seemed to cherish no malice. They could suffer physical pain with more equanimity than mental. To make one dullard study, the teacher had tried the rod in vain. As a last resort I placed on his head a dunce cap. This caused much merriment in the schoolroom, but the poor little fellow, with the tears trickling down his cheeks, sat in speechless humiliation. At last his little sister ran to him and throwing her arms around his neck, spoke words of comfort to him while she wiped the tears from his cheeks with the hanging end of her turban. From that day he was one of the most studious scholars among them.

They were not disposed to be lazy and very cheerfully did whatever was required of them in the way of manual labor or special duties connected with the mission station. We had a call-bell, and all on duty knew their numbers and always promptly and cheerfully responded.

The saintly Ofeekee of Ejahyay memory, being now a widow, took up her abode in the mission compound. She was of much service in looking after the young people, was really the matron of the girls' department, in fact. She was also a thrifty trader and contributed to their support. Mary or Osuntala, also took lodgings in the girls' dormitories when she first came, but she was still young and comely, and she soon had a suitor in a pious Sierra Leone man. She was little inclined to marriage and discouraged him for many months, but her modest shyness only made her lover the more persistent, and one day she asked me with downcast eyes, if I thought she would act wisely in marrying again. I rather encouraged the idea and the union proved to be a very happy one. I will notice in this connection that the relation of our mission station in Abeokuta to the civil power was singularly unique. In Ejahyay, when a ruffian on one occasion pursued our mission children into the station yard, stoning and cursing them, Areh had the offender severely whipped by the *bale* of his compound. But in Abeokuta, the government was such a strange mixture of patriarchal, monarchical and republican that we did not know sometimes to whom to apply for protection. In each of the numerous chiefdoms was an Ogbonee lodge to which everybody but slaves belonged. The presiding officer of each lodge was elected by that lodge and was called an elder. At the death of any chief, the lodge of his chiefdom elected his successor. The chiefs and the elders chose the *Alake* or king, whenever they chose to have such an officer. This action, however, needed to be confirmed by the people assembled in mass meeting on Oro day. Declarations of war which are always made by the chiefs and Ogbonee elders conjointly, are also confirmed by this popular assembly. The chiefs were fond of power, and they always elected a man as *Alake* who let them have their own way in matters of importance.

The *Alake* under whose sway it was my fortune or rather misfortune to live, passed most of his time in playing "warree" (a favorite native game) with the Ogbonee elders and other boon companions and left the administration of justice largely to a favorite slave, a young Foolah, who was almost white. This young man generally decided cases in favor of those who gave him the largest sum of money. It was in vain to appeal from him to the *Alake* or king, for no one could see the king without the consent of this unworthy representative, and he gave his consent only when it suited his convenience.

The government of this *Alake* was a good exponent of his character. He would issue a decree and the town crier would publish it throughout the city, but in a few days the people would entirely ignore it, and the fat, lazy old fellow, who issued it, would go on playing "warree" and dandling his babies and not trouble himself about the matter. Coming from under the vigorous administration of Areh, I found it difficult to feel anything like respect for so weak a ruler. His cowardly character and his general indifference to his duty as a sovereign, came near involving me in a tragedy.

Just before I arrived from Ejahyay, a gigantic American ship-carpenter named West came up from the coast and asked for shelter and work. He claimed that he had been put on shore at Lagos because he was too sick to work. Mr. Phillips believed him and granted his request. He proved to be a consummate hypocrite, also a drunkard and a desperado. Some weeks after his arrival, when my wife was confined to her bed with serious illness, he got crazy drunk and "cleaned out" the native part of the mission premises by chasing everybody he met while holding an open knife in his hand. The frightened girls took refuge in my wife's room.

The presence of so many persons in this room under the circumstances, greatly aggravated her illness and I twice went out to find where the brute was hid. It was so dark that I could not see him until he had crept close to me, and twice I was exposed to his murderous knife. Once he walked by my side the whole length of the piazza threatening to kill me, but by a side leap through a door, I escaped him. At last I found him in such a position that I succeeded in getting all the girls safe into their house. The boys had all fled the compound, one of them narrowly escaping a thrust of West's knife. Mr. Phillips took a seat in my room. I had hardly taken my seat from seeing the girls safe, when I heard the maniac say with a hiss, "If you move, you are a dead man." In another moment, with a loud yell, he leaped through an open window into the middle of my wife's room. He remained standing where he was for a few moments, tearing his clothes and making drunken threats as to what he would do, and then with another yell leaped back through the window again.

Mr. Phillips sent to the *Alake* asking for protection. He replied that he was not the ruler of white men and that Mr. Phillips could do as he pleased with the man. But, fortunately, we were not called on to use desperate measures. The third day, his liquor being exhausted, he became sober enough to apologize for his conduct and left apparently with the intention of doing better in the future.

A few days after this, however, I received a note from him saying that he was coming to kill me, and Mr. Phillips immediately notified some Ejahyay men who happened to be in the compound. West entered the gate on horseback but dismounted and approached the place where I was, in the piazza, with his hand resting on a dirk in his belt. Mr. Phillips detained him a few moments to reason with him while my brave Ejahyay fellows gathered to my right with their weapons in their hands. The ruffian saw his peril and began to tremble. He then beat a hasty retreat, remounted his horse and galloped away. But the old *Alake* drank and dozed and played "warree" and cared for none of these things. I never saw West again. He happened to interfere with the two Liberians who went in search of me during my trouble in the interior, and they gave him the option of dying or leaving the country, and he wisely chose the latter.

23

A Narrow Escape

Although things were pleasant on the whole, serious illness, the rude alarms of war, and many other things often broke suddenly in on the quiet routine of our daily life. Of all our unpleasant experiences in Abeokuta, the most terrible was a Dahomian alarm. It was the settled custom of the king of Dahomey to make an annual excursion with a large army and to take and destroy some town distant from his capital. The very old and the very young were butchered, but any other captives were carried away to be sold as slaves or to be offered in sacrifice to the *manes* of the king's father. In this way many thousands of people miserably perished every year and the name "Dahomee" was associated in the minds of the people of neighboring nations with everything ferocious and terrible.

It was not a mitigating circumstance, that a large corps of the Dahomian army was composed of amazons, for these female warriors were nothing better than human tigers. One of their favorite amusements was to see which of them could first get through a high circle of thorns and kill a helpless prisoner tied to a stake. Though their limbs were shockingly torn by the spikes, they thought it excellent sport. I was also informed that when one of them sneeringly said to another, "You are nothing but a man," only the death of one or the other could settle the difficulty. All that I heard about them tended to convince me that they were past human feeling and that the shedding of human blood was their chief delight.

When the Egbars united with the English in breaking up the slave trade, the Dahomian king came with a large army, including 7,000 amazons, to destroy Abeokuta. They stormed the city with great fury but received a bloody repulse, leaving from eight to ten thousand of their bravest warriors under the walls. From that time until the time of my coming to Abeokuta, the king of Dahomey had been vowing vengeance against the people who had shown that he was not invincible. The amazons especially were eager for revenge. He had entered into an alliance with Ogumulla and had agreed to attack Abeokuta at the same time that the latter attacked Ejahyay, but for some reason this covenant was broken. He came within a hundred miles of Abeokuta with an army the size of which may be imagined by the fact that he had forty amazon generals on his staff. But after destroying another large town he returned to his country to await the next "dry season." That time had now come and the people of Abeokuta were not surprised to learn that a large army had left Abomey and was coming east. Scouts were sent out to watch the movements of the Dahomians while every preparation possible was made for the anticipated assault. After some days the mounted scouts returned and reported that they had gone three days' journey and could find no trace of a Dahomian army.

Supposing that the king had again decided to go in another direction, the people returned to the farms or addressed themselves to their usual business in the city, giving little thought to anything else. The *Alake* had been greatly stirred up at the prospect of danger, but he again gladly returned to his accustomed ease. A feeling of perfect security prevailed everywhere, while the Dahomian host was within a few miles of Abeokuta.

About ten miles west of the city on the road leading toward Dahomey was a town of ten thousand inhabitants named Eshagga. This town was really a part of Abeokuta, many people having homes in both places, living in either as their business required. About four o'clock one afternoon, while sitting in the back piazza of the mission house, I noticed great masses of black smoke boiling up from beneath the western horizon. Soon I heard something which seemed to be a prolonged moan coming from the Eshagga gate of the city about four miles away. This sound increased in volume and pitch, like the roaring of a mighty wind, until it spread left and right all over the city and all around me, and I found that it was a wail of loud lamentation coming from the women and children. Then one of the female converts rushed into the house screaming, "Dahomee! Dahomee!" Her countenance was distorted and her eyes were literally protruding with terror. Rushing out and calling upon all the women and children to stay where they were until I returned, I ran to the great rock in the centre of the town and took a view of the situation.

The whole city was in a tremendous stir and uproar. Thousands were rushing to the walls and thousands of resolute men already lined the walls on the Eshagga side for many miles and the line was made bright by the glitter of weapons in their hands. Along the narrow paths across the extended plain, couriers were riding at full speed calling in the farmers from the fields. I could see no Dahomians and observing that everything was being done that could be done, I returned to the mission house greatly encouraged. Here I was further strengthened by learning that the city was under the military command of Shokanoo, one of the most efficient and warlike chiefs of the nation, and that he would still have at his command a very large proportion of those capable of bearing arms if he could get them all in before the attack. Besides these, the old men and the boys were all rushing to the wall, sword in hand.

It was nearly dark when I got back. I found that all the females and the smaller boys had packed up to flee, but I urged them to remain where they were until God in His providence should show them which way to go, for we did not know from what point the attack would come. To this they finally assented and on their knees awaited the coming assault. My wife remained on her knees most of the night. With so many of God's people praying through the town, I felt fully assured of God's protection.

After leaving instructions that I should be awakened when the firing commenced, I offered a fervent prayer, threw myself on a bed and fell asleep. I awoke about daybreak and learned that the Dahomians had not made their appearance. For some time it was supposed that the wily enemy was hid in the high grass waiting a favorable opportunity to storm the city, but trusted scouts informed Shokanoo about noon that they were certainly gone. They brought in a deserter from the Dahomians who explained how it was that so large an army succeeded in getting so close to Abeokuta without being discovered, and why it was it had returned without taking advantage of so favorable an opportunity to capture the city.

A large forest lies between Dahomey and Eshagga. This man said that the Dahomians had entered this forest in single file at many places and that they had cut their way through it, step by step, until they reached Eshagga. It had taken them a month to do this and, during this time, they were not allowed to make any noise which would distinguish them from the wild denizens of an African forest. If any one forgot himself and spoke in an audible voice, he was instantly slain. Even orders were given in grunts or barks like those of monkeys. In this way they made several miles a day and finally united all their columns just before coming out of the forest at Eshagga. The scouts had followed the ordinary routes or else the secret paths of the hunters and therefore had seen no sign of the presence of hostile forces. They succeeded in getting into Eshagga through a very singular custom of the Yorubans.

When soldiers are going to war, they do not salute any one, and it is a gross insult for any one to salute them. The Dahomians came out on the road between Eshagga and Abeokuta about dark. It almost took my breath away when I learned this; because we were then completely in their power if they had only known it. But the king of Dahomey thought it unwise to leave so strong an enemy in his rear and determined to destroy Eshagga that night and assault Abeokuta next day. When the people sitting at the gate of the former town saw a detachment of the Dahomians hurrying along, they supposed that it was a body of Egbars on their way to the war at Ejahyay; but their customs did not allow them to speak to the soldiers, and they had no way of learning anything about them.

The Dahomians quietly filed into the town and camped in a market-place in the centre. In the meantime, the people of the town felt all the more secure on account of the presence of the soldiers, and retired that night, as we did in Abeokuta, utterly unsuspicious of the sword that was at their throats. During the night the rest of the enemy surrounded the doomed city, the gates were opened and the slaughter began. Excepting a few hundred spared to be offered in sacrifice, everybody but one man perished. This man jumped over the walls but was found and left for dead. Though terribly hacked up, he succeeded in getting to Abeokuta that afternoon and in giving the alarm. But it would have been too late to save the city, if the Dahomians had carried out their original plan. The deserter declared that the king was so well satisfied with the slaughter he had made among the Egbars and was so suspicious that the king of Abeokuta knew of his presence at Eshagga, that he decided to return to Abomey until another season. When he reached this decision, we did not know that there was a Dahomian within a hundred miles of us. God put into his heart to wait until Abeokuta was ready to defend itself. He returned next dry season but there was no surprise this time, and he received a repulse even more bloody than the first.

What a benefit the French conferred on mankind by destroying this cruel power, the following *verbatim* extract from the report of a British naval officer will show. It was made upon the testimony of a German merchant who was forced to remain at the Dahomian capital and witness the bloody scenes which followed the return of the Dahomian army from its murderous expedition to Eshagga. The report was made by the commander of H. M. S. Griffin from Little Popo. The last portion reads as follows:

"Mr. Euschart was next brought to the market-place where he was told many people had been killed the night before. He first saw the body of Mr. Doherty, a missionary and church catechist at Eshagga. The body was crucified against a large tree—one nail being driven through the forehead, another the heart, and one through each hand and foot. He was then taken to the market-place where the king was seated on a raised platform and was talking a great 'war palaver' with the people. He promised them an attack on Abeokuta in November. Cowries, cloth, and rum were then distributed. In front of the market-place there were rows of human heads fresh and gory and the market-place was saturated with blood. The heads belonged to some of the

Eshagga prisoners who had been killed during the night after having been tortured in the most frightful and cruel manner. Mr. Euschart was then ordered to remain quiet in his house and not to look after sundown.

"When the ground shook violently from the earthquake felt at Accra, Mr. Euschart was at once brought to the market-place where he again found the king seated on a raised platform surrounded by amazons. The king told them that the "ground-shaking" was the spirit of his father complaining that the "customs" (bloody rites) were not made properly. Three Eshagga chiefs were then brought before the king who told them that they must go and tell his father that the "customs" would be better than ever. A bottle of rum and a head of cowries were then given to each and they were immediately decapitated. Twenty-four men were then brought out bound in baskets with their heads just showing out and were placed on the platform in front of the king. They were then thrown down to the people who were dancing, singing and yelling below. As each was thrown down, he was seized and beheaded, the heads being piled in one heap and the bodies in another. Every man who caught a victim and cut off his head received one head of cowries.

"Mr. Euschart was then taken to another part of the town where similar horrors were being perpetrated. The next day the platforms were taken down and the programme seemed to be singing, dancing and firing guns. There were no more public sacrifices for ten days, but it is supposed that many took place during the nights. He was then taken to see the "Grand Customs" at the palace of the late king. At the gate of this, two platforms had been erected. On each of these, sixteen men and four horses were placed. Inside the house was another on which were placed sixteen women, four horses and one alligator. The men and women were all Sierra Leone people captured at Eshagga and dressed in European clothing. Each group of men, bound in chains, was seated around a table upon which were placed glasses of rum. The king then ascended the platform and *adored his fétiche* and seemed to make obeisance to the prisoners whose right arms were then loosed that they might drink the king's health. After this, the effects of the late king were paraded and worshipped by the people as they passed. A grand review of the army then commenced. As each company passed, the king harangued them and promised the sack of Abeokuta in November. Nearly the whole of the troops wore firearms. A few select corps had rifles, but the majority had flint locks. The number of the troops altogether could hardly be less than 50,000, including 10,000 amazons.

After the review the prisoners were beheaded, their heads being hacked off with dull knives. At the same time the horses and the alligator were killed, particular care being taken that their blood should mingle with that of the prisoners'. All being over, Mr. Euschart was permitted to leave Abomey after having received as presents, eight heads of cowries, one piece of country cloth and two bottles of rum."

As this letter declared that British subjects had been deliberately murdered by the king of Dahomey it caused much excitement in England. But this part of Mr. Euschart's story was a mistake. The man crucified and those beheaded, while dressed in civilized clothing, were civilized Abeokutans. Mr. Doherty was captured and went through some dreadful experiences, but the king found out that he was a British subject and thought it would be wiser to release him than to have a war with so powerful a nation.

After Doherty's release he told how the king was disgusted with the ten commandments when, at his own peremptory command, they were read to him by his Christian prisoner. The command, "Thou shalt not kill," he seemed to take as a personal affront. Thus he received his first and probably his last message, from his Creator. I afterward saw a wax statue of this king in London. He was seven feet tall, nearly white like a Foolah, and dressed in the uniform of an English general. Doherty said that he was the most godlike man in appearance that he ever saw and that he was not surprised his people worshipped him as a demigod.

He carried out his promise to attack Abeokuta, but so far from sacking the town, he received a defeat from the Bashorun's veterans that greatly weakened his power and made him willing to let the Egbars alone forever afterward. The amazons, however, fought with such fury that they broke the line in one place and scaled the wall. Some of them were found dead in the heart of the town. It was said that none of them turned their backs until a retreat was sounded. One of our mission boys distinguished himself by killing one of these furies in a hand-to-hand fight. He was standard-bearer of the converts and an amazon endeavored to wrest the standard from his hand and kill him with her short sword.

24

The Human Sacrifice

The mourning for the destruction of poor Eshagga had not ceased when Ejahyay fell. For six months after I left, there was no fighting. In the meantime Ogumulla had it circulated among the slave-hunting peoples that Ejahyay would soon fall. Then eager for prey, thousands of recruits joined him from neighboring nations until they formed three great camps, probably numbering 50,000 men in each. The allies could hardly muster one-third of that number, but they continued to make a bold stand until the last day, when the soldiers of both allied armies broke camp and fled leaving the people of Ejahyay to their fate. Aborgoonree, Areh's head slave and by the influence of the Bashorun, his successor, escaped with the Egbar army, but Areh-Argo and other Ejahyay leaders committed suicide. All the leading men among the captured were slain, but the rest of the people were held as slaves to be sold or redeemed. A few escaped to Abeokuta, Illorin and other places friendly to their cause.

Among the captives was my faithful interpreter, John Thomas, who was carried to Ebaddan and held for redemption. He had been assured by the Bashorun that, should the Egbars decide to give up the fight, he would be duly notified of the fact; but for some unexplained reason, he failed to receive this notice. We could get no communication with his captors and, after being kept in irons for three years, he was released. But this mercy came too late to save his life. His nervous system was completely shattered like that of my companion in the Ebaddan adventure, and he soon died and was laid beside that other victim of Ogumulla's cruelty who had lost his life by being true to me in time of need. Both died in the full assurance of faith; and I humbly hope to meet them in heaven. They had wandered from God, but these troubles brought them back again and proved in the end to be a great blessing to them.

The houses and the walls of Ejahyay were broken down and a decree issued that the town should never be rebuilt. There is now a smaller unwalled town outside the forest, but the site of the old town is a feeding ground for wild elephants.

The allies continued to flee until they reached Atadee, fifteen miles from Abeokuta. From this place the Bashorun sent a message to the *Alake* simply saying, "We are coming." The laconic brevity of this language implied a threat and the *Alake* was much frightened. Through my interpreter, I had known that some very unpleasant correspondence had taken place between them before the fall of Ejahyay. The Bashorun even declared that the *Alake* would like to see him and his army captured or killed that the *Alake* and his people might inherit their possessions. I, therefore, felt quite uneasy for several days, but when the army entered the city there was no serious disturbance, neither was there any disposition on the part of the people to criticize the conduct of the Bashorun and his army at the seat of war. The truth is, I never saw on the battlefield braver deeds in any country, than I saw during the siege of Ejahyay. With equal weapons, any people would find Yorubans foeman, worthy of their steel.

But the heroism of their conduct was soon tarnished by one dreadful act—the offering of a human sacrifice to Ogun, the god of war. This horrible deed was as unexpected to us as it was appalling. When the Abeokutans formed an alliance with the English to dethrone Kosoko and to open up the country to legitimate trade, they entered into a treaty to abandon human sacrifices. But war had greatly demoralized them and the priests took advantage of this state of things to persuade them to return to the old ways and to offer up the accustomed sacrifice to the war god, saying his favor would be restored to them and he would crown their arms with victory as he had done in the past. Influenced by this advice, the chiefs and Ogbonee elders decreed that a slave should be purchased in the market and offered up as a sacrifice in a fearfully wild spot near our mission house on the road leading to Ejahyay.

The unusual excitement which suddenly seized the women in the market-place near our house, was the first intimation that we had of what was about to take place. When they heard of the decree and that the victim had arrived at the spot designated, they sprang to their feet with shouts of joy, ran to the spot and engaged in a kind of frantic dance to a wild, glad chant of praise to Ogun. Many of them also addressed prayers to the man asking for some earthly good or sending messages to departed friends. They also cast to him choice articles of food. These the victim ate with apparent relish and seemed to feel honored by the attention shown him.

The women showed a physical endurance and a madness that was really terrible to behold. They seemed to be possessed of the devil and I have not the slightest hesitation in believing that they were. With amazing rapidity, they went round and round encircling the victim until the ground, which had been previously covered with high grass, was as bare as a floor and quite smooth.

The place was partially enclosed by several large boulders, and in the rear of the enclosure thus formed were several others nearly as large as a house. These made narrow, dark alleys leading to little courts. The whole place was as complete a "devil's den" as could be imagined. Previous to this event, I had called it, "Pan's den," but I now changed it to the first name.

While the women were singing, dancing and invoking the victim as a god, as I have already described, the officiating priest placed two upright forks about seven feet high on each side of the entrance and across these laid a pole from which a fringe of palm leaves was suspended. While the maniac dance still continued, the victim was laid on his face and beheaded. The people then dispersed and the head was placed in a fantastically marked earthen pot in one of the little courts in the rear; other offerings were placed in other parts of the den and all was over but the horror of the deed.

I was warned not to go too near while all this was going on, and I did not see any of the ceremonies or hear what was said, but when the people were gone I cautiously entered this infernal temple to see for myself whether it was really true that a human sacrifice had been offered. The headless trunk removed all doubt on the subject. It was some time before some of the English would believe the story. One of them, however, visited the spot with me and took a sketch of the victim's body and of the place. This was sent to England.

While the chiefs and Ogbonee elders and a majority of the people favored this deed, there were very many who did not, but they were powerless to interfere. When the English sent a consul to live among them that they might be kept in mind of their agreement on this subject, they ordered him to leave the place in two hours under penalty of death, and he left at once. This treatment was a defiance to the English, but they did not resent it at that time, and their forbearance on this occasion exalted the Egbars very much in their own estimation, the more because they soon afterward, by the assistance of the Emir of Illorin and of the king of the Ejayboos, forced the Ebaddans to sue for peace. Both Ebekoonleh and Ogumulla seem to have died suddenly on their return to Ebaddan, and the people being left without an efficient head and being cut off both from the coast and from the interior, were soon reduced to great straits, and forced to end the war for the time by asking terms of peace.

25

The Stolen Child

The man who did the most for the military supremacy of the Egbars at this time was an inferior chief named Ogudookpeh, the same who afterward carried away one of the mission girls. He was a giant in stature, and on the battlefield, seemed to know no fear. He was always in front and his bearing was so lion-like that he could hold the men together and induce them to stand when no one else could. He sometimes disdained to retreat until he was left entirely alone.

One of Ogudookpeh's striking peculiarities was that he never smiled. This eccentricity was said to have been caused by an unfortunate event in his early life. To commit suicide in the presence of another is one of the ways the Yorubans have of revenging a gross insult offered to them by that person. This is called "dying on his neck." You cannot frighten a Yoruban quicker in any way than by threatening to "die on his neck," though I was never able to find out the reason for this. Ogudookpeh grossly insulted the wife of one of his young companions and the latter, after reproaching him for his base conduct, committed suicide in his presence. From that day Ogudookpeh was never seen to smile. Remorse seemed to have banished the song entirely out of his life. Yet he did not seem to be incapable of a kind of grim humor.

To help them fight the Dahomians, somebody sent the Egbars a cannon, but no one knew how to fire it. One day, there was a thundering report and a ball came crashing through the houses of the city. Ogudookpeh had succeeded in shooting off the big gun. Fortunately, nothing but a horse was killed, but when the owner demanded damages, Ogudookpeh exclaimed, "Why, you fool, you ought to pay me for knowing how to shoot the gun." Once, this savage humor assumed a very dangerous form. Seizing his bow and quiver he ran out into the streets of his chiefdom and began to shoot at everybody he saw, ordering them back into their houses. The people thought that he was for the time possessed by Oro and that Oro was thus expressing his displeasure. They could more readily believe this because he held an office in the Ogbonee lodge in which he represented the avenging power of Oro and in which his own person was sacred. He could, therefore, do with impunity what others could not.

I was the victim of one of his harmless jokes, and I was the more readily taken in because I supposed that he was incapable of such a trick. He wanted to exchange cowries for coin and he desired to make the bargain in person and not through an agent. He knew that I would not come to him on such business any more than he would come to me, so he resorted to stratagem to bring me to him. Instead of sending a messenger with a staff, he sent a mounted military courier who dashed into the mission yard and in an excited manner shouted that his master wished to see me immediately. Ogudookpeh's very name was a terror to the people, and fearing that some of the inmates of the mission compound had fallen under his displeasure, I hastily mounted and told the courier to lead the way. This he did at full speed, his loose tobe spreading out on each side like wings, and the loose end of his turban band streaming out behind. Thus we went through the city and thus we came to Ogudookpeh's house.

I found him dressed in a silk stove-pipe hat and velvet shocoto, standing outside his gate under the shade of a large tree calmly smoking his pipe. He was a perfect picture of repose and cool impudence. As soon as I saw him I knew that nothing serious was the matter; but I was so relieved that I did not lose my temper and everything passed off very pleasantly.

Another of his peculiarities was that he would not own slaves and made it a capital crime for any of the people of his chiefdom to own them. But he would sell all captives in war to meet the expenses of that war, and in this way was indirectly a slave owner. His vengeful, ferocious temper showed itself once in the murder of his own child. When the mission girl whom he had kidnapped escaped to Lagos, leaving her son to his mercy, he called the child to him and cut off its head with his own hand.

I have always thought he was partially insane, especially as he believed that he would never die. He did seem to bear a charmed life and survived the most of his contemporaries, after having passed through untold perils on the battlefield. He imagined himself a demigod, and that some day he would go up to heaven like Shango.

I would have been afraid of this savage if it had not been that he was subordinate entirely to the Bashorun, and the latter had never failed to show himself a friend whenever I needed his services. The Bashorun was really the supreme ruler of Abeokuta, and the fact that he was known to be my friend saved me from serious oppression by a powerful and very cunning chief named Artumbala, who lived near the mission compound and who claimed to be its protector. Being greatly impoverished by the war, he sent to "borrow" some cowries from me, but I had been reduced to the same condition from the same cause, and was forced to deny his request.

Whenever the government at Abeokuta desired to accomplish something that needed much diplomacy, they generally employed Artumbala to represent them, and he rarely failed to successfully execute his mission. As he supposed that my refusal was caused by covetousness instead of necessity, he at once undertook to get the money out of me by a cunning trick. While he was returning from a council of chiefs with many of his warriors around him, he passed by a place where many of the children of the mission compound were playing. After the company had passed with a great beating of drums and other deafening noises, the mother of a three-year-old boy fell at my feet with loud lamentations, saying that the Egbars had stolen her child. I found out that one of Artumbala's men had taken up the child and had given it into the hands of his chief who had in turn passed it to another, thus authorizing the deed.

It was now clear that the old fox intended either to sell the child or to force me to redeem it with a large sum of money. I had had some acquaintance with him in Ejahyay, and had also learned much about his methods from missionaries in Abeokuta, and this information convinced me that I could not circumvent him by diplomacy. I, therefore, determined to deal with him in a straightforward manner only, for his habits of thought would leave him utterly unsuspicious in that direction.

Taking the weeping mother with me, I went at once to his house. I found him sitting in state with his officers and many of his warriors around him. A large crowd of people were also in the compound evidently awaiting my appearance. The mother fell moaning at his feet and I informed him of the cause of her grief.

"Why do you come to me, white man?" he asked, seemingly in angry surprise.

"Because your men took the child," I replied, sharply.

"How can you prove that my men took this woman's child?" he again asked in a louder tone as if he was getting more angry. The soldiers murmured indignantly. Rising to my feet and looking him sternly in the eye, I emphatically said, "*You* know it, Artumbala, and *I* know it, and that is enough." For a few moments nothing could be heard. The chief pretended to be furiously angry, and the soldiers talked so loudly that everything was utter confusion, but my last reply completely took the old fellow by surprise and was a home shot. Then talking loud enough to be heard above the din, I told the chief that I was going to take all the children to Lagos and tell the English people that Artumbala stole my children and would not let me live in Abeokuta and that he was the enemy of the white man. This was another home shot, for at that time he had become quite famous in England by pretending to be a convert of the Church of England Missionary Society. Having said this, I hurriedly left the compound with the howls of the people following me.

I found great consternation in the mission yard. Everybody was looking for Artumbala's men to come and destroy the mission house and seize all the Ejahyay people as slaves. I had hardly quieted them when Artumbala's messenger came in a trot and said the child was there, but it had been taken by Ogudookpeh's men and that Artumbala was afraid to give it up until I sent the price of the child to Ogudookpeh, for if the latter should get angry with me, he would come and kill everybody in the compound. I then threatened to take the whole case before the Bashorun. The messenger immediately returned from Artumbala and said that I must not take the matter before the Bashorun, that he did not want to see me get into trouble and that he himself would satisfy Ogudookpeh's men, and that if I would come down he would give me the child. I took the mother and went. The crowd was still there but very silent. The mother threw herself at the feet of the chief in mute supplication. In another moment he took the child from some one behind him and handed it to me and I placed it in the arms of the mother. She received it with many expressions of joy and of thanks, and hurried away. I also thanked the chief but I did not give him a cowry.

When I came out next morning, I learned that Artumbala had come with some of his men early that morning and gone to the chapel and passed several moments on his knees and then had gone away without saying anything to anybody. I suppose that he intended this to be a kind of dignified apology to me and also to assure the converts that he meant them no harm.

About noon while I was walking the piazza, he entered the gate with some attendants and, coming into the piazza, threw one of his arms across my shoulder and walked up and down with me for sometime, talking about the hard time he was having on account of the war, his friendship for the white people who had lived in that house, and the way he had protected them in all their troubles. He then hinted that some return for all this kindness on his part would be proper and acceptable. On this new tack, the wily old diplomat completely captured me, and if it had been in my power, I would have given him anything in reason. But I had nothing to lend or give away without taking the bread out of the children's mouths, and when I succeeded in convincing him of this fact, he went away seemingly satisfied.

A short time after this, however, the old fox made me feel his displeasure in a case of litigation before him. One of the converts was guardian for his little niece and, with the mother's consent, gave me the child to educate. I did not accept the trust until the guarantees were given which the native law provides, that the child would remain in the mission school until she had reached a certain age. In the presence of the mother and other witnesses, the uncle placed the hand of the child in mine and formally delegated to me all the rights of a guardian.

This arrangement was very satisfactory both to the mother and her brother, until the mother married a Mussulman. The stepfather insisted that the child should be brought up in the faith of Islam, and persuaded the mother to demand its return. I felt that it would be a sin to return the child under the circumstances, and refused to comply with the demand, telling her that she could come to see her daughter whenever it suited her convenience, but that it must remain in school according to the contract.

The Mussulman then sued me before Artumbala for the possession of the child. He presented his side of the case first and, if there was a single fact in any of his statements, that fact entirely eluded my observation. When my turn came, ignoring the falsehoods of the plaintiff, I made a plain statement of the facts of the case. Knowing that I could prove what I had said, the plaintiff tried to circumvent me by asking if the laws of my country would allow me to act as I was doing in this controversy. To this I replied, "I am not before a court of my country, and I am not being judged by its laws. I am in your country and I am being judged by its laws. Do you despise your own chief and the laws of your own country?" This unexpected reply filled the lying fellow with confusion and he fell on his face before Artumbala and cried out, "No, no I honor my chief and the laws of my country." The chief laughed heartily at the man's discomfiture and pleasantly told me I could go, for I was right in the matter. A few days after this, the mother came early one morning and took the child away without my knowledge or consent. I knew that she would not have dared to do this without the consent of Artumbala, and I let the matter drop. The Mussulman had probably given him a sum equal to the redemption price of the child and then been permitted to kidnap it with impunity.

26

Improvements

At the end of my second year in Abeokuta, most of the young people in the school could read in their mother tongue and had taken a course of study as far as its translated literature permitted. The Bible, of course, was their principal text-book and they knew more of this book than many children of enlightened parents in so-called Christian lands; for it is a sad truth that while there is much show of studying and teaching them among us, comparatively few outside the ministry and those who have been specially trained as Christian workers, have anything like a complete and systematic knowledge of the Holy Scriptures.

Even when used as a text-book in schools, the Bible is often more valued as a treasury of ancient literature than as a source of religious light. It would be a good thing for some highly educated young people if they were so placed for a year or two that they would have nothing else to read but that Book of books. Not only on the subject of true religion but on many other subjects, they would have broader and more enlightened views, and would not be so quickly infatuated with all sorts of fanciful notions and vagaries current among many of the cultured in enlightened countries.

It is one of the merited punishments inflicted on those who allow science, literature and the news of the day to make them neglect the Bible, that they are left to grope in spiritual darkness, to believe the most absurd things, and, in all sorts of ways, to make fools of themselves until even those who have emerged from paganism regard them with amazement, if not with contempt.

But the Bible was not by any means the only text-book when they had learned sufficient English to take up a course of study in that language. As the English spoken by the average Sierra Leone people at that time was "pigeon English," I much preferred to hear their own musical language and did not encourage them to speak a mutilated form of my own. It was quite ridiculous when they first began to adopt the dress and manners of the white man in preference to those of their own people. In full dress, they always wore creaking shoes, and the more racket these made, the better they liked them. Utterly worthless was the shoe that had no "cracklin." A note from a Sierra Leone man at Lagos to one of our boys, who had bought a pair of shoes from him, contained this sentence, "You say shoe no good because it have no cracklin, but I am thankful that I have the honor to say that shoe have much cracklin." To this I was able to testify, for whenever he put them on, the "cracklin" loudly proclaimed his approach.

This strange fancy obtained even among educated Sierra Leone teachers and I suppose our boys got it from them. Our teacher was really a very intelligent and worthy man, but he had a finished Xantippe in his wife. She was young and comely but had many of the mental and moral characteristics of a heathen concealed by a rather thin veneering of European civilization. She seemed to take pleasure in worrying her husband because he could not punish her as the heathen men punished their wives. After frequently reprimanding the teacher for tardiness, I found that he had been detained by the childish perverseness of his wife, even though she knew he was in danger of losing his position by such neglect of duty. One Sunday morning, when he was in a great hurry to get ready for Sunday-school, she sat down on his clothes and refused to allow him to have them, so that he might be late and get another reprimand. She held in her hand a switch used in driving goats out of the house, and tauntingly invited him to whip her. To her amazement and rage, he accepted her invitation. Her cries brought the other women of the compound to her rescue, and they brought her to me to complain how badly she had been treated. The poor teacher came also to apologize for giving away to his temper and acting in such an unmanly way.

For the sake of Christian civilization, I affected to be quite indignant, but in my heart there was much sympathy for the poor husband who had been so dreadfully humiliated while trying to do his duty for her sake. This incident convinced me that there can be nothing like Christian homes in Yoruba until native ideas of home life have been thoroughly eradicated from the minds of the girls, and been replaced by those inculcated in Christian teaching.

Having passed through a severe acclimation during the first two years, I did not have fever so often as I did in Ejahyay. Once only was I very ill, and was greatly pleased to hear that during the critical period of my sickness, the converts had spontaneously assembled in the chapel and prayed for my recovery. My wife was twice brought to the brink of the grave, and if we had not had the services of an experienced English physician, I think she would have died. The grief and anxiety of the people and the school children were very pathetic and were only equalled by their joy when she began to recover. They sincerely appreciated her self-denial in living among them and in sharing their sorrows as well as their joys.

The strain on her nervous system by these two attacks and by the incidents of our last year's life in Ejahyay, greatly weakened her constitution and, at the end of our second year in Abeokuta and of our fourth in the interior, Mr. Phillips having returned from England, I determined to return for a while to America. While preparing to leave, I heard that marauders, taking advantage of the disturbed state of the country, had appeared on the Ogun river and were robbing canoes and maltreating those found in them, even selling some for slaves. Especially on account of my wife, this news was naturally very disturbing. Besides, I had agreed to take the two children of Enigbio to Lagos. In leaving Africa, I did not want to undo any good I might have done if it was possible to avoid so great a misfortune, and I hesitated to place myself in a position in which common humanity might force me to resort to deadly weapons.

My first thought was to apply to the Bashorun for an armed escort, but when I came to consider the moral effect such an application might possibly have, I decided not to do so, but to go on trusting in God alone, as Ezra did under like circumstances, using only such instrumentalities as Christian prudence should suggest and God in His providence should seem to appoint. After having taught these dark-minded people for four years to trust in our God alone, it did not seem to be the right thing to act as if I myself did not believe in Him; and our trip down the river was attended by some special providences so remarkable that the memory of them has been a source of spiritual strength to me ever since.

27

Cast Among Robbers

One bright morning in November, after an affecting parting with the converts and children, we came to the bank of the Ogun on our way to America. It was now the end of the rainy season and the river was wide, deep and swift, and presented an appalling scene. In addition to the two canoemen and my wife, I had in our dugout a young native convert to act as interpreter and messenger and the two native children previously mentioned. Besides the necessary provisions, I took some presents for the marauders including a large box of brown sugar. This, I placed by my side in the prow of the canoe, and under the blanket on which I sat, I placed my gun. I had found that a very good way to prevent violence among these people is to show that we are ready for it. Peace is promoted among them, as it is among nations more civilized, by an exhibition of superior or at least equal strength.

During the first forenoon, I do not remember seeing anything of special interest. I was surprised to hear that a dead manatee was lying on the bank at one place. I suppose it had come up from Lagos and been entrapped by some fisherman. Early in the afternoon, I learned that we had come to the border of the district infested by the robbers and it was decided to stop until next day; for if we went on, we would have either to camp in the dangerous district or to travel in the night, and on account of the darkness and floating trees, the latter would be as dangerous as the former.

Too keenly alive to the responsibility I had taken on myself to sleep much that night, I often and fervently prayed for guidance and protection during the coming day. All the forenoon of next day, I sat in the prow of my canoe watching right and left for some sign of the enemy. As we came around a bend of the river about noon, my heart gave a jump at the sight of an armed sentinel standing on a bluff overhanging the river. I knew we had met them at last. They had a number of canoes and were prepared to pursue us if we attempted to escape, so I ordered my men to steer directly for the spot and show them that we intended to surrender. As we approached my wife securely hid the children.

As soon as the prow of our canoe touched the bank, the sentinel gruffly ordered us to come ashore. I lifted my wife from the canoe, we ascended the bank, took a seat on a log and awaited the issue. The countenance and manner of the sentinel were anything else than reassuring and nobody else had yet appeared. Presently the leader and some of his men came out of the bushes. I was greatly puzzled to observe that the former seemed to be much embarrassed. Then I recognized in him a former officer in the Ejahyay army. He expressed much pleasure that I had not attempted to pass without stopping, saying that if I had done so his men would have fired on us. He then told me that I must give his men something to satisfy them. This was very manifest, for they had begun to grumble and to scowl very ominously when they saw how friendly their leader was to me. I got my messenger to bring them a large quantity of sugar and this seemed to thoroughly sweeten their tempers.

In the beginning of our conversation, the leader had shown a scar on his arm marking a place from which I had taken a bullet; and now to show his appreciation, he offered me some chickens and some rum. The latter, much to the dissatisfaction of the canoemen, was declined but I gladly accepted the poultry. He then gave me a feather upon which he had strung three cowries, saying that there was another band down the river, but when the chief saw the feather and cowries he would allow me to pass without trouble.

We parted quite pleasantly, shouting salutations to each other as long as we were in hearing. Shouts and yells down the river, about an hour afterward, told us that we were approaching the other company. In a few moments more our eyes were greeted by a perfect pandemonium. In a large clearing on the bank of the river were scores of half-naked men running about, dancing, leaping, yelling and utterly crazed by alcohol. Although the spectacle was so appalling, I thought it best to go straight for them. At first they regarded us with drunken surprise, then began to clamber into the canoe.

While the messenger was gone to deliver the symbolical letter to their leader whose tent was near the bank, I was occupied in trying to keep them out of the canoe where my wife and the two children were. They were beginning to get angry, and it looked as if a display of violence was imminent, when a man leaped from the bank into the canoe, seized my hand and shook it with drunken hilarity, making, at the same time, many protestations of friendship. He then told the men trying to get into the canoe that they would touch me at their peril. He showed me the place on his wrist from which I had taken a bone after the defeat of the Egbars in Ejahyay, and was telling me about his troubles since that time, when their chief suddenly appeared among them, rod in hand, and struck right and left over their naked shoulders, storming at the same time, "Don't you see me? Don't you see me?" My friend fled with the rest, but I was now safe. Again "man's extremity had been God's opportunity," for I was becoming desperate and was about to resort to something violent when the Ejahyay soldier appeared and helped to restrain the crazy mob.

Having dispersed, for the moment, his drunken followers, the chief excitedly shouted to me that the message was all right and then urged me to hurry away as quickly as possible. Even after the canoe had gotten some distance from the bank, a crowd ran down to the river and demanded all sorts of things from us. When the uproar had ceased, the children showed their perspiring but happy faces. It had been a severe ordeal to them, for if their presence had been discovered by the robbers, nothing but a fight could have saved them. They had not only been greatly frightened, but had nearly smothered themselves in trying to hide.

It was not long before they had to crawl back to cover, for we saw men with guns running along the bank of the river in the edge of the forest. They were evidently hastening to reach a point where the swift current would carry us close to land, but when we swept past this place, we neither saw nor heard anything of them again. But I would not like to say how fast my heart beat, as we darted by the dangerous point. What they were after, I never found out. It was another unsolved mystery like the incident in the Ebaddan forest at Lahlookpon.

About sundown we came to a little village inhabited by a people called the Parraquoi. Thinking that we were now out of the dangerous district, I stopped here to salute the chief and to request permission to pass the night at his town. The landing-place was a strip of cleared ground and to the right was a very tall bluff on which the village was situated. I sent my messenger up to this village to call the chief, and while I was waiting for him, a man in a soldier's dress came out of the forest and dipped up a bucket of water. While doing this he closely inspected the canoe and then sullenly returned without paying the slightest attention to my courteous salutation. This silence was a declaration of war.

While impatiently awaiting the return of my messenger, I noticed other men moving about behind the bushes and I also saw guns. It was now clear that we had been drawn into an ambush, and the robbers were waiting to see what we were going to do before making an attack upon us. When the chief of the Parraquoi came down, I saw that he was excited and disturbed, and I merely paid my respects to him and requested permission to go in peace. He laid his staff on my shoulder and solemnly bid me go in peace. Poor old man! Those kind words were his death warrant. So soon as he had spoken, the robbers rushed altogether from their covering and dragged the canoe with us in it, out upon the bank. Then there was a fierce hand-to-hand struggle for the mastery between the followers of the chief and the band of robbers who acted in concert but did not seem to have any leader. They fought with clubs mostly, but the din was so deafening, I could give no orders to my own men.

After a brief struggle the Parraquoi got between us and our enemies, and with the assistance of the canoemen pushed our canoe back into the water. I could not hear what anybody said, but as we were hastening away, I saw one of the canoemen gesticulating to me and pointing toward the bank. I turned and found that a number of the robbers were aiming their guns at me and I heard one of them say, "Duro, awa yin ebon si nyin." (Stop, or we will shoot you.) Resistance being useless, I held up my hand in token of surrender. Just here, when I could see no way of escape, God sent us a deliverance as strange as it was sudden. Before the prow of the canoe touched the bank, some of the Parraquoi women, who had been watching the fight from the top of the bluff, ran pell-mell down the steep descent and seized the guns in the hands of the robbers, while others above besought us, both by words and gestures, to hurry away. The men whirled the women through the air, round and round, and even thrashed them against the ground, but could not break their hold. So plucky were they that my wife seemed to forget her fears in admiration of their courage and cried out, "Look at the women! Look at the women!"

While the men were cursing and yelling, because they could not release their guns, and the other robbers were kept back from the river by the Parraquoi men, I took the advice of the women above us and escaped. The brawling continued as long as we were in hearing, being sometimes emphasized by the report of guns. We seemed to be pursued for a while, but I did not see any one, only heard a call behind us. I do not know how many were hurt, but I learned from the missionary at Abeokuta that the chief of the Parraquoi was killed.

The sun had already gone down when we escaped, and soon it was intensely dark. To guard against floating obstructions, as great trees, I stretched myself, with hands extended, on the prow of the canoe. We met with no accident during the remainder of the night, but the hideous bellowings of great crocodiles in the inky blackness greatly disturbed my already nervous wife. Several times we saw lights and heard voices on shore, but we went swiftly and silently by without getting again into trouble. Hearing the nine o'clock gun at Lagos, we knew we were in the boundaries of the English "protectorate" at that time, and we felt secure enough to stop and wait until the moon rose.

Next morning, just as the sun rose in all its tropical splendor, worn out but happy and thankful, we came out of the mouth of the Ogun into the broad and beautiful lagoon upon which Lagos is situated. During our stay in the interior this town had become an English colony and, materially, had greatly changed. This revolution, together with changes physical, mental and spiritual, which had taken place in myself during the eventful four years of my residence away from civilization, made me feel as if I had been absent a long time—almost a lifetime. After enjoying the hospitality of the missionaries and the governor of Lagos, we took the mail steamer for Liverpool, crossing the raging bar in a little tugboat. This was a very pleasant change from the old canoe or surf boat, for the bar at Lagos in the rainy season is the most terrible landing-place I ever saw. Early in the morning, at times, the roar of the surf on the beach sounds like the booming of cannon.

28

The Colony of Lagos

Leaving my wife in America to follow when her health would permit, I returned alone to Lagos; but here I learned that, on account of a difficulty with the governor of Lagos, the Bashorun of Abeokuta, instigated by Shookanoo, who cordially hated the whites and was a counterpart of Ogumulla, had broken up the mission stations and that all our people who could get away with Mr. Phillips, were then in Lagos.

For two years, I waited for an opportunity to get back to Abeokuta, but was never permitted to see the place again, a serious illness compelling me to return, at the end of that time, to America. Before bidding adieu to the reader, I will say something of my life in this now beautiful town and of the present state of things in this part of Western Africa.

When I returned from America, things were on a "boom" in Lagos, and comfortable dwellings could not be rented for any price and, after living for a while in the elegant dwelling of the absent negro postmaster, I was forced to take up my residence in the original mud hut of the American Baptist Mission. In this house I learned more of the *fauna* of this part of the coast in two years than I could now learn in many years if I were occupying the elegant brick residence which is now home of the Baptist missionary. The house was a good illustration of the kind of houses occupied by pioneer missionaries in this part of Africa. The ceiling was like that of native houses—palm poles covered with mats and with earth. The floor was made of boards from split logs. The walls were of *adobe* and the windows were holes in the walls closed by shutters made of split boards. The house had become old and the ceiling was either gone in some of the rooms or had been replaced by loose palm poles through which the lizards roosting up there frequently fell into the sleeping-room at night and got up a great "rumpus." One night I heard something fall, and not hearing the usual scuffling which followed such a mishap to one of my saurian pets, I lighted a candle and investigated. I found that it was a species of centipede. The legs were large and far apart; it was about a foot long and had a long, sharp spike at the end of its tail. When I pinned it to the wall with a sword cane, it proved to be very tenacious of life and struck right and left in a most savage manner. The natives say that its spike is very poisonous, and I felt very thankful that I did not get it into my foot.

The ordinary species of centipede is very numerous in the sands of the streets, and are so sociable that I frequently, on retiring at night, found one snugly ensconced between the white sheets. Rats and snakes contested for empire under the floors, and as the last were full of holes, the rats spent much of their time in the rooms of the house, even contesting with me for the food on the table. One bold marauder took bread from the table while I was eating. The snakes were often large, but I could not learn much about them. The natives were much afraid of them, but I did not hear of a single instance in which any one was killed by a snake, though I heard of one instance in which a white man was nearly frightened to death by one.

There were many varieties of ants and beetles, some of the last being not only of great size but of wonderful beauty. The large lizards (of which mention has already been made) had the freedom of the house. To keep them out was too much trouble and they were useful in destroying the young of the centipedes. More than a hundred slept on the loose bamboo poles over my bed.

In a field back of the house were many ant-palaces, some of them seven or eight feet high, and it often afforded me most pleasant recreation to study their wonderful structure. While wandering about among them, I sometimes came upon amphibious saurians three feet long whose mad rush for the water made me perform some extraordinary gymnastic feats. At night, large bats, about the size of rats, would flit through the trees around my shanty. At a distance they appeared to be hawks.

But my circumstances were forgotten in the pleasant social intercourse, not only with the English missionaries, but with educated natives among whom I had valued acquaintances. One of these last, was Bishop Samuel Crowther. In my last desperate illness which compelled me to give up my work among the people of Africa, the last voice of prayer at my bedside was that of this devoted servant of God as he pleaded for my restoration to health.

The history of Mrs. Davis, another native acquaintance, was almost as remarkable as that of Crowther. When a little girl, she had been sent as a present to the Queen of England by the bloody King of Dahomey. The queen felt the responsibility and gave the young slave girl the best education her kingdom afforded for girls, and the accomplishments of the young captive were quite marked. She was a musician, poetess, linguist and brilliant conversationalist. At her marriage with a wealthy native merchant, the queen thought fit to be present, and the bride was given away by the Duke of Cambridge, her representative. Like Crowther, she was jet black and had the tribal and family marks deeply cut into her face. Educated Yorubans have greatly multiplied since then, but the history of these two is quite sufficient to show that there are great possibilities before the Yoruban race.

The civilization of Lagos, however, can be of little use to Yorubans so long as its influence is counteracted by the rum trade. It is to be regretted that this is not discouraged, at least, by the authorities at Lagos. On account of the revenue which it brings in, they are said to rather encourage it.

Mussulmans, especially Haussas, are greatly favored by the Lagos authorities. About fifteen millions of people speak the Haussa language and a professorship in it has been established in Cambridge University. This gentleman is said to prophesy that English, Arabic, Suaheelee and Haussa will, in course of time, be the only languages generally spoken in Africa. I hope, however, it will be a long time before any other supersedes the musical Yoruban tongue.

The Haussas make excellent, dashing soldiers, and are the chief reliance of the English in their wars with the natives in this part of the continent. They are the Sepoys of Africa.

The favor shown the Haussas has drawn Moslems of other nationalities to Lagos and, out of a population of nearly one hundred thousand, they probably constitute one-half. The shrill cry of the muezzin and the loud prayers of the priests, which literally pierce the skies, never fail to break the stillness of the early morning.

Pagan rulers sometimes get Moslem priests to pray for them. The prayers offered up by the priest of the Bashorun in the camp at Ejahyay, could be heard all over the city. This shows that religion among these people is often a strange mixture of paganism and Mohammedanism. Yet I had little success in my labors among Mohammedans because they regarded me as an idolater. For this reason my time, while in Lagos, was chiefly occupied in training the refugees from Abeokuta and in laboring among the heathen population. Among the refugees, we had some very interesting converts who have since become successful missionaries to their people. Among these is Moses Ladejo Stone who was one of the children at the Abeokuta orphanage previously mentioned. He now has charge of the Baptist station at Lagos and is an able preacher and consecrated Christian.

The English, after some bloody conflicts with the Egbars and other Yorubans, have obtained political control of this part of Africa, establishing a kind of autonomy except in the case of Abeokuta. That town is still independent through treaty rights, but doubtless will not remain so very long. This supremacy of the English gives to the missionaries of that nation, especially the clergy of the Church of England, a great advantage over those of America; but the work of the missionaries of the Southern Baptist Convention has been attended by marked success. For Rev. C. E. Smith and Rev. W. T. Lumbley and their native co-laborers and any others who may yet follow them, we hope our Christian readers will often think to pray.

This part of Africa being now "pacified," foreign enterprise and capital will soon open it up to commerce. The English have already commenced a railroad which is intended to connect Lagos with the Niger, passing through Abeokuta, Ebaddan, Ogbomishaw and Illorin. In a few years, this wonderful innovation will probably be completed.

The author may not be permitted to travel on that road, but so long as he lives, he will often in imagination revisit the scenes so hallowed by precious memories. It is humbly hoped that this simple but true story of life among those who dwell in pagan darkness, may lead some reader to carry to their dark souls the light of the true knowledge of God.

THE END

Transcription of Original Sources

[Editor's Note: The text of Stone's book is faithfully transcribed from the 1899 edition originally published by Fleming H. Revell Company, New York. The following correspondences of Stone have been taken from original sources. The Journal is housed at The Virginia Historical Society at the University of Richmond and the Letters and Missionary Papers are housed at The International Mission Board, Southern Baptist Convention, Richmond, Virginia. The transcription of the work is as close and accurate to the original as possible].

JOURNAL OF REV. R. H. STONE: 1858–1859

The Voyage

Left Brother William Crane's of Baltimore today [November 4, 1858] and came down to the wharf in a hack in company with Brother James, Seth Taylor, and my wife. There we found a steamer which brought us with the other passengers to the Caroline Stevens which had dropped down the stream about two miles below Fort Henry. Arrived safely along the side of her, and passengers and baggage were soon transferred; the gentlemen climbed up the side of the ship holding a rope in each hand while the ladies were drawn up by a pulley attached to a chain. After the confusion of arranging baggage was over, religious services were held on deck. They were opened by singing "On Greenland's Icy Mountains," followed by prayer and "How Blessed is the Tie That Binds." The services were closed by a short and impressive address and an effective prayer by two of the Baltimore ministerials and were rendered doubly impressive by the surrounding scenes and incidents. Steamers were rushing to and fro around us while ships and schooners under full sail dotted the waters as far as the eye could see. We lay opposite Ft. McHenry from which blood red streams of fire spouted piercing columns of silvery smoke as cannon balls threw up great columns of water and danced along the surface. The voices singing "From Greenland's Icy Mountain" sounded discordant.

We have immigrants on board bound for [page torn-top next page says:] in this life we sometimes tremble for fear that we have not been called of the Lord without whose blessing all is vain. But a review of all the circumstances, which have caused us to go convince us again that it is a temptation of the devil. May the Lord lay us out for purposes of His own glory and sanctify us with every grace which will qualify us for the work.

November 5, 1858. Weighed anchor this morning and was towed down into the bay, a distance of eighteen miles. There was something cheering in the merry chorus of the sailors as they drew up the ponderous mass of iron. At twelve the steamer left and then the canvass was spread and the ship set sail, we are now several miles below Annapolis whose tall spires are in sight during the day. We passed down the bay this evening at the rate of seven knots an hour, but are now at anchor. Besides our daily religious exercises in the morning and evenings, we have made arrangements with the captain, who is said to be a Catholic, to have an hour's prayer meeting at four o'clock. We held one this evening apparently to the enjoyment of all. I think we have a goodly company of fellow passengers; there are ten missionaries besides ourselves, six gentlemen and four ladies, one of whom, Miss Kilpatrick, is single. We are having a most agreeable time on board. May the Lord who knows our wants bless our association to our mutual spiritual good and to a better qualification for the work to which he has called us. The missionaries are respectably sustained by the bureaus of missionary associations, Protestant Episcopal Board, New York, and the Methodist E Board.

Sunday, November 14, 1858. My poor journal has been lying a neglected book for nine days owing to seasickness. Mrs. Stone and myself have been sick nearly the whole time, and how dreadful it is. Sue is yet confined to her birth but much convalescent. We bid adieu to the shores of America on Sunday the seventh, and since that time excepting the two first days, we have had squalls every day and a rough sea all the time. Those who have not been to sea before have had a most uncomfortable time. Seasickness has come in some instances amongst the ladies to an alarming extent. The ship sometimes rolls dreadfully. We have spent some most disagreeable nights in our births; moveable things have been dashed about quite promiscuously, making at times quite a jingling and rattling discord. On Wednesday the tenth, directly after a squall, a waterspout was formed near us and considerable alarm was felt as it was to the windward and was approaching the ship. The captain loaded a gun to fire into it but it broke up in about thirty minutes. Thursday, November the eleventh a death occurred in the steerage in the person of an infant of one of the immigrants to Liberia.

Her little remains were committed to the mighty deep in the evening of the same day.

We have kept the regularly appointed religious exercises during the whole time though once or twice they have been thinly attended. We have had preaching, singing, and praying, and caring on both Sabbaths during the passage. Messieurs Seys and White officiated the first Sabbath, and Bishop Burns and myself the next. I neglected to mention the names of the missionaries on the boat. They are Messieurs Rambo, Messenger, and Hubbard with their wives, Episcopal missionaries; Miss Kilpatrick and Bishop Burns for the Monrovia Methodist Mission. Bishop Burns is a colored man and has been head of his mission for many years. He is a cultivated and good man and has lately been ordained in Ohio. There are also Messieurs White and Miles for the Mendi missions, Presbyterian and Congregationalists, respectively. The Reverend John Seys goes out with us as the U.S. Agent. The last three gentlemen have left their wives behind. Judge James of Liberia, a pious cultivated man, and a colored doctor with his wife are among the cabin passengers. The sea has been very rough today and several short squalls have occurred. Last night the moon shown brightly and the view on deck was surpassingly beautiful. A few days ago, the captain shot a chicken hawk from the deck when we were six hundred miles to the nearest land. He fired several times in vain but again and again the poor bird returned with weary wing to rest upon the ship merely to have the death barrel leveled at her life. A storm must have blown her out in the ocean untill it lost its course. We are today in about Lat. 28″.10′.

Monday, November 15, 1858. The sea rather smoother today. Directly after morning prayers were over, the startling cries of, "man overboard!" rang through the ship. The deck was soon crowded. The poor sailor was about a hundred yards from the ship swimming the great billows which were bearing him rapidly away. The sails were loosened, the boat was let down and oared by six hardy seamen, and it was soon riding on the billows in pursuit of the drowning man. He was at last picked up about a mile to the windward. When the joyful news was announced by those aloft, "Thank God!" burst from the lips of nearly everyone present. I am too sick to relate all the particulars. While I attended this incident, an experienced voyager remarked that it was the most thrilling one that ever came under his notice. May God sanctify it to the spiritual good of the other seamen. For his salvation we are now earnestly praying and laboring.

Tuesday, November 16, 1858. Very pleasant on deck this morning on which most of us were engaged in instructive and amusing games. They were introduced and led principally by Brother Seys, a remarkable missionary who knows how to be cheerful as well as grave. He is one of the

Methodist connections and is very affectionate, edifying, and pleasant in his conversation. Have a slight headache this morning. Sue quite seasick but was able to go out on deck this morning. May God sanctify her afflictions to her spiritual good and a better preparation for the work to which He has called her. She enjoys her religion more than she ever did, she says. A stiff gale is now blowing and we are going at the rate of at least ten knots per hour. Lat. 33".03' Long. 51." 31'.

Wednesday, November 17, 1858. Went very rapidly all night last night. Slept in the cabin on account of unpleasant smell of bilge water from my birth which is the upper one. Rested well. Felt well all day but a little seasick tonight. Sue has been able to go up on deck but has been quite sick all day. Her food will not digest for nausea. We are now in Lat. 33." 28' Long. 47."1'. Have been going at the rate of twelve knots this evening. Made 220 miles from twelve o'clock yesterday to twelve o'clock today. Sea quite high. Waves sometimes break in the ship and give some merriment by ducking same. Tremendous billow struck the ship tonight and broke over it which made considerable fright and commotion. We had a very interesting meeting this evening. Some interest is found among the sailors in answers to our prayers. The carpenter, a Catholic, desires an interest in our petitions at the throne of grace. A sick sailor is much concerned for his soul. He is visited and prayed with. I had a conversation with a Catholic sailor in which I endeavored to impress upon his mind the necessity of prayer (the necessity of a change of heart). God bless him and bring him to a knowledge of the truth as it is in Jesus Christ. Had also a conversation with the mate, who is Swede, on deck—a beautiful moonlight night and endeavored to impress divine truth with illustrations from surrounding objects. May the Lord make me the humble and prayerful instrument of doing some good to these poor sailors.

Thursday, November 18, 1858. Today Lat. 32." 32' Long. 42." 20'. Have felt unusually well. Sue is nearly well and very cheerful. Nothing extraordinary has occurred today. We spent our time variously in walking the dek, inventing games, talking, reading, writing, and in anything by which we might advance the spiritual good of the unconverted around us. The sick sailor mentioned yesterday is experienced on the subject of religion and has expressed a resolution to endeavor to serve God. Saw much seaweed floating. Some was taken and was very curious and beautiful in its structure. It decomposes out of water after a short exposure. Went very rapidly this morning but the wind has slacked off very much now. Close my journal today by expressing my unfound gratitude to God in restoring the health of not only myself and my wife but of all the other passengers.

Friday, November 19, 1858. North Lat. 31." 21' West Long. 40." 2'. Felt much better this morning. Sue's health much improved. Spent one hour after breakfast in reading and discussing the Psalms. We have agreed to do this daily taking them in order until we get through then read some other portions of the Bible in similar manner. We do this separately from our private reading. Spent most of the morning in reading Liberia As I Found It by the Reverend Alex Cowan of Kentucky. I found it very interesting because it described to the mind minute details. Two sails were in sight early this morning. Both were bound southward. Our course being E.S. East North Lat. 29."30′ Long. 31." 23′ West. We are now going Southeast and expect to fall in with the trade winds in a day or two. We had a formal discussion tonight after tea. The Reverend John Rambo in the chair, Mr. Messenger as secretary. Subject: "What prominence should schools take in Protestant missions?" It was quite edifying to myself and apparently interesting to all. We expect to have another next Friday evening with the subject "Should Polygamists be Admitted into the Church?" It is now nine o'clock p.m. and I have just returned from on deck. The moonlight is surpassingly beautiful. The moon shines brightly and we are going at the rate of eleven miles an hour. How proudly and defiantly does our noble ship dash through the foaming deep.

Saturday, November 20, 1858. Very little breeze early this morning though tonight there's a facsimile. It is now nine o'clock p.m. and having to defer our usual prayer meeting, we have just closed it. We had quite a warm time, and I felt greatly in need of grace as I have done all day and requested the brethren to join me in prayer for an especial out-pouring of the Holy Spirit that we might be filled with zeal and love and be sanctified for tomorrow's service. This was followed by a brief and effective message by Brother Burns relative to his early life and Christian experience which caused the tears to flow freely all around. The deep feeling continued, until after rejoicing over our hope and the work we were engaged in, and singing a doxology, we broke up. Attended the prayer meeting in the steerage this evening. The interest among the steerage passengers has considerably increased. Addressed a meeting, with other brethren. The sick sailor in the steerage says that he loves the Lord Jesus Christ, and is going to serve him. Sailors have a great knack at waving a religious conversation by telling some amusing, appropriate anecdote calculated to turn gravity into mirth. We have a very hard case in that regard on board this ship. I often individually draw out from them their personal history, and find that a sailor's life is a most excellent commentary on the old proverb "Truth is stranger than fiction."

Sunday, November 21, 1858. Cloudy this morning but a stiff gale from starboard quarter bore us rapidly over the foaming billows. Had preaching in steerage at ten a.m., the Reverend John Rambo giving us most edifying discourse. Similar services were appointed to be held in the cabin at four p.m. but it was so stormy that it was considered prudent to defer them. After supper, the sea having become much smoother, we held a prayer meeting in the cabin. The Reverend George Hubbard gave us his religious experience and so interesting is it that I would like to put it down for my journal. He is a native of the West Indies: inherited a fortune; squandered it; went to sea; followed a life of dreadful hardship: became the master and owner of a vessel. Was engaged in trafficking with the Fejee Islanders when the Holy Spirit suddenly cut him. Was cordially received by the missionaries; forsook his evil companions: had religious exercises and order on his ship: lost his vessel in Australia, had hardly enough to carry him to America, whither he took a passage; had great consolation in his religion; resolved to become a missionary; now on his way to Africa to preach "the riches of Christ."

Monday, November 22, 1858. A most lovely day; the weather quite warm. No breeze of any account, have traveled very little today. We spent our time most agreeably on deck talking, exercising, and in various other amusements. Just after sunset a very striking phenomenon occurred. The sun having sunk behind a black cloud, its crimson rays were reflected from a cloud above upon the gently rippling ocean making it look like a furnace of molten gold. A bird passed by the ship about dark supposed to be one of "Mother Carey's chickens." Listened to a very edifying discourse from Brother John Seys this evening. Sue's health is much improved. She walks the deck with me today. For this and God's other mercies I feel grateful. Talked with the rescued sailor mentioned before. Was pleased to find him very piously disposed, if not even a Christian. He is a Swede and may God sanctify this narrow escape to his and the other sailors' spiritual good. Took the autographs of my companions as seen in the front of the book. The reckoning today at twelve o'clock was North Lat. 29.″ 30′ Long. 31.″ 23′ West. The night as beautiful as it can be.

Tuesday, November 23, 1858. North Lat. 27.″ 44′ West Long. 29.″ 56′. We are now 716 miles from San Antonia of the Cape de Verde Islands. Most lovely weather untill late this evening when there was a little rain. It is now nearly clear, and we are going very rapidly as we have been doing all day. Feel well physically but my heart lacks the quickening influence of the Holy Spirit, and I do not feel as spiritually minded as I would like. Sue complains of the same frame of mind and is quite unwell today though she did not lie in her birth. Besides my religious reading and exercising, and some bodily exercise in various ways, I was principally employed in looking over the "African Repository" and learning music.

Wednesday, November 24, 1858. Beautiful weather and fine breeze. A sail was perceived on our lee-bow about ten o'clock, and as it was very small and was evidently intercepting us, the captain thought it might be the escaped from some wrecked vessel and came to and bore down upon her. She was a beautiful little schooner, and even though she put up English colors and professed to hail from London, there is very little doubt to all in the boat but that she is not engaged in fair trade. We also passed at twelve a British mail steamer from West Africa to Liverpool. We exchanged salutes but did not come in speaking distance with each other. I forgot to mention that a few days ago we passed a vessel bound west but though we were near enough to exchange signals we were prevented from finding out who each other were by the captain not having the necessary signals. The strange economy of the American Colonization Society, the ship was not provided with these important articles. Our regular prayer meeting was interesting this evening. Very encouraging reports concerning the religious interest amongst the sailors were made. Have been reading The Life and Adventures of Captain Canot.

Thursday, November 25, 1858. Nothing extraordinary. Saw a sail on the weather bow. Very beautiful weather but little breeze. It is now eight o'clock and we are rolling lazily from side to side scarcely moving. All of us seem to be hearty. Sea-sickness has entirely passed away. The Reverend John Seys made and delivered an address to the immigrants giving them information concerning their anticipated home. We are enjoying ourselves very much but all seem to feel a want of grace, and it is the burden of our prayers during our social worship. May God receive our hearts and prepare us for all our work. We passed into the tropics this morning. It is very interesting to see florescent light in the wake of the ship. The rudder on a dark night seems to move in a mass of lava.

Friday, November 26, 1858. Beautiful day but little breeze. We have rolled all day on the long and lazy swells of the ocean hardly making any progress. Four sails have been seen today; one of them seems to be nearing us. Nothing can equal the splendid sight the ocean sometimes presents in the reflection of the sunlight. It glitters at times as if it were full of the most sparkling gems then again the horizon looks as if the sea was made of great masses of bright melted silver rolling, breaking, and glittering incessantly. Several young dolphins were around the ship this morning: they seized the bait once or twice but none were caught. I have a toothache this evening; my heart aches also because of the coldness of my heart in the service of God. Lord, revive me!

Saturday, November 27, 1858. Weather most agreeable, and breeze very fresh. The flying fish has been in his glory to-day; schools of them flying through the air at the same time. A few mornings ago the Reverend John Seys composed and read at the request of the passengers a humorous poem in which our names were made to rhyme. This caused a very witty and well-written piece of poetry to come from one of the sailors complaining that they were neglected and requesting that a similar piece should be composed and read reading their names. This request was complied with and all hands were assembled to hear it read. They were much delighted and after singing some appropriate songs the meeting broke up. The sailors' hearts are evidently being reached in this way and the religious impressions made on their mind by associating so familiarly with missionaries will probably be blessed to their souls' salvation.

Sunday, November 28, 1858. When I say that a clod of earth would have been refreshing to my eyes, my feelings may be somewhat imagined. When looking out of my stateroom I beheld the base of the towering mountains of San Antonio, the largest of the Cape de Verde Islands. Arranging my toilet hastily, I went up on deck which I reached just in time to behold the sunrise in all its tropical splendor, its golden light cast an air of enchantment over the whole scene and it will be hard for me to forget the feelings produced by the occasion. Services were held morning and evening in which the gospel was preached. I feel painfully in need of grace and go mourning all the day. If I attempt to pray I can find no utterance to sing praises that fall helplessly from my lips: "Give me a clean heart O God, and renew a right spirit within me." I feel very unwell today, and I endeavor to attribute my spiritual coldness in some degree to that.

Monday, November 29, 1858. Beautiful morning, sailing finely. Saw a porpoise six feet in length minutes ago. It is now ten o'clock, and we have prospects for a beautiful day. How balmy and delicious is the morning tropical air; it is a luxury merely to breathe. Eight o'clock p.m. We are moving very briskly. This evening a large school of porpoises seemed to be racing with the ship. They are a large fish from three to ten feet long having very long noses something similar to swine. They were continually leaping out from the water displaying their full proportions. None came near enough to be harpooned.

Tuesday, November 30, 1858. Beautiful day. Trade winds carrying at the rate of eight miles per hour. Flying fish abundant. Very interesting prayer meeting this evening. As we looked around on each other, the question arose in our minds, who will be the first to fall? Who first to explore the blissful realities in the unknown mysteries of the "kingdom of God." Tears begin to flow but we all expressed our confidence in Christ and resolved by His grace to fall with our armor on. How happy is the missionary even if he is apparently going into the jaws of death. How real and substantial is the religion of Jesus Christ.

December 1, 1858. Trade winds bore us on very briskly. Some sea birds around the ship this evening. To a "landlubber" like myself their presence suggests that land is near, but alas, how does he find himself deceived when he learned that they probably had never seen land. Sue little unwell but myself quite well.

December 2, 1858. We have one of Paddy's most dreadful hurricanes this morning. It blows straight up and down the mast; or in other words, almost a dead calm. Eight o'clock p.m. A most beautiful day but dead calm has prevailed, and there is no prospect yet for relief. Had a very interesting though brief sermon this evening from the Reverend John Seys from the text "Bless the Lord, O my soul and forget not all His benefits." It was to commemorate the day of Thanksgiving, an anniversary held in the United States on this day. There were addresses from the other brethren also pertinent to the occasion. The ship presented a very interesting scene this evening. All the cabin passengers were assembled on the quarter-deck. Some were talking, some singing soft melodies, some reading, some engaged in relaxing pastimes or rejuvenating exercises, all apparently happy and cheerful. Vainly endeavoring to persuade Sue to follow me, I clamored up the side of the boat to look quietly upon the scene around me. Scarcely a breeze ruffled the glassy surface of the ocean. The sun was setting with splendor remarkable even for the tropics, a splendor perfectly indescribable. Nor was the quarter-deck the only interesting scene on board. The main-deck was crowded with the immigrants. The old were engaged in grave conversation, the young were interesting each other with lively chat and singing accompanying; I detected the sound of guitars, while the merry sports of the children made the air resound with their mirth. The sailors also who were not on duty made no small part in the drama. Their voices rose from the forecastle deck in plaintive song which I was not familiar to hear from such hearty men. I am unwell tonight and will have to stop with this ugly scrawl.

December 3, 1858. Paddy's hurricane somewhat abated. Passed two vessels to-day, one a whaler and the other a French merchantman. Saw a large school of porpoises this morning, some of them appearing to be fifteen feet in length. One shark was caught this morning. Had our regular Friday discussion on deck tonight. Subject was "How Far Should the Missionary Engage in Secular Employments?" Was very much enjoyed.

December 4, 1858. All day the ship has rolled around and round on her keel in a glassy ocean in a dead calm. Went forward to the forecastle deck this evening to mingle with the sailors assembled there. Some were singing pathetic love songs; some were drawing nautical objects; some reading instructive religious and scientific books. Some were engaged in witty conversation while others were out on the jib-boom endeavoring to catch the dolphins with a hook or harpoon. A large school appeared this evening sporting in their usual way. Took a saltwater bath. We have a bathroom. The ladies avail themselves of this tropical luxury on Fridays, the gentlemen on Saturdays. It refreshes us very much.

Sunday, December 5, 1858. Had preaching. Sunday is quite an interesting day on board. The bell rang at ten o'clock. The main deck soon became crowded with a motley congregation of sailors, immigrants and cabin passengers. Nearly every grade and occupation in life was represented. I cannot say the assembly was seated in the same order as if they were snugly stored away in velvet pews, nor were they even as deacons as they might have been where books and papers are not allowed to be read and conversation carried on. A barrel covered with a plank over which was spread a flag constituted a pulpit. Bishop Burns took his stand before this and gave us an edifying discourse. Going a little this morning, but from twelve yesterday to twelve today, we did not make six miles of longitude. School of porpoises seen today.

Monday December 6, 1858. All well. Warm. A beautiful butterfly flew about the ship today. The sight of this companion of my childhood in the sunny meadows of summer caused a thrill of pleasure to dart through my heart.

Tuesday, December 7, 1858. Ten o'clock a.m., dead calm. An infant of one of the steerage passengers died last night and was buried this morning at eight. As the sound of the mournful hymn echoed in the glassy deep, I felt a desire to consecrate myself anew to Christ. The ocean is alive. Large schools of various kinds of fish are rushing about making the water boil like a cauldron. A "sucker" was caught a few minutes ago. It derives its name from the peculiar construction of the top of its head which enables it to adhere to hard substances so closely it takes the power of a strong man to remove it. It was about fifteen inches long.

Wednesday, December 8, 1858. The pleasant sound, "Land O!" was heard about ten a.m. this morning. Many miles of coast are in sight, but we are considerably above Sierra Leone or rather Freetown. As several of us will leave this vessel at Freetown, a missionary meeting tonight was held in the cabin, and a very interesting and affecting affair it was. Each encouraged and exhorted the rest. All were much moved and tears flowed freely. We agreed to remember each other in our prayers early every Sunday morning. A large dolphin was caught; this is about the most beautiful fish in the sea. They are sometimes found to be poison, and to discern when this is the case, the cooks boils a piece into which has been inserted a silver coin. If the silver is made black, there is poison; but if it remains untarnished, the fish is palatable.

Thursday, December 9, 1858. We are now lying at anchor before Freetown.

The pilot met us about ten miles from Freetown and conducted us in safety. Some natives dressed in the simplicity of nature's attire came alongside before we were in port. The bay as we came up was spotted with maritime fishing boats, and the mountains surrounding Freetown looked like a grand picture. Many natives came on board this evening seeking employment and bringing various kinds of tropical fruits for sale which were obtained for a trifle. A woman also came to obtain washing for the passengers. Messieurs Miles and White left us this evening.

Friday, December 10, 1858. In company of the Reverend John Seys went on shore this evening. Visited the market, the Wesleyan Mission House, a church grammar school and singing school, and also the American Consul. Went again this evening to obtain the American Consul's advice about a certain matter of importance. The captain, to save port expenses, has determined to leave it and anchor at sea. While I was on shore the vessel left, and I was compelled to hire a Kroo boat, a great expense, and overtake it.

Saturday, December 11, 1858. Went on shore this morning in company with my wife and other missionaries and their wives to take breakfast with our friends the Reverends Brown and Chester. We spent our time most agreeably in visiting various portions of the city and returned the evening reaching the vessel seven miles from town at seven. Made arrangements to preach for Brother Brown of the Baptist Mission tomorrow. Found myself under many obligations to The Reverends Brown and Chester of the Wesleyan Mission with whom we breakfasted.

Sunday, December 12, 1858. The captain has been compelled by the government to be farther from town, and the vessel now lies at anchor sixteen miles from it. This occurrence has entirely broken off my engagement to preach in town. Services were held this evening on the main deck, but there was no preaching this morning on account of the disturbed state of all on board. The captain being thrown back by some accident desired the men to work today, to load the brig which he had chartered to carry the cargo up into port, but they refused and rebellion was brewing when fortunately he withdrew his command.

Monday, December 13, 1858. This has been a day of some excitement. Our attempt to bring the two vessels alongside that we might unload, they came into collision carrying away our main-royal-mast and mizzen channels and causing the same injury to a large portion of the bulwark and jib-boom of the brig. The cargo is now being discharged in small boats.

Tuesday, December 14, 1858. The Reverends Mr. Seys and Mr. Burns who have been on shore since last Saturday returned today both quite indisposed. They informed us that a great appointment was given out for us all to meet at one place on Sunday and give some account of the revival in

America, and a boat was chartered and sent after us, but as we had gone so far down the river, we could not be found. Bishop Burns preached Sunday night to a congregation of fifteen hundred, and only the missionaries with him were civilized. During service some children near the door set the grass on fire and shouted, "Fire, fire!" The confusion which followed was such a Babel of languages and can better be imagined than described.

Saturday, December 18, 1858. Left Freetown yesterday morning; had quite a severe tornado last night. It thundered, lightened, and blew in quite an appalling manner. Weather cloudy and cool. Brisk breeze this evening. Quite indisposed. Sue well.

Sunday, December 19, 1858 Had preaching morning and evening. At eight this evening the vessel dropped anchor before Cape Mount. The moon is shining brightly and under its enchanting rays the densely verdant mountain is distinctly visible. The incessant and hollow roaring of the ocean on the beach disturbs the silence of the evening air.

Monday, December 20, 1858. Went on shore this morning. Sue and several of the missionaries, ladies and gentlemen were of company. The surf on the beach was very bad, and we had the opportunity of witnessing the skill of the Kroomen in passing it. When we had safely passed through, we were hastily seized in their brawny naked arms and safely borne up on the dry beach before the succeeding surf reached us. We passed up by a winding path to the receptacle for the immigrants, many of whom were awaiting us and gave us a cordial reception when we arrived. After a pleasant conversation with Captain Moore's family and some cool and sweet water, we visited the Methodist Mission House where we were cordially received by Mr. Williams, the present occupant. He lived in a house built somewhat on the native plan but furnished with many civilized conveniences. Leaving my friends here I proceeded by a narrow path winding through thick high grass and shrubbery to the Baptist chapel which is used by a minister located at Monrovia. The location is a most excellent one but the building nothing more than a pen of large crooked sticks with tiled roof and gabled-ends. The seats and pulpit were in harmony with the rest of the house. Returning from this to the mission house, I again found my friends and after some pleasant conversation, we left for the receptacle where we took dinner and then came on board with unfound gratitude to God especially for preserving us from the surf as we went and came. I forgot to mention that the celebrated "Mama Sally" visited us at the receptacle.

Tuesday, December 21, 1858. The freight for the place is being busily unloaded. A young native bullock was brought on board and slaughtered. Received a pressing invitation from Mr. Weir of the Presbyterian Mission to take dinner with him but not feeling like going ashore, declined.

Wednesday, December 22, 1858. Nothing very extraordinary today. A large shark prowling around the ship was enticed by bait and hooked. He was drawn up untill he swung then lassoed and fastened to the side of the ship where he was slain by cutting off his tail. All well.

Friday, December 24, 1858. Dropped anchor before Monrovia this morning. Going, coming, meeting, and parting the order of the day.

Saturday, December 25, 1858. Went ashore. Preached at the Baptist church. Took dinner with Brother Yates, vice-president of Liberia.

Sunday, December 26, 1858. Preached in the morning; listened to a sermon from Davis in the evening. Took dinner with Brother Yates.

Monday, December 27, 1858. On Monday we rested.

Tuesday, December 28, 1858. Dined with the Reverend John Seys.

Wednesday, December 29, 1858. Dined with ex-president Roberts. Spent the remainder of the week visiting about Monrovia. Among other places going to the Senate Chambers and House of Representatives, both were in session. Went to the "Palm Palace" where the agricultural fair was being held and to the office of the Liberian Herald.

Sunday, January 1, 1859. Listened to a sermon from Brother Weir. Attended in the evening a Sunday School concert held at the Methodist Church. Reports from the various schools gave a total of nine hundred of which number three hundred are Congoes and Kroos.

Monday, January 2, 1859. Attended a Sunday School picnic with Sister Cooper. Visited for the last time an afflicted man with whom I have been in the habit of conversing and praying.

Tuesday, January 3, 1859. Took dinner with Sister Ellis, hostess of the "Navy Hotel." Visited Judge James and went up to the "Lighthouse" in the Cape. Thursday took dinner with the President; Friday with the Baptist high school. Friday took dinner with Bishop Burns.

Sunday, January 9, 1859. Listened in the morning to a sermon from Brother Cheeseman. Preached in the evening.

Monday, January 10, 1859. Took dinner with Sister Cooper. Visited for the last time an afflicted man with whom I have been in the habit of conversing and praying.

Wednesday, January 12, 1859. Set sail for Bassa yesterday. A tornado struck ship last night. Ran below Bassa in the night and did not get into port untill late this evening.

Thursday, January 13, 1859. The cargo is being discharged. Some of the passengers are going ashore. Bassa is notorious for its bad bar, many persons have been drowned in it and devoured by sharks which infect its surf. These sharks were formerly fed by the annual human sacrifice offered by a native king. They are less numerous since this bloody rite has been abolished.

Sunday, January 16, 1859. Set sail this morning for Leone. Had divine service this morning and evening. Understand that Brother Vonbrum, a native minister of this place has recently baptized twelve native converts.

Tuesday, January 18, 1859. At anchor. Thirty men have been sent ashore. One of them was furiously opposed to leaving the vessel and had to be swung down by rope and pulley and fastened to the boat.

Wednesday, January 19, 1859. Received our invitation from Brother Roberts to dine with him and to preach to his congregation this evening, but as the captain anticipated getting the vessel underway by four p.m. I declined accepting it. We did not, however, get way untill eight p.m. and are now moving rapidly. Some new passengers were added this evening to our already crowded cabin.

Thursday, Jan. 20, 1859. Cast anchor before Cape Palmas at three p.m. Our cabin and deck which a few hours ago were full of life and mirth are now silent, lonely, and desolate. Sue and myself intend remaining on board as long as possible to avoid sleeping on shore before reaching Lagos. We are now writing beside each other and find much solace in each other's society after so sudden and great a vicissitude in our ship's society.

From Sierra Leone to Lagos

The tornado, terrible thunder and lightening, three hundred pounds of gun powder, Cape Mount, the shark, the lacerated Kroo man, the surf—its roar like the report of a cannon, loudly roaring billows, running away with the ladies, the receptacle, my walk, the meeting house, Mr. Williams, the expected war, the children bathing in the surf, Monrovia—pleasant times spent there: kind treatment, dining about with various people, the senate and the representatives, the agricultural fair, the Sabbath School picnic description, walk upon the lighthouse, snake, maritime enemies, the president and other dignitaries, the convicts in the street, the schools preaching, the preachers, soldiers, statesmen, teachers, down the coast, Liberian passengers, old colored missionary, the oranges by Brother Williams, the bar and the death of the son of Mr. Seys. Massacre. The character of the natives. Sassawood. Witchcraft. Inability of young even to rise in the world. The Kroo-children stuffed with rice. Cape Palmas. The orphan asylum. The cast and crew. The pleasant walks on the sea beach and point of the cape. Episcopal mission and missionary. The native wars. Sister Drayton's story. The Krooman and the boat. The gun and steamer "Hope" down the coast from Lagos. View of the coast. The surf. The first pillow. The doctor and others. The baptism. Various places. Lagos. The shark. Bar and accidents on it. Mister Turner. Brother Harden. Strange appearance of things—housewall. The rat and biscuit. Preaching, walking, and contemplating.

ACCOUNT OF A RETURN JOURNEY FROM ABEOKUTA TO IJAYE, APRIL 1859

The Journey to Ijaye

April 26.th. This morning we all started for Ijaye in good health. We are now stopping at a native house in a little town called Itadi. We have quite a comfortable little room, but the pleasure of having such comfortable lodgings is greatly diminished by the indisposition of my wife, who is groaning with pain. In this very room I passed a sleepless and delirious night, in my first trip to Ijaye, and the same fortune now falls to my companion.

Wednesday 27.th. We arrived this evening, at a little town called Illugun where we have been accustomed to stop for the night. When we entered the house of the man of whose hospitality we usually partook as regular shelter, he became, from some unaccountable cause, furiously angry and compelled us to leave his house. Though we were all greatly fatigued, and my wife so sick and feeble that it was with great difficulty she could walk. We were compelled to take shelter under an old shed belonging to the "bale" of the town. Here we lay until Bro. Phillips returned from a search for a better house, and informed us that, a man in the farms had consented to let us stay with him. On arriving at this place, we were kindly received, and had a very good, though dirty room to sleep in. While lying in the wind under the old shed, I contracted fever, and my temples throb with fiery blood.

Thursday 28.th. We reached Ijaye this evening. Our joy when we came in sight of the town, can better be imagined than known. It was greatly increased when we reached our house and were surrounded by our affectionate family who deeply sympathized with us in our afflictions. I arose this morning very sick. At first I rode in a hammock, but this making me worse, I mounted my horse. Nausea, vomiting, and feebleness soon overcame me, and I was compelled to take the hammock again where I remained in a state of prostration untill we came within a few miles of Ijaye, when I rode my horse the remaining distance. After leaving Illugun, Sue became very sick also. She became completely prostrate, and was afflicted with a most distressing nausea and great vomiting. She is still no better, but I thank God, who has brought us all safely home, and who has given her a comfortable couch and house.

May 6.th. My wife and self so much convalescent as to take a ride on horseback.

Saturday 7.th. Great Mohammedan celebration yesterday. Returning from market yester evening I met a company bearing a woman who was walking most piteously. I understood that this morning that she was beaten by her husband, and is now dead. If caught, the man will probably be sold as a slave.

Thursday 12.th. Bro. Phillips was waked early this morning by someone at his door crying, "Blood!, blood!" in the Yoruba tongue. On demanding an explanation, he was told that a man and his wife who lived in a neighboring compound, were fighting, and that his presence was desired to settle the difficulty. The wife had bitten off a part of her husband's lip, but appeared repentant. Her husband visits us as a patient.

Saturday 14.th. Bro. Phillips gone to Abeokuta. Pay day. All our cowries are nearly gone, and there is no prospect of getting more very soon. The chiefs of Ijaye, Abeokuta have closed the gates against our loans on account of the bad conduct of the E. Nigerian Expedition, and I am not able to buy here. I sent to the chief to borrow some.

Sunday 15.th. Have preached twice today, but this has been a day of sadness, care, and labor. Early last night, Sue was seized with a vomiting which continued with but little intermission all night. This morning it assumed the black form, and was very profuse, so that I felt it my duty to send immediately for Bro. Phillips. By diligent application of remedies, she is now much better. A rogue has taken all our provision cowries.

Tuesday 17.th. Yesterday the milkman came for his pay, and took nearly every cowrie. But last evening two men came. I bargained for $30 worth. I've been much engaged having them counted today.

Wednesday 18.th. We were greatly surprised late last night by the arrival of Bro. Phillips. He came the whole distance from Abeokuta in one day. He came alone and was pursued by a wild beast supposed to be a leopard.

Saturday 21.st. Had "roasting ears" for dinner. Disturbed by a rogue last night. He knocked at the front door to see if we were all asleep, but vanished at the sound of our approach. Bro. Phillips gone to Abeokuta again. Sue is sick again with nausea, chills, and fever. Many heathenish noises are around us tonight. The rolling of the drums, the wild song, the shouts indicate that they are at their ancestral revels. Occasionally the wild wail of mourning women, breaks upon the night air, telling that death has come, and making a significant discord with the sound of mirth. All is deathly silent about the house, and nothing breaks upon the profound stillness but the measured ticking of the clock, and an occasional sigh or moan from Sue, sleeping in an adjoining apartment.

Monday 23.rd. Preached twice yesterday. Sue was up, but taught children, and had fever and delirium all last night. The chief [a.k.a. Areh, Kumee, Kumi, Kurunmi] sent his messenger today saying that if I was in need of anything, to send to him for it.

Wednesday 25.th. Recd. the mail from America. Sue's face was like an April shower day—sunshine and showers, but alas, for me, I did not receive a letter from any of my friends. Sue nearly well.

June 4.th. A day of overt rejoicing in America. Bro. Phillips returned from Aboekuta on the 31.ˢᵗ ult. and found us both sick in bed. I am now in excellent health, and Sue is convalescent.

June 12.th. Preached today in the parlor. It is amusing to witness how pleased the children are to get on their Sunday, American clothes.

Wednesday 15.th. Among the people who visit us daily is a quite interesting Mohammedan from the interior, to whom Bro. Phillips preaches in Yoruba. I hope he will scatter the word. All of us are in the enjoyment of excellent health.

Friday 24.th. Lightening struck a house this afternoon, and the Shango are catching everything they can find outside of any compound, to sacrifice to him.

July 7.th. Called on a compound to salute a bride. She was entirely covered with cloth, so that I did not see her face. A bit of music connected with her wedding. She had intended to elope with a young man connected with our family, but the scheme was frustrated. Bro. P. and myself have been suffering much with the toothache. In endeavoring to have mine treated, it was broken off.

Saturday 9.th. After visiting a sick girl, we all went to the market. Sue and I sat down under a tree and Bro. P. preached under another. The crowd of people around us was so dense that we could not see him, but he soon came over to our sides, and mounting a large root, called the attention of the people by requesting silence, and then proclaimed the everlasting gospel in their native tongue to our attentive and numerous audience. A word here and there indicated that some things, especially the mercy of God, was assented to. Returning, Sue had to be carried across the branch. One man made an effort to lift her, but utterly failed to the great contempt of another who lifted and bore her off, as if she had been a child. This was a sight probably never seen in Ijaye before.

Tuesday 19.th. Rode out to "the bush." Was thrown from my horse; my gun kicked off blood from my nose, and I received a good dunking from the clouds besides.

July 26.th. All in excellent health. I had a walk this morning. We made a call upon a friend, who is by profession a weaver. All appeared glad to see us. A woman gave us a mat to sit on. When the barly came, he gave us a cola nut in a calabash. This is a token of friendship, and I divided it among ourselves and himself and friends. When leaving, they followed us to the gate saluting us, and exclaiming, "Ijawo 'abo, ijaw 'abo," [white man's bride] as if they wld. never weary calling her name. As we came home a company of children followed us to the gate of our compound, where they took leave of us as if greatly grieved in having to part. They crowded around, taking possession of hands and shaking them with more cordiality than grace.

July 27.th. Have laid aside Yoruba Theology for awhile to read my mail from America. How delightful is "good news from a far country." We all visited the chief [a.k.a. Kumi, Kumee, Kurunmi, Areh] this afternoon. When we entered the front courtyard, a crowd was collected in each side of the chief's gate door awaiting him to hold court. What kind of justice is sometimes dispensed at these courts was implied by a frame standing near the chief's door into which criminals are placed for execution. Though a cruel man, Kumi appears to be a man of great justice and impartiality in his judicial decisions. Among capital crimes may be mentioned adultery and theft. For the latter crime the chief once beheaded two of his own brothers. He invariably beheads with his own hand, and does it with a single blow.

The drums having informed him of our arrival, we soon were in pleasant conversation with him. While thus engaged he privately called his confidential messenger, who after prostrating himself at the feet of the chief and receiving a secret command, departed. Before leaving, the mystery was explained in the present of a goat. Kumi is a man of very superior intellect and policy. He inspires the greatest reverence and fear among the people of Ijaye. Once when I went to salute him, he appeared very angry about something. As we were leaving, crowds of people came and prostrated themselves at a distance before him. When we reached the gate we met a man who had a dirty head and terror-stricken countenance, showing that he was in great danger of losing his head or being sold as a slave.

R. H. Stone

LETTERS AND MISSIONARY PAPERS

Sparta, Ga. Aug. 31st '58

Dear Bro. Taylor,

Yrs. of the 25 inst. is before me, and as nothing of more importance intervenes, I will proceed at once to answer your questions in the order that they are proposed.

1st. I was twenty-one on the 17th of last July.

2nd. I am not constitutionally delicate, and have been in the almost undisturbed enjoyment of excellent health for the last two years. I am now remarkably well. The Lord who healeth all our diseases, has given me faith to believe that he will take care of me as long as he has any use for me.

3rd. I am not a graduate, though my education is somewhat classical and has been considerably improved by private study. I do not apprehend any material difficulty in the acquisition of the Yoruban language; but it may be because I do not fully appreciate its philological difficulties and peculiarities.

4th. Though I have been the subject of my strong religious impressions from a tender age, yet, I did not feel any important or radical change of heart until the Autumn of '52. This last impression, the one which I humbly trust has been blessed to my soul's eternal salvation, was brought about by reading in conjunction with Bible, Wayland's "Obligations to Love and Serve God." For a long time I was the subject of much mental distress but the Holy Spirit was pleased not to cease its work upon my heart, until it had formed in it "Jesus Christ, the hope of glory," and had given me the faith which is the "evidence of things unseen," and which filling the soul with light and with "joy unspeakable and full of glory," lifts it far above sense and time. I concealed the fact of my conversion until the following summer, when being convinced of my duty to "put on Christ" by public profession and by baptism, I determined to unite myself with the Baptist church. Through the mistaken kindness of my parents, however, I was prevented from doing so until the summer of '56, when I had the inexpressible happiness of being "buried" with my Savior, and of uniting myself with those whom I believed to be the true church.

5th. I felt I was called to preach the gospel, even before I was united with the church, but as I entertained the idea of graduating at the University of Va., I concluded to defer taking up the cross until after that time. Having consented to the requests of my father, to teach a year before I entered college, through the influence of some friends in Ala, I obtained quite a flourishing school in that state. But though I was located in an intelligent community I found that religion was at a low ebb. This condition of affairs made me think of taking up the cross at once, but I continued to postpone the idea until I could not conscientiously any longer delay, and having obtained a license to preach from my church in Culpeper, Va., I entered the pulpit during the first part of last April. I felt then, and still feel the answer of a good conscience to my feeble efforts to proclaim the truth.

6th. There's nothing strikingly remarkable in the call which I think I have received to preach the gospel to the heathen. During the latter part of last year, and the first of this, I began to be deeply impressed about the lost condition of the world generally, about its moral misery and wretchedness, and the dreadful destiny of those who did not obey and those who have never heard the gospel. This frame of mind was principally brought about by an interest in the Holy Scriptures, which was rather sudden and remarkable, and which caused a prayerful,

continual and undivided study of them night and day. Through this
enlightening influence, I became more widely awake to the painful
realities of life and to perceive how dreadful is our existence in this
probationary time. The natural and reasonable consequences of such
feelings, was that I became earnestly desirous to devote myself to
the service of God and there do something to alleviate the misery of
this "vale of tears." My mind became very much and even painfully
exercised upon this subject. I did not know what to do; and to obtain
an answer to this question was the burden of my prayer day and night.
Whilst sitting in my room one gloomy evening, and thinking over my
future destiny, feeling that an answer to my prayers must soon come, a
paper was handed to me, and looking carefully over it, observed a notice
that the Washington Assoc. of Ga. had agreed to sustain a missionary
in Central Africa and desired the man. I laid aside the paper without
once thinking or rather reflecting that probably this was an answer to
my prayers; but suddenly the thought flashed through my mind that
this might be so, and I immediately threw myself before the throne
of grace imploring God that He should show me if this was what He
wanted me to do. It is in vain for me to attempt to describe the feeling
that followed. I remember now that the impression, "I am going, I am
going," involuntarily burst from my lips as I arose from prayer. I do not
possess significant command of language to be able to give a correct
idea of my feelings on the following day. They have made an indelible
impression upon my mind, and will be a source of rich consolation in
all those afflictions which must inevitably await me in Central Africa.
All secular cares were removed from my mind; the aspirations of my
vain heart, were lifted, from the earth to the skies; all the ties which
bind me to my native country were severed; my mouth was filled with
songs, the expressions of a heart full of light and joy. If you will allow
me to adopt the language of the old African when trying to express his
feelings at his conversion, "I felt as light as a feather."

You have now a plain and brief sketch of my religious history in
answer to your questions. You perceive there is nothing remarkable in
it. The working of the Divine Spirit in my heart has been quite simple,
yet at the same time influential and inexorable. The finger of God's
providence points me to Africa, and I hope to spend at least the first
part, if not all my life, in that benighted country. I do not know that I
could have a greater sorrow in this than to be prevented from going;
and I anticipate feeling greater happiness preaching the gospel to men
who have never heard it before, than I can derive from anything else

in this life. I do not think I am either an enthusiast or a sentimentalist.
In looking over the history of modern missions which began with
Carey, I find that they have been, indeed, most wonderfully blessed,
but I sometimes am disposed to think that if our young missionaries
had less of that religious romance that came near driving—to—when
first the idea of being a missionary entered his head, and more of that
humble, reassuring, patient and plodding spirit of Carey, their labors
would have been more blessed. Yet this may be a notion resulting from
my inexperience. I know that tribulations await me, but if I am called
to give a full expression of my feelings upon this subject, I must say
I am determined to go as soon as you say is possible for me to do so. I
am often painfully conscious of unworthiness and weakness, but while
I can do nothing without Christ, I can do all things with, and I am
desirous of giving my quota to the great work which was stopped by
Mohammedan ferocity and Roman superstition which will now go on
untill "All the Kingdoms of the earth shall become the Kingdoms of our
God and his anointed."

Aff. Yrs. in Christian faith,
R. H. Stone

Paoli, Oct. 20 Wednesday 1858

Dear Bro. Taylor,

I arrived home safely, and was much gratified by the reception of
my kindred and friends. I expect to be married tomorrow night. I am
now at home, but will go up tomorrow. My mind is a little perplexed
by several queries, some of which are quite important, and I write
especially to ask your advice.

1.st It is impossible for my friends to make up all the cotton I
purchased. What must I do with the remainder? Would it be of any use
to me in Africa?

2.nd Father has given me liberty to purchase goods at Culpeper let
House to the amount of $150, and I am not informed as to what I had
best purchase. Please give me an inventory in your next.

3.rd What day had I best start for Baltimore?

December 30th 1858
Ship M. C. Stevens, off Monrovia

Dear Bro. Taylor,

After being detained at Freetown for a week the vessel set sail for Cape Mount on the 17th ult. From this time I notice my journal saying as follows:

Saturday Dec. 18th. A tornado struck the ship last night. It rained heavily during this time, and blew, thundered, and lightenend in a severe manner. Weather cloudy and cool.

Monday 20th. In company with Mrs. S. and the rest of our party, I went ashore. The moon being full, the surf is quite bad here now, and we had an opportunity of witnessing the skill the Canoemen possess, in passing it safely. We first went to the Receptacle, where we met and were entertained by the Steward. We then proceeded to the Methodist Mission house, now occupied by Mr. Williams. On our way we passed the chapel, which is a frame building, with a thatched roof. The dwelling house is of the same construction, plastered with mud. Leaving my friends here, I went to see the Baptist chapel. It is a small, open hut, built of crooked poles, but has a tiled roof. The school was not in session, and I did not have the pleasure of being with Bro. Bacon or Wilson, the latter being absent at Monrovia. The American Colonization Society has a school in the Receptable. The Methodist also have one in the same place. From the teacher of the former, I learned that these two number about 40 scholars each, but that the Baptist school did not have so many. The classics are not taught in any of them. Mr. Williams informed us that there is great need of an orphan Asylum here. They are bound out by law to persons who are not able to take care of or educate them.

Saturday, 25th. Cast anchor before Monrovia early yesterday morning. In company with our party, went ashore this morning. Mrs. S. and myself went directly to Bro Yates' house where we had been invited. We received a cordial reception from his good lady, he being absent at the Senate Chamber. Services were held today in church, and at the request of Bro. Day, I preached. After services, I made the acquaintance of several of the ministering brethren, amongst them Bro. Vonbrun of Basso, who is a native. From church, we visited the "Palm Palace," where an agricultural fair is now being held. Every department indicated a growing prosperity. From this place, in company with Bro. Yates, the Vice-President, we paid our respects to the President. He seems quite sanguine of soon having a communication between Liberia and the Niger.

Sunday, 26th. Preached in the Baptist Church this morning. The congregation was a very good one, the house being nearly full. Had the pleasure of listening to a sermon from Bro. Davis of the Bassa mission;

this evening dined with Bro. Yates. On the beach, as we were leaving, I observed a little Kroo boy who had a cap made of the leaves of a large Bible.

Monday, 27th. Visited the Methodist High School. The classical department is not now in operation, owing to the absence of Mr. Horne, the teacher. A teacher was in one of the rooms, drilling some children for a celebration which is expected soon to take place. From here we went to the Senate, which sits in the second story of a stone building, from whose top floats the Liberian flag. We found them engaged in debate over some important bill. The senators, eight in number, sit before plain red desks, similar to those used in school rooms, but a little differently constructed for this peculiar use. The speaker sits upon a rostrum covered with red cloth. There is no galley for visitors, but they sit on benches placed in the end of the room. Everything seemed to be conducted with becoming dignity, and in the usual parliamentary manner. From here we went to take dinner with Rev. John Seys, the U.S. agent for taking care of the re-captives of the Echo. We visited his charges during the evening. We found the males, 180 in number, sitting in circular rows in the kitchen yard of the Receptacle, taking their dinner. After this was over, all, both boys and girls, were assembled in the passage to hear "God-man's palaver," which was a school sermon by Rev. J. Rambo of the Cavalla Episcopal mission, delivered through an interpreter. This interpreter is also a Congo, and was recaptured several years ago. He followed the speaker by reading and singing a hymn, thus showing what may be done for these poor creatures. He is said to have found a known brother amongst them. Mr. Seys thinks of endeavoring to establish a sort of manual labor school for their benefit.

Wednesday, 29th. In company with our party, took dinner with E. J. Roy, who is originally from Newark, Ohio. The subject of the Orphan Asylum came up again, and I learned that there was great necessity for such an institution, located somewhere in Liberia. The Episcopalians have me at Leap Palmas, in which about 24 children find an asylum and receive secular and religious instruction.

The American bark "Exchange" is about to leave this post for Baltimore, and I take the opportunity to make a report.

Thursday 30th. Visited the House of Representatives. The same simplicity found in the senate chambers was also observable here. Quite an important question concerning a national college is now before the House. The society for establishing the college is located in America, and through their trustees in Liberia they had all even begun to erect the building, but a difficulty with the government concerning the location, has put a stop to it.

From the House we visited the "Palin Palace," where premiums were being delivered by the president. The highest, $25, was awarded for cotton cloth and a barrel of nice brown sugar. The sugar cane grows to an immense size here, as my own eye proved. From here we went to Ex-president Robert's, where with the rest of our party, we were invited to dine. Mr. Roberts lives surrounded with all those luxuries and conveniences which wealth affords in America. The dinner also showed that there are some who *live* in Africa.

December 31st. I have to close my letter this evening, and hasten to drop you a valedicting line. I find Monrovia a very different place from what I anticipated, quite enlightened and hospitable. The society here is very different from that in Freetown. In the latter place, nearly the whole population is composed of uncivilized natives. These are divided into several powerful tribes or parties and it is said that nothing but the English guns, keeps them from open war. One who is a stranger, is, however, astonished to meet so many with tattooed faces, who have been converted from degraded heathen to meek and lowly ministers and followers of Christ.

There was a concert at the Methodist High School last night. Tomorrow, which is New Year's day, a Sunday school picnic will be celebrated on the cape. I understand my unworthy name is amongst those who will deliver addresses on the occasion. We hope to meet the steamer at Cape Palmas, if not we will have to await the one of February. We are both very well and quite hopeful. Mrs. Stone desires to be remembered.

Yr. In Christ
R.H. Stone

Lagos Febry 7.th 1859

Dear Bro. Taylor,

We arrived before this place on the 3.rd and came ashore the next morning. We came around the coast in the "Hope," a steamer irregularly connected with the mail line. We had a pleasant passage of six days, stopping a day each, at Elmira and Cape Coast. Your kind letters came duly to hand, and we are both very grateful for the edifying and paternal advice it contains. Satan sometimes endeavors to persuade us that we have not the Lord's commission, but a prayerful consideration of the motives which prompted us to come, soon puts all such doubts to an end. This hope cheers us amidst the apparent dangers which are rising up in our path. We have arrived in somewhat troubled times. Kosoko is said to be on his march to this place, and the new King of Dahomy, to be preparing to attack Abeokuta. All the chiefs, excepting one, are said to be in favor of Kosoko, and the King of Lagos, who seems to be an irresolute man is very much alarmed, even shedding tears at times. I suppose the whole movement, is a renewal of the league between Dahomey and Kosoko, to revive the slave trade. The bloody rites attending the inauguration of the new King of Dahomey, is said to have consisted of a thousand human sacrifices. I fear the missionaries at Abeokuta will not fare well in the hands of such people.

I accompanied Bro. Harden to our chapel Sunday morning. Though the chapel was situated in the midst of the town, and crowds were continually passing and repassing, not a single heathen or Mohammedan designed to enter and listen for a moment. They seemed to be wholly taken up with the things of the world, and had no desire to hear the "good news." Perhaps the condition of political affairs occupies their minds. The services were conducted partly in Yoruba and partly in English. Bro. Harden seems to have made considerable progress in the acquisition of the former. The congregation consisted of a few professed Christians and two little children.

On our way to the chapel, we passed two little heathen mud temples, the object of worship being a curious kind of tree which shaded them. We also passed a stump covered with shaggy fragments of mats, which I was informed was an idol. The people here are excessively superstitious, and the King squanders nearly all his revenue in sacrifices to the sea, small shells, oyster shells and such things.

We expect to start for Abeokuta on Wednesday the 9.th inst. The boatman engaged at first promised to start to-morrow, but they still say they will reach the city at the time appointed, which is Saturday. I have received a letter from Bro. Phillips, and have sent a messenger by land to Ijaye to inform him of our arrival.

We are well and hopefull. Mrs. Stone desires to be remembered affectionately to you. I hope you will ask the prayers of the church in behalf of their missionaries, especially when Satan seems about to make vigorous attempts to strengthen his waning power in this country.

Yours in Christ,
R.H. Stone

P.S. We have lost one of our boxes, and some of our flour is much spoiled.

Yrs nc
RHS

Ijaye, February 26, 1859

Dear Bro. Taylor,

We arrived at this place on the 20th inst, and are now comfortably fixed. A journey of five days brought us from Lagos to Abeokuta. The canoemen used as much dispatch as possible travelling both day and night. This was voluntary on their part, as they promised to reach Abeokuta in four days. Our bed was placed in the canoe and an awning of mats placed over it. Under this covering we lived day and night, only, when the sun was not shining during the day. The sandbars gave us much trouble, often detaining us for an hour or more. The forests along the banks of the river are very old and picturesque, and resound during both day and night with a great variety of noises, some of them appearing to a stranger, quite unearthly. The parrot and the trumpet-bird seem to lead principally in the concert. Perhaps some incidents by the way would not be uninteresting.

February, Wednesday 9th. Left Lagos this morning. The lake being rough, Mrs. S became very seasick and the nausea was by no means relieved by the hot sun pouring down on our little shelter. At 2 P.M. the canoe entered the mouth of the creek. After proceeding nearly a mile through a thick bamboo jungle, the familiar sight of a small field of Indian corn and a cheerful cockcrow told us that human inhabitants were near. We soon reached a little village where we determined to partake of a frugal meal and signify it with the name of holiness. When about finishing our meal, the King of the town sent to inform us of his displeasure in not being saluted on our arrival. I was somewhat annoyed when he returned with the messenger sent for this purpose. As the object of his visit was to get a "dash," I gave him some palm juice over which he smacked his lips with affected satisfaction. I was sorry to perceive the villagers were very eager to obtain rum. This evening hundreds of monkeys were along the river bank having come to quench their thirst.

Thursday 10th. This evening we stopped at a village to take some refreshment. The people were engaged in worshiping the river, and were beating drums incessantly while we were there. During the repast crowds gathered around us, the object of their greatest interest appearing to be Mrs. S's little rocking chair. They were much afraid the chair would turn over with her. As the canoe pushed off, we merrily exchanged parting salutations crying, "O de gbosha, O de gbosha!" [good bye].

Friday 11th. While taking our dinner under a shady tree at a village we received a visit from the chief. He was dressed in a yellow robe ornamented with cowries and beads. His presence drew a crowd, which before to our great satisfaction had stood off. While reclining on a mat near us, and talking to his companions he seemed to be struck with the charms of a woman in the company, and immediately declared that he would make her his wife. She objected and told him that she already had a husband. He replied that he could take her away from her husband. She again remonstrated by saying that he was the chief of the town, and such an act would be unworthy of him. The chief then invited her to draw near as he had something secret to tell her. She came with a fondling laugh, evidently highly pleased with the honor done her, and sitting down by him, received an "old-fashioned hug" while something was whispered in her ear. They sat lovingly together untill the company was broken up by our departure. Our interpreter explained the matter to us, but he could not say whether the chief was sporting.

Saturday 12th. We stopped a few moments to-day at an Abeokutan farm, where they were busily engaged in loading and sending off canoes for Lagos. I was struck with the business deportment of these people. I had the opportunity of observing their extreme politeness. In their salutations when meeting, the younger always prostrated himself before the elder unless the former is of higher rank than the latter. A messenger in this country never salutes anyone by the way, with his body. This fact gives some light on the command the Lord gave the messenger of the gospel when sending them out, saying, "Salute no one by the way." As they bore an important message, he desired them not to loiter on the way and to carry the tidings of the Kingdom of God with as much dispatch as possible.

This evening we crossed a party of hunters on the banks of the creek. They were armed with guns and crossbows, and drove their game with dogs, as sportsmen do in the States.

Sunday 13th. We slept at Augbomaya last night. This town is fifteen miles from Abeokuta and has much distinction for being the place where most of the exports are started for Lagos. The sand beach was crowded with people, and contained heaps of articles ready to be placed in the canoes, of which thousands are running up and down the river, carrying native clothes, palm oil, and cotton; and bringing in exchange, European merchandise. I noticed many bales of cotton among the articles before mentioned. They were regularly ginned and pressed as in the Southern States.

At 2 P.M. [we arrived] at Aro, a little town one mile from Abeokuta. We managed to obtain a little native home and a man's saddle for Mrs. Stone, and led by one of our canoemen, we started for the town. After passing the gate, a half-hour's walk brought us to the Wesleyan Mission house. As the Baptist house was more than four miles from this place, and I was now exhausted and fatigued, I borrowed a horse here. He proved to be a lively little creature, just capable of elevating my feet above the ground. Darkness soon overtook us, but through the assistance of our guide, we got safely along. We passed through the market, and had an opportunity of hearing and seeing this little Babel under favorable circumstances. When about two miles from the mission house, we met a company sent for us by Bro. Priest, which through mistake, had gone to Augbomaya, and thus missed us. When we arrived at the house, all was silent and dark, but the door was soon thrown open, and we were cordially received by our good brother and sister. The chief of the township came to salute us tonight.

We both had the fever while at Abeokuta, and did not entirely recover untill we reached Ijaye. Three days of easy travelling brought us here. We slept in native houses on the way. The last night, I slept in Shango's room. I was compelled to drink the water used to obtain a favor. I suppose he did not get thirsty, as we rested quietly. Since our arrival, we have visited the chief [Areh] of the town who is a man of much power. He received us kindly and presented us with a goat, for which in turn, we made him a small present. This man has a bloody name, and is a terror to the inhabitants of Ijaye; but I think, for the sake of Bro. Phillips, who seems to be popular with him and the people, he will be our friend. He sends daily to salute us. The people here seem to be wholly given to idolatry. Religious processions are continually going about the streets. While in the chief's compound during our visit, a large one entered and commenced dancing to the beating of drums around an orisha. They also appeared to be worshiping a painted child.

We are at this time enjoying good health, and have every temporal comfort that is reasonable for one to expect in this country. We feel grateful that the Lord has called us to labor in this part of his vineyard. We have not been able to see much of the town yet. Whenever we go out Mrs. Stone is an object of great wonder, and crowds of women and children follow us. Occasionally they run before us and peep timidly up in her face, as if they were disposed to think her not human. Bro. Reid is here, and all of us together have much social enjoyment and religious comfort in each others' society. A heavy rain fell yesterday evening, and I was much surprised when we discovered it to be largely mixed with hail, some of which was gathered in a cup, proving its identity beyond doubt.

Remember me to Bro. Poindexter.

Yours in Christ,
R. H. Stone

Ijaye, March 26, 1859

Dear Bro. Poindexter,

I am grateful today that we at this time are well, and much pleased with our new home. The work of the Lord appears to be prospering at this station, and we are much encouraged by the prospect of success. Faith in prayer, patience and toil, however, is the only medium through which we expect success. Since our arrival in Africa, Mrs. Stone has had fever twice. I am now recovering from the third attack. Following are some extracts from my journal.

Monday 28th. Visited the big market this afternoon. While sitting under a tree, a crowd numbering not less than five hundred, gathered around us. Their wonder and admiration appeared to be excited by Mrs. Stone's dress, as those who spoke complimented her for the quality of cloth on her person, and the children following us returning, were continually shouting, "Look at the cloth! Look at the cloth!" It is amusing and surprising sometimes to witness the manner in which even men retreat from her and ask with fearful and doubtful countenance, "Is that a woman?" The simple creatures are ignorant of the mysteries of crinoline.

During our walk we passed several barber shops where men, women, and children have their heads shaved. We saw the operation performed upon some infants, who screamed and kicked rigorously during the time. The heathen mother, though proud of her children, and much flattered when they receive particular attention, possesses little or no maternal tenderness. When the Yoruban mother feeds her infant she inclines its head downward, and places the mouth in her hand full of a kind of sour drink called "eckaw" which is sucked down the gasping throat through the forced respiration caused by its uncomfortable position. This practice is not as cruel as one about Cape Palmas where infants are stuffed with rice to a certain distention, which condition, the loving mother ascertains, either by thumping the body or putting her finger in its throat. They are then greased and laid out in the sun. The mother in a Christian land has much cause for gratitude to God for the domestic happiness which she receives from the enlightening influence of divine truth.

Tuesday, March 1st. In a ride out into the farms this morning we passed a creek near the gate where men, women, and children were bathing together. Yorubans, though neat in their dress, appear insensible to modesty.

Thursday, 10th. Bought a horse and from his savage looks named him "Bucephalus." Visited a funeral celebration. They were drinking "arte" or native wine and beating drums. An orisha sat at the foot of the grave which is always in the piazza of the dead man's house, and all the poor man's effects were displayed to excite sympathy. After declining to partake of the festivities we retired; the mourning women raising a cry of lamentation as we passed the gate of the compound. The gospel was preached in the compound before returning.

Saturday, 12th. Prayer meeting imploring the blessing of the Lord upon our labors for the conversion of the heathens.

Sunday, 13th. Preached to a very good congregation. The chapel not being finished, services are held in our dining room. Bro. Reid preached in the evening. The Sunday School exercises are very interesting. Our senior class, composed of converted females is able to repeat from memory the 3rd, 6th, 7th, 8th, and a part of the 9th chapters of Matthew. They also repeat other distinguished portions of scripture. As they are taught orally, the class is sometimes much increased by those who desire to learn something of the word of God.

Monday 14th. While Bro. P. was preaching this afternoon to a company of men who came to visit us, one of them tried to excite a disturbance, saying, "Don't let us listen," but being silenced by the others, became interested in the end. The miraculous birth of the Savior causes considerable discussion among them. Great fire in town this evening. Thousands were collected in a field near it, many of them weeping and mourning over their desolate homes. The little girls who have been working on the chapel were paid off finally today, each receiving an extra present of a piece of white cloth. Wrapping this around them, they ran wildly into the street, singing and shouting, "We are the children of the whiteman," and caused a great sensation. This was done in revenge upon some wicked people who were continually insulting them, saying they were the white man's slaves, and he would steal them and sell them.

Wednesday, 16.th One of the chief's daughters, a most interesting girl, is becoming much interested in the truths of the gospel. A young man who has been before with the especial request to hear the word of God, came again today. When asked if he ever prayed and how, he replied in the affirmative and said he asked for cowries and to be a great man. This is a good specimen of all heathen praying. They ask and have not, because they ask to consume it unto their lusts. The spirit within them lusteth. They know nothing of the charity which seeketh not its own.

Thursday, 17th. Received some insulting language from Mohammedans in the market, but charity softened them and we parted with expressions of courtesy. There is little hope for these people as they will neither reason or care to reason. A very interesting case, however, is with us; a convert under Bro. Phillips' ministry sometime since April contemptuously asked, "What is sin," but when it was more fully explained, he fell on his knees and said, "I am a great sinner, pray for me." From that time he became greatly interested, and Jesus Christ was the prime subject of his conversation. He visited us a few days since and in some remarks on his favorite subject said, "Jesus has done all our work for us." During further conversations he said, "When I wash my face in the morning I pray to Jesus, at noon I pray to Jesus, when I lie down to sleep I pray to Jesus." He is the son of the former King of Yoruba, and but for his rank, his Mohammedan brethren would probably have killed him. Returning from market, was saluted by a man at the door of his compound. A crowd collected, and I preached "Jesus Christ and Him crucified."

I have not been able to obtain an interpreter, but have the privilege of using Bro. P's since the chapel has been finished. I have studied the language a little. I believe this is the time for us to make the quarterly report, and I hope you will consider these brief remarks as sufficient.

Yours in Christ,
R.H. Stone

Ijaye, March 31.st 1859

Dear Bro Poindexter,

Since the date of the enclosed letter, Mrs. Stone has had a slight bilious attack of fever; but she is now in a state of convalescence. Unless there is a relapse which is improbable, she will be able to resume her accustomed domestic occupations in a few days. Except imprudence should give a malignant form to this fever, I do not regard it as the least dangerous. It does not give my mind more care than a cold would in America.

As I before indicated we are both very grateful that the Lord has directed us to labor in this part of his moral vineyard. Many incidents are continually occurring to encourage us and to warrant a belief that the hand of the Lord is with us. The gospel is not popular in Ijaye nor would I have it to be; but some wandering sheep appear to be beginning to hear the voice of the good shepherd.

When returning from preaching in the market yester-afternoon two men by the way desired to hear the word of God. The interpreter told them it was late, and invited them to come to the mission house the next day. This afternoon they came in and prostrated themselves according to the custom of the country, and when we desired to know why they were interested in the gospel, one of them, an humble looking man, replied that he sought peace; that he had been a Mohammedan, but their way was dark and he could now see that the ways of his father led to evil, and that he wanted another way. His countenance seemed to indicate sincerity, and if he is in earnest, he is evidently seeking to know the right way. I endeavored to show him this way, and told him of the glad tidings of the grace of God in Jesus Christ. Before leaving, he expressed himself much gratified, saying that he believed the word, and by the help of God would endeavor to do it. After receiving instruction concerning prayer, he departed declaring it his intention to return again. Such incidents as these encourage the missionary greatly, and render his life a very pleasant one though he may be sometimes the subject of afflictions and temporal privations.

In preaching in the market the Mohammedans often endeavor to stop us, and the heathens sometimes object and say "We will serve our gods as our fathers did"; but the sheep will hear the shepherd, and the gospel needs no "auxiliaries" to destroy the works of the Devil in the world, and to make all things subject to Jesus.

Remember me affectionately to Bro. Taylor and the brethren. May the Father and Son in whom dwell the treasures of wisdom, give them grace so that all their counsels may resound to their glory.

Yours in Christ,
R.H. Stone

P.S. Please subscribe for The Religious Herald

R. Stone

Ijaye, June 28, 1859

Dear Bro. Poindexter,

I was too much indisposed from fever to write by last mail. I had another light attack but am thankful to be able to say that we are both quite well.

Bro. Phillips is now absent at Abeokuta as Bro. Priest's departure makes it necessary for that station to receive particular attention. Bro. Reid is now with us and we all have, much comfort and pleasure in each others' society.

As the Abeokuta school has been transferred to this station, our school is now in quite a flourishing condition. Four of the scholars can read the Bible in the Yoruba language. The most interesting one, a boy about twelve years of age, has been taken from us by his father who lives in Lagos and who is opposed to having his son so far from him. He can read and speak English fluently, and was studying geography, arithmetic, and the Bible in the same language. I hope he will unite with Bro. Harden's school in Lagos.

I have nothing to write relative to our missionary labors, more encouraging than usual. I hope and believe the work of the Lord is progressing slowly but surely. A woman who is the wife of an American man petitioned yesterday to unite with our church by baptism. She has been a regular attendant at the Sabbath services, but as she was formerly under Wesleyan influence, I fear she has wrong ideas about church fellowship and have deferred her indoctrination untill Bro. Phillips returns from Abeokuta.

Bro. Phillips' interpreter has now become our teacher, and as I have never yet been able to obtain an interpreter, I can preach only on the Sabbath days. I am diligently engaged in the study of the language, as I earnestly desire [to] be independent of an interpreter and be able to speak to this people at any time, "The Whole council of God" "in words easy to be understood." Remember me affectionately to Bro. Taylor, and other brethren of the Board.

Yours in Christ
R.H. Stone

Ijaye, Central Africa
August 2nd 1859
Rev. James B. Taylor
Richmond, Va.

Dear brother,

Yours of May 21st is before me. I am grateful for the expressions of sympathy it contains. You ask if I cannot use the language of the

Apostle when saying, "I thank Christ Jesus, one Lord, that he has counted me faithful, putting me into the ministry." In reply, I must say that my unfaithfulness often troubles me, and I deeply feel that I am not a good steward of the grace of God yet, I feel humbly grateful that I am permitted to preach "the everlasting gospel" and a holy, unearthly joy fills my heart when I think of the "crown of righteousness" which is laid up for me, and which "the Lord, the righteous Judge shall give me at that day, and not to me only, but to all them also who love his appearing." The world and its excellencies once appeared to me very desirable, but how much like "drops" are they, when that faith which is "the evidence of things unseen," contrasts them with the "inheritance incorruptible, and undefiled, and that fadeth not away, reserved in heaven" for me. I again have the pleasure of saying that we are all well. Indisposition occasionally visits us, but we are soon up again, engaged as if nothing had happened.

I have not yet been able to employ an interpreter, as the wages we have been accustomed to give, are not now sufficient to obtain a worthy one. It is more profitable to engage in trade. We are now diligently engaged in the study of the language, but I am not yet able to preach or pray in its words. I am exceedingly anxious to be independent of an interpreter, as it is very inconvenient to have communication with the people altogether through them, and much is lost by preaching through them. When well enough, I preach on Sabbath days, using an interpreter. I preached last Sabbath to a very good congregation in the chapel. Bro. Phillips preached in the afternoon in Yoruba. He has dismissed his interpreter, and made him teacher at his request. I hope you will continue to exhort the brethren to pray for us. When Christians are writing to each other it is very common in closing to say, "pray for me." This, some think is a nice pious way of closing a letter, and is practiced merely for the sake of form. Under such an impression, they give only enough attention to it, as will enable them to read it. But if they knew how the missionary wrestles in prayer with God, and how he prays that God wd enable his brethren to feel an interest in him and his work and pray for him, they wd then know that [it] is with an earnest and anxious heart he writes that short sentence.

Sue sends her love. Remember me affectionately to the Board.

Yours in Christ
R.H. Stone

P.S. Why do not we receive the publications of the Board?

Ijaye, Sept. 1st, 1859
Rev. James B. Taylor
Richmond, Va.

Dear brother,

Yours of June 29th is before me. I will not mention the pleasure it gave me. I am happy to welcome you to the mission rooms again where you may resume the privilege of comforting, encouraging, and advising those who are so far from their native country and its advantages, and are so frequently the subjects of affliction, temptation, and perplexity. We rejoice that the Lord has put it into the hearts of some to carry the gospel to the brethren. We are waiting patiently for Him to move the hearts of some to give themselves "a living sacrifice, holy, acceptable unto God" by denying themselves the comforts of a civilized country and obeying the Macedonian cry which has so often come from Africa. Our affairs are about the same as when I last wrote to you. We enjoy much good health, but occasionally are prostrated a few days by fever, during which time we endure much suffering. But I can truly say we are happy and contented, and nothing is further from my wishes at this time, than a return to America. Your devotion, the cause of Christ, renders an explanation to yourself unnecessary.

I still devote the most of my time to the study of the language. I am able to express myself in short sentences about the ordinary affairs of domestic life, and upon a few religious subjects, but my tongue is better trained to speak than my ear to hear. It is probable I will not have the privilege of preaching or praying in Yoruba for 8 or 10 months yet. Remember me affectionately to Bro. P and to the Board, also to Sr. G and family. Mrs. S. sends much Love.

Yours in Christ
R.H. Stone

Ijaye, Oct. 31. 1859
Rev. James B. Taylor,

Dear bro.

The mail of this month has failed to arrive and we are denied the pleasure of receiving a letter from you or Bro. Poindexter. Since last writing, I have obtained the services of an interpreter, Bro. P. having engaged him in Abeokuta the last time he was there. I am now permitted to preach almost daily, either in the streets, houses, or market.

From what I have heard, I think, though our numbers are so few, our mission is in more spiritual prosperity than it has ever been. Since its establishment the people have had time to think, and the consistency of the conduct and doctrine of the whiteman, have in some degree removed their prejudices, and they are beginning to think the whiteman really means to do them good. We have now eleven children living with us; and two of them—a boy and a girl—are so small that they sleep and eat in the house with us, and not with the other children and people of the yard. They are very interesting and sprightly, and give us much amusement and pleasure. The congregations in the chapel are increasing, and among those who attend the services, may often be observed the aged and thoughtful, paying fixed attention to the word of God.

Rumors of great wars are afloat, and among them this town is very prominent. The C. Missionaries of Abeokuta have published a paper in the Yoruba language. I am able to read the scraps of news, but not the long articles. I now find myself able to read the gospels without much difficulty. My wife and I are quite well, and I hope sincerely interested in our work. Remember us to the brethren.

Yours in Christ
R.H. Stone

Ijaye, December 1st 1859
Rev. James B. Taylor
Richmond, Va.

Dear bro.

Yrs. of Sept 30th is before me.

Being full of comfort as usual, it gave me much pleasure.

Though I have been enjoying good health, and am now feeling very well, I do not feel much like writing by this mail. On another page you will see some extracts from my journal which will give you a very good idea how I pass my time among the people. Mrs. S. is not now very well, though nothing serious is the matter. She has been enjoying excellent health of late. We frequently recreate by riding into the country. I sometimes go fishing or hunting before breakfast, returning before 7 o'clock.

The interest of our mission is increasing. One young man was baptized here last Sabbath. Another has professed conversion at Awyaw. The two young men are of remarkably studious and sober habits and bid to become faithful followers of Christ. The congregations at the chapel appear to be increasing.

All is well. Let the brethren who feel a sincere interest in this mission be encouraged.

Yours in Christ,
R.H. Stone

Flight from Ibadan
Feb. 22, 1860
Fragment of Letter

We were afraid we would be pursued by Ogumulla's horsemen, and either killed in cold blood or carried back into more binding captivity. But we reached Lahlookpon in safety and found lodgings in the chief's compound, in court of which we secured our horses. I soon found my horse was known to all, and my circumstances through him. This made me feel somewhat uneasy, and also heartily wish "Bucephalus" was where he came from.

A queer chamber. A storm coming up about 7 o'clock, I was not able to log in the prayer, but was compelled to seek shelter in a dirty corner where the chickens were used to roost. They set up a chirp of dissatisfaction at first, but not being further disturbed did not express themselves again. With a mat for a bed and my saddle for a pillow, I forgot all my heart-bleeding somehow for a few hours, when I was awaked by a great tumult in the compound. We at first, thought the house was attacked on our account, but discovered it was caused by the sickness of the chief's child, which was supposed to be dying. I prayed earnestly that the Lord would preserve its life, and hinder Satan from imposing upon the beliefs of the people that they were punished for giving shelter to a wayfaring and persecuted child of God. The child revived and all was quiet again. We rose early and commenced our journey as soon as it was light. We feared an ambush or that spies had gone on in the night and we would be detained in the larger town Ewo which was before us. We reached the Oba by noon. The ford is the place of collecting toll, the gate of Ewo not being more than a mile distant.

We were treated politely, but some remarks addressed by a richly attired Mohammedan to our guide showed that our character was known. Our guide carried us to the house of a Church Scripture Reader. We passed the house of the Ibalogun who was sitting in state surrounded by turbaned courtiers, Ewo being a Mohammedan town. His compound was surrounded by exceedingly high walls. Being obliged to stop to salute him, we received a courteous reply.

An English Bible. Our host, lived like a native, and the only evidence that he was not a heathen, was his kindness and ability to talk a little English. From him we obtained a genuine English Bible. How precious and surprisingly lovely did the Psalms appear to me. With this we had devotional exercises in a little room given us to sleep in. Having discovered that I loved the [creatures or creations] of this world more . . . I obtained that night a peace of mind which greatly lightened my burdened heart.

Ogbomishaw. We intended to go from this town to Awyaw which is said to be only a day's journey distant, but when we arrived we learned that the road to Awyaw was not passable, unless we took a guard and guide from the King. Great was our disappointment on hearing this for we, at first, expected to have to return to Ibadan. But I refused to seek direction from the King, preferring to commit my way to the King of Kings. So after much annoyance from lying sharpies we resolved to go to Ogbomishaw which was said to be only two days' journey.

Having borrowed fifteen cents worth of cowries from our host we passed through the gate early Sunday morning Febry. 26th on our way to Ogbomishaw. It was a beautiful morning and our hearts were much revived. We passed through some strange looking country and saw strange looking birds, and tracks of wild animals. Once we startled a buffalo which was lying near the path. Our guide seemed [to] never tire, walking swiftly ahead of us with a drawn saber in his hand, and we pressed on so rapidly that by 2 o'clock we came to the farms of Ajebu, a large town where we were directed to pass the night and which was one day's journey from Ewo. The children in the farms on the first sight of us ran in great fright and hid themselves, and no persuasion could make them return but only made them go back farther. We stopped a few minutes under a shady tree in the town to take some refreshment of native food, and then hurried on to pass the night in some little town nearer Ogbomishaw. By inquiries on the way, we began to entertain the hope of reaching Ogbomishaw the same day. Darkness, however, overtook us in the farms, and we began to think we would have to camp out in a stormy night, but we presently came to a light which, by approaching it, we found to our great astonishment and delight to be the gate of Ogbomishaw. When we thought ourselves many miles away; we found ourselves within ten steps of the gate. After wandering through the town, for about a half-mile, we came to our mission house. A light glimmered through the windows, and two horses stood in the yard. On entering, we found that Dr. Delany and Mr. Campbell had just arrived from Illorin. These, you probably recollect are the colored gentlemen who have been sent out to explore the country.

They gave me plain civilized food, that night. I had the exquisite pleasure of sleeping on a good bed. My heart was very sad all the next day when I looked at the things in and around the house. Every convenience for a missionary and none willing to come. I earnestly prayed that God would not let the lamp of His word in this place go out but would supply it with fresh outpouring of the oil of His spirit.

Tuesday morning. After remaining one day in Ogbomishaw I started for Awyaw, the capital. I was compelled to leave my Liberian friend in charge of his friend, a young man who had charge of the mission house, as he was not well enough to travel. Messrs. Campbell and Delany started with me, but being unencumbered, I soon left them behind. About 12 we reached the Oba, and while my men were refreshing themselves, attracted by monkeys, I walked a little way in the forest to see their pranks and watch their ludicrous gestures as they would break and cast twigs.

Suddenly I was startled by a deep but loud roar as of some great wild beast. Hurrying back, I told my people to start quick, for a wild beast was coming. They only replied with a roar of laughter, exclaiming "Aja, aja ni!" [a monkey, it is a monkey!]. They had hardly spoken this when we heard a loud monkey laugh in the forest, as if the monkeys greatly enjoyed the fun of seeing a whiteman run. How such an animal was able to make such a noise, I leave for naturalists to say.

Once, on the way, I thought we were attacked, but the persons proved to be hunters, in pursuit of a wild beast which came toward us. It appeared to be a wild boar. One man had taken a beautiful black antelope.

ARRIVAL AT AWYAW

After about an hour of sun we came to the plain before Awyaw, whence we had a fair view of the towers of the King's palace. It was with some misgivings I entered the town, for I feared that spies from Ibadan would influence the King to detain me as a spy. But before I reached Bro. Reid's house, I perceived that I had nothing to fear. When I came in sight of the mission house Bro. R and his people came running to me with great joy, showing that they knew of my misfortune, and were expecting to see [me]. I was surprised at this until I heard that Bro. Reid had just arrived from Iwo [Ewo] where he had been in search of me. I could not refrain from shedding a few tears at once more meeting with brethren and friends who deeply sympathized with me.

It was with great joy that I heard that the road to Ijaye was open, and that a man had come several days before bringing information of my loss and also of my wife who, he said, was resigned, but once sunk under her grief, when, on the day that messengers were sent in search of me, she heard them talking in a low tone of voice at the door at midnight. Bro. Reid accompanied me part of the way next day. We passed a place where they had been fighting the day before. The Ijaye people of the stronghold Esan through which I had to pass endeavored to make me give some information of what I had seen, but I positively refused to do so.

As I approached Ijaye, my horse seemed to partake of my feelings, and yielding to a slight touch of the spurs set forward in a swift gallop. Thus I passed the gate and through the town untill I came to the mission yard walls. Fearing the effect that a sudden revelation of myself would have upon my wife, I approached cautiously, and looking over the wall saw my interpreter lying at his door. Gently calling him, I endeavored at the same time to cause him to keep silence by making gestures, but in vain. As soon as he saw me he leaped to his feet and came running and screaming as if he were mad. The children of the yard and others soon joined him, and I became almost as bad a prisoner as when among the Ibadans. Struggling to free myself, I met my beloved wife, pale and almost fainting, leaning upon the arm of Br. Phillips. Here I drop the curtain.

I found Bro. P nearly recovered from his sickness, and that my wife had been so much overcome by her sorrow as to be attacked by bilious fever. She was soon well, however, after my arrival. Many people came crowding in to see me. I was much affected at the tears of joy of one of our native sisters.

After much importunity on his part, I at last consented to go and see the chief the evening of the same day. He received me in the strictest privacy and by many artifices endeavored to draw some information from me of what I had seen, but in vain. I explained my character and relations to the Ibadan and Ijaye people. This put an end to the interview. Concerning this, Kumee and the present war, I will perhaps, hereafter say more, when I think of the deliverances which I have received from the merciful hands of God, my gratitude is inexpressible. I feel an increased zeal in my work, and earnestly pray that a sense of God's goodness to me, may make me endeavor to be more faithful and like my redeemer.

Yrs. In Christ
R.H. Stone

Ijaye, Africa, June 21st 1860

Rev. James B. Taylor,

As Bro. Phillips will write about the camp—its perils, excitements, and bloody & shocking scenes, I turn, with pleasure, from such details to those of a more agreeable nature. You will doubtless be interested in an account of the persecution of the widow and her son. The boy was even threatened with the loss of his birthright and of his liberty, but encouraged by his heroic mother, he has refused to the last to comply with the heathenish customs required of him by his relations. Let us pray that he may receive a nobler birthright, and the glorious liberty of the gospel of Jesus Christ. His father was an anomaly. Though he never confessed that he believed the gospel, and though bitterly opposed by his family, he seemed determined that we should have his children to educate in the nurture and admonition of the Lord. Yet I fear his doom was of one who "often reformed, hardeneth his heart." I was quite affected, when the news of his death arrived, to observe the grief of two of his little children who live with us—a boy & girl, ages respectively 6 and 4 years. They sat down by each other, and wiped the tears one from the other's eyes, as they wept.

Under the head of this man, I may mention another—an old man who lived within a few yards of the chapel. Though I do not remember ever to have seen him in the chapel, he was, nevertheless, well acquainted with us, and the word of God. He died suddenly and unexpectedly a few days since, and from certain circumstances under which I was led a few months since to talk to him, it is reasonable to be supposed that his mind was very dark. One evening my attention being attracted by a turmoil before the door of this old man's compound, I observed a small boy, approximately 8 or ten yrs. of age, come out from it, holding in his hand a bunch of dried grass which he lighted at a pot-fire, and then rushed back with it flaming in hand, the crowd following, screaming, and begging at the top of their voices. Fearing for the safety of our chapel, I hastened to the spot, but before I could definitely learn the matter, the little incendiary had again lighted his torch and was about to enter the house when I rushed at him. Frightened at this unexpected and [?] onset, he dropped his torch and fled, hotly pursued by me untill he sprang through a hole in the house wall. The exclamations of the people soon informed me how sacrilegious had been my conduct, for they then told me that they supposed the boy was inspired by "Shango" the god of thunder & fire, and that this deity required a sacrifice of them which was to be given to the boy. Fearless of "Shango's" wrathful thunderbolts, I told them that a flogging would take such inspiration out of him, and supposing the matter ended, I left. But a Liberian who passed the house directly afterwards, informed me that this old man and all the people of the house were prostrate before the little imp of Satan, (for I know no better name for him), imploring him to cease, and promising in answer to his enquiries what they would give him, that they would give him anything they had, if he demanded it. Shocked at this information, I went to his house early next morning and preached to him and all his family who would listen. He thanked me, and said the word was true & good, but his manner was such as to imply that he was not thoroughly convinced of his folly, or did not like to confess it so. Cannot those who have received the benefits of divine revelation, sympathize with the dark-minded people.

Still nearer the chapel than this old man lives another, a young man, who is the master of the house and was wounded in the first battle. He had never been our friend, untill he experienced at our house when wounded, the novel kindness of Christianity. A few weeks since, when his wounds were nearly healed, he was seized with the "tetanus." For a time it seemed impossible for him to live. But while continually administering the proper remedies, I prayed fervently that God in his mercy might spare one who had so long been regardless of his word, and that He would still give him time to repent. My prayer has been answered, and the terrible disease broken. As soon as his mind is strong enough to justify it, I expect to go to him as the messenger of God, and beseech him in Christ's stead to become reconciled to God. Attended and am still attending another man exactly in the same situation, only he lives farther from the chapel and his father has been our enemy. He is now nearly well, and when so, I expect to go to him as to the other. May God bless His word, and deliver them as brands from the burning. One day while I was leaning over the latter, his father seeing my sympathy exclaimed, "Who would have thought it, that the whiteman is so kind! Once we feared and suspected him, but now we know that his word is true."

I mention these instances to show that though war fills the land, and "fear and the snare, and pit are on every side," yet we are encouraged in our work.

Thirteen children are living with us, and some of them are very young and pretty. I cannot think that the Lord will permit them to be torn away from us by violent hands and carried into captivity & slavery. At this time it would require but short residence in this country to make anyone detest the slave trade, especially if they are torn from their homes and friends, as I have been and as many are daily being done [this sentence has been partially marked through, as if edited]. A few days ago an old man and his little son—probably his little Benjamin—were caught and brought here. The Egbas took one and this people the other. As they were separating the little boy raised his tearful eyes to his father's face and said, "Father, farewell! It is war that thus breaks our hearts." War! War! The thunder of battle almost daily echoes over Yoruba's plains, so fertile, and well adapted for the ploughshare. May the day hasten when men "Shall beat their swords into ploughshares and their spears into pruning hooks," and, "nations shall not lift up sword against nation, neither shall they learn war anymore."

I am still in the enjoyment of uninterrupted health, though, through the sickness of my wife once, and that of my interpreter on the remaining occasions, I have failed to perform my part of the Sabbath services twice, and my regular Wednesday service once. Mrs. Stone is now well and sends love.

Yrs. in Christ
R. H. Stone

Ijaye, Central Africa,
August 28th 1860
Rev. A. M. Poindexter:

Dear Brother,

I am informed that a caravan will leave this place for Abeokuta tomorrow, and as no other opportunity will occur before the mail leaves Lagos, I now use the present one to write my monthly letter.

Yours of May 16th reached us. Like you, we all hoped that the confusion which filled this country would soon come to an end, but by this time, I suppose, you have been informed otherwise. Since the great defeat of the Egbas before the Ibadan camp, no fighting of importance had occurred until Monday the 13th of this month. Skirmishing and kidnapping occurred almost daily in the farms, and frequently the enemy appeared in force as if about to attack the town, but after the day had been passed in skirmishing between advance parties, both armies would retire to their camps without any serious loss or engagement. On Sunday the 12th, they approached unpleasantly near the walls—even burning the watchman's house, but on the appearance of the Ijayens, they retired across a creek, at a ford of which, and also along its banks, a sharp firing continued through the whole day. On Monday the 13th, however, they advanced in manner not to be mistaken. It was evident they intended to make an effort to take the town. They were allowed to pass the ford before mentioned, when they were taken in flank by the left wing of the Ijaye army, and received a most single and bloody defeat. The command given by the chief on this occasion, reminds me of one delivered at Bunker's Hill: "Tell them," he said, "not to throw away my powder." They were equally and fearfully obeyed. The heart becomes sick and would turn away in horror from such a scene, but there is a terrible beauty about a battle in Africa which fascinates the eye. As the mellow light of the declining sun falls upon the wide-spreading, intensely verdant, and palm-dotted plain which surrounds Ijaye, its beauty is indescribable. Imagine you have a far-extending view of this plain on a clear evening; hear incessant peals of rattling thunder echoing over its hills and through its vales; see silvery clouds floating in the bright light of a tropical sun, above the dark hosts engaged in combat, and you have in your mind what, alas, is too often realized by us.

The Bashorun of the Egbas frequently visits us. From him I hear all the particulars concerning the war. He is very sanguine of success. The Ijabus, a people on the South of Ibadan, and the people who furnished the Ibadans with arms and ammunition, have joined with the Egbas in the war, and nearly all the towns on the West side of Ijaye have submitted. The strength of the enemy now consists in the Dahomians, and the towns on the North side of this town. The duration of the war depends principally upon the movements of the Dahomians. It is to be hoped, however, that they will not attack Abeokuta, as I hear that the British lion has shown them his teeth.

Not being able to provide for them here, I have sent two more of our children to Abeokuta, since Bro. Phillips' departure. Four now remain with us, one of the original seven having been taken home by his relations because we were not able to make them any presents. Brother P. has not yet been able to send us any provisions, as everyone desires to bring food for himself. The Lord has daily provided such things as we have needed, and we continue to trust Him with unwavering faith. Through the kindness of the Bashorun and with what I have been able to buy here, the children have thus far been provided for, but we are now in a great strait for cowries, and I expect to have to send our remaining children down, if not go ourselves, to Abeokuta. I do not like to think of this, and will not go until the hand of Providence plainly points, and firmly urges me to do so.

Though surrounded by what some people call unenviable circumstances, Sue and I are in the enjoyment of health, and are very happy and contented. The Lord has placed us here, and we have no desire to be anywhere else, until His providence leads us elsewhere.

Though so few of us remain here, everything goes on as it did before. The confusion now prevailing is not favorable for street preaching, but fit opportunities are used to tell the "good news" to such as are willing to hear. A semi-weekly service is held in the Chapel. I preach twice on the Sabbath, and every Wednesday evening endeavor to strengthen and edify our converts. I have been praying in this language for two weeks, and hope to be able to preach in it, before the year ends. My wife teaches the children. She is much pleased with the progress they make; she is now able to teach very intelligibly. We are much interested now in our work here, and not favorable to the idea of leaving Ijaye, unless Providence directs in a way not to be misunderstood. We cannot realize the consolations which the word of God affords until placed in circumstances for which it was intended. His promises now appear to us as living words, and His providence as a living hand.

We have not heard from Brother Reid since I left there last February, but I suppose he has written to you by way of Ibadan, as that way was open before the Egbas declared war.

I am awaiting anxiously for the return caravan, as I hope it will not only bring us provisions, but the information that reinforcements are coming.

Yours, in Christ,
R. H. Stone

Ijaye, March 2nd 1861
Rev. A.M. Poindexter,
Richmond, Va.

Dear brother,

Since writing under date of February 20th a very hard fought and bloody battle has been fought here. The enemy, dividing into two parties approached both camps of the allies. They came within almost musket shot of the Egba camp and by yells, savage songs, and by firing a few muskets in advance, endeavored to draw the latter outside their entrenchments. But the Egbas desired to draw them nearer and did not sally, when the enemy retired to assist those who were fighting the Ijaye army and drove the latter into their entrenchments before the Egbas, who had attacked the rear of the retiring enemy, could come to the rescue. A dogged conflict then took place upon which the fate of the town hung. The enemy fled, but not untill they had given as well as received heavy losses.

The war is growing more desperate every day. Our friends in

Abeokuta are becoming alarmed, but we continue to trust in the Lord. We would not needlessly expose our lives, and I hope if we are ever taken captive or suffer any evil by this war, that our brethren will not attribute it to rashness but a desire to do our duty, and to serve the Lord faithfully without fear. We earnestly beg your prayers. Under present circumstances every hour may bring the most painful vicissitudes. But I know that "The Lord of hosts" is with us and the God of Jacob our refuge. There is sweet consolation in the words of the psalmist: "God is our refuge and strength a very present help in trouble. Therefore will not we fear though the earth be removed and though the mountains be carried into the midst of the sea."

One of our children died a few days since, but Mrs. Stone still has thirteen scholars. We hope that we are both profitably employed. The renewal of the war, has given some more patients to visit me, and to be visited by me. I hope the sisters who are interested in the mission will not fail to assist us by sending clothes for the children. I am by no means a beggar. If anyone should think so, I hope that one will neither give nor send anything. In such we would take no pleasure.

May the Lord avert the impending calamities in America, and may the day soon come when spiritual and not carnal weapons will produce all the change which occurs in the world to hasten the progress of truth.

Mrs. Stone sends love.

Yrs. aff.
R.H. Stone

Abeokuta, April 1st 1861
Rev. James B. Taylor
Richmond, Va.

Dear brother,

Your kind letter of January 29th came safely to hand. The condition of our country is truly distressing. But we earnestly pray that God may forgive our national sins, and avert the impending calamity. These difficulties place us in an embarrassing condition, but the same Lord who has brought us through so many dangers and trials, will continue to show his mercy to those who trust in Him. These things are not in vain, but they are intended to be a part of that series of events which will consecrate the glory of God in the world.

I suppose you can easily surmise why I am here. Since the secession movement in America was likely to cut off our usual supplies, we supposed it not only prudent but necessary to proceed at once to husband our resources by adopting the most economical method of carrying on the mission. As the maintenance of two families was likely to be attended with more expense than if they were united into one, and as the transportation of provision to Ijaye during the rainy season would have been attended with heavy expense, it was supposed to be best for us that we should all live together at Abeokuta. There was no particular inducement to remain in Ijaye, as the men were engaged in war and the women in transporting provision. We had as many children as we supposed we could support, and all the disciples came down with me. We had no idea of leaving Ijaye untill we left for America, untill the last letter from the Board arrived. I would not have left any of the disciples behind under any consideration.

We left our house about midnight on the 4th ult. and slept in the Egba camp. Just as we arrived, the enemies' camp took fire making a great conflagration. This caused much excitement and rejoicing among the young men, but the old veterans supposed it was a ruse and acted accordingly. The night passed quickly, the silence occasionally being broken by the shout of the watchman, the sound of the patroll drum, and the wild and savage war-song.

The caravan was to have started on the rising of the moon but it being cloudy, we did not start untill light. Scouts were sent ahead to examine all the most dangerous places, and when they made their report, we started in a great hurry and traveled very rapidly that the most convenient places for attack might be passed before the enemy could receive information of our departure. The road to Ase was formerly very safe, but is now rendered very dangerous by the proximity of the enemy's camp. We, however, reached there in safety by 11 A.M. Sometimes imagination would transform a white tree into an Ibadan warrior. Here we overtook the principal part of the caravan for they had left us behind. Having partaken of some refreshment we again started hoping to reach Okee-Magee by the night. We traveled very rapidly, and I occasionally relieved Sue by letting her ride my horse while I walked. There is one dangerous [place] in this part of the road called Abis which was a former camp of the Ibadans and situated at the junction of this road with one leading to the Ibadans camp. I was made aware of our approach to this dreaded place by a reproof from one of my men when I called aloud to someone behind. We began to overtake those detachments of the caravan which had preceded us and when within a hundred yards of the spot we were compelled to lead. A most profound silence was observed. Occasionally I would ask in a low tone of voice some question relative to the vestiges of the camp which was situated in a strip of wild looking forest and extended along both sides of the road for nearly a half mile. When fairly out of danger, the chattering and laughing were renewed as if nothing had happened. About 5 P.M. we were overtaken by a terrific hurricane. The atmosphere was so thick that we were almost suffocated. I began at one time to be seriously alarmed. Some of the carriers were thrown down, and an oil cloth afforded no protection against the torrents of rain which drove under it, and thoroughly drenched the body. About dark we reached the two mountains. Through these we defiled with great caution owing to the great rocks which lay in the road. The hammock bearers continually relieved each the other quarrelling, and encouraging and saluting each the other all the time. The scenery was the wildest I have ever beheld in Africa. The narrow and rugged path lay on the banks of the Ogun which severed the bases of two craggy and wild looking mountains. The deepening darkness much exaggerates the scene. As we approached the Egba camp which was situated at the entrance to this pass on the opposite side, the reports of muskets magnified by the water and echoing crag into the roar of a cannon came pealing along the rocky bed of the river. When we entered the camp it was pitch dark. With much difficulty we found our way to the Bashorun's tent. We were shown two small and indifferent tents (which were no protection from the wind and rain) and I decided to lodge there. Our condition was now anything else but endurable. Sue and I were both thoroughly drenched by the storm and no other prospect appeared before us but to sit up all night in the wind and rain with our wet clothes on. To add to my trouble, the news came that two of my boys were found, lying exhausted on the road side, and that my interpreter and the disciples were no where to be seen. The carriers—thirty in number—came and put down their loads at my tent door and left them to my care. Things remained in this condition for a while when the Bashorun sent for me. He had some hot yams prepared for us—an agreeable surprise. I obtained a very comfortable little room from him, and we had the pleasure of exchanging our wet for some dry clothes. Here we slept, and though we only had a thin grass mat to lie upon, the night was passed by us in profound and refreshing slumber.

The next morning we found all right, except that a partially blind woman who was of our party was lost. The disciples and my interpreter came in early and the two lost boys by daylight. We sent a hunter in search of the lost woman, and left cowries for her use if found. I had a good view of the camp by the light of day. It is situated in the midst of a dense and majestic forest which has been so cleared as to make it a beautiful grove. Being in a valley, every sound is greatly magnified, and that night the flash and report of muskets, and mirth of thousands of warriors, gave the place an appearance not easily described. We had a pleasant journey to Atadi the next day. We traveled at our leisure no longer fearing an attack. Sue would occasionally get out of the hammock and I dismount from my horse, and we would enjoy the variety of a pleasant walk. Though we feared no enemy, yet we were often in danger in endeavoring to cross the deep beds of dry rivulets whose perpendicular bands were made very slippery by the rain on the previous evening. The path for an hour or more led us through a majestic forest along the banks of the beautiful Ogun.

After resting a half-day at Atadi, we arrived at Abeokuta about 10 A.M. the third day. When about a mile from town, we met a party of the girls who came at the top of their speed with arms extended and screaming with all their might!

This journey was less fatiguing than any we have ever made, and we arrived here in fine health. My wife has since been sick, but is now nearly well. As for me—with profound gratitude to God I mention it—I have not had fever for more than a year, and I am now in excellent health.

There is a very interesting state of things here. Many of the larger children—their ages ranging from 12 to 14 and 16 years, also several of the people who are working for us, appear to be deeply repentant.

We baptized two young men several Sabbaths ago. We had to go down to the river Ogun and it was an interesting scene. As the prayer for these peoples went up from us, many of the people who happened to be present being employed near the place, exclaim, "Oseun! Oseun!" [you are kind]. The candidates were the young man, my interpreter, and the youth who was received several months ago at Ijaye. I am here compelled to cut short my letter.

Yrs. affectionately,
R. H. Stone

Abeokuta, April 29th 1861

Dear Bro. Poindexter,

Yours of Dec. 23rd has arrived. We still hope that our country will be spared the horrors of civil war by a collision between the Federal government and the new-born Southern republic. Our hope and consolation is that the Lord reigns and He is a God that judges in the earth. I have faith to believe that this important revolution is one in that series of events both small and great by which the glory of God will be consummated in the world.

While your hearts are saddened by financial embarrassments, ours are made to rejoice by manifestations of divine grace in our midst. Many among the largest children, both boys and girls and several women are inquiring earnestly—even with tears, what they must do to be saved. Some of the youths of both sexes, and one or more of the women give evidence of conversion. Is not this encouraging? Will our brethren forsake us under such hard circumstances? I feel they will not; but if they do, the Lord will not. He will sustain, when even father and mother forsake.

The political prospects of this country—the war notwithstanding—are as bright as its spiritual ones. The present disturbance in the states and consequent suffering among factory hands, and loss of capital by manufacturers in England, have made the manufacturing and mercantile community of that country sensible that a dependence upon the South for a steady supply of cotton, is very precarious. They have, therefore, resolved to encourage by their influence and capital the art of cotton planting in every country that it is practicable. The extent to which this article has been cultivated here, has made this country one of those to which they will give their attention. The troubles in the states are, therefore, likely to develop the resources of this and other countries which have been hitherto almost neglected. The Consul, Col. Foot, formerly English consul at Neamgua, visited this town a few weeks since. He seems determined to make an effort to entirely overthrow the Dahomian kingdom next year. A difficulty with Porto Novo has already caused a collision and the matter will probably be extended to the destruction of the Dahomian monarchy—an event over which I suppose the whole civilized world will rejoice. The Counsul visited us during his sojourn here. He assumed the protection of our interests under the English treaty. He appeared much interested in our missionary operations and contributed $5 for the support of the children—a very unexpected donation.

It is difficult to conjecture how the present war will terminate. By faith, however, we expect the humiliation or destruction of such powers as destroy the peace of the country and hinder the progress of the gospel. The enemy has divided their forces and are preparing to act against the [Ijebus?] as well as Ijaye. No fighting has occurred since I left, the first month being occupied in fasting, and the remaining time in military preparations for the future. Two very severe conflicts, which I did not mention, took place before I left. Both times the Ijayens were completely routed before the Egbas could arrive to their assistance. When the combatants would rush almost upon one another's gun, the roar of the musketry was so terrific that it was heard here at Abeokuta and thus announced the battle before it ceased. When it is remembered that Ijaye is between sixty and seventy miles distant from here, some idea of the contest may be formed. One long line of wounded, dead, and dying issued from both sides during the whole time of the fight. Men with blood gushing from bosoms would walk back firmly, sternly, and evenly proudly to their camp.

Twice, before we came down, the enemy drew themselves up in battle array almost in musket shot of the Egba camp, and just before our door. They yelled, beat their drums, blew trumpets, fired muskets, but the Egbas declined fighting outside their walls, and we were thus spared the sight of a contest right before our door. There was a little skirmishing, and the Egbas returned with two heads, but this occurred as the enemy was retiring to support the diversion sent against the Ijaye camp. The Ibadan army is immense, the allied forces not numbering a third of it. Sometimes the front ranks of the latter could not retire to load but were compelled to do so in the same place they stood when they fired. During these dreadful times we were often on our knees in private and prayer meeting capacity, praying to the Lord, that if it were His will that He would spare us and the people. He has heard us thus far, and I hope to be able to go back when the rainy season is over. The chief sent to tell us not to leave him altogether but to come back again. My former interpreter, whom I baptized, and whom I sent to take charge of the station from the hands of the first man, I left there, is now laboring among the people—holding prayer meetings and also talking with the people in their houses. I hope his labors may be much blessed. We are much pleased and gratified by the sympathy of those little children mentioned in the Commission. I hope I am still improving in my knowledge of this language. When I preach, the people affirm that they distinctly hear and understand every word I say. I am still in excellent health. Sue's health has improved much since her last sickness. She now enjoys excellent health. I have received my sewing machine, but it is not yet in successful operation. Our love to the brethren of the Board.

Yours, in Christ,
R. H. Stone

Abeokuta, May 27th, 1861
A. M. Poindexter, Cor. Sec.
Rev. James B. Taylor

Dear Brother:

Your favor of March 27th came safely to hand. I am thankful to hear that peace continues to prevail. It is difficult for me to comprehend how coercion is compatible with republican government.

Since I came to this country, I have never been so much encouraged or interested as I am at present. The Spirit of God is evidently in the midst of us reproving "of sin, of righteousness, and of judgment." After every Sabbath evening service the room is crowded with those inquiring after the way of life. The most of them are youths and children who are connected with our family; but many are of those who work here or visit the house. Some of them declare with tears and expressions of joy, that they have found peace in believing.

I have been preaching in the houses and streets of that portion of the town which is absent to us. The people generally leave their work and gather around me. Occasionally one mocks, but such a one I remind of the coming of the Lord in the clouds of heaven, and of "the great white throne" set for the judgment of all men according to the Gospel. I also remind them that they despise the love of God in the gift of His Son when they mock at the word I speak. The mocker sometimes looks frightened at this, and is also reformed by those around.

I also incite the people to come to family, or rather, to the chapel service that they may hear more fully. Sue sent out two of the female converts one Sabbath morning to talk to the women, and to invite them to come to the chapel also. They now go out every Sabbath morning, except something beyond their control prevents. Their labors have been attended with some success. Several have been induced to come to church regularly morning and evening. They are by their [exhortations], example and prayers quite efficient native agents. We also have four youths and young men of much promise—Ejinde, Onashe, Albert, and Elbert. Ejinde was baptized by Brother Philips last year. Since that time he has learned to read in his leisure hours, and is a diligent student when opportunity permits. He is now a sawyer by trade, and is native of Ogbomishaw, aged 21. Onashe was one of those baptized by me this year; can speak English very well, reads fluently and has much liberty in prayer, also earnestness in his daily walk. Has studied English and elementary arithmetic, aged 19. Albert is our cowry disburser, and is strictly honest and correct. He is an excellent financier. He has not been baptized, but gives good evidence of conversion. He can read fluently and is a daily student of the Bible. He also talks English very well and can cypher a little, aged 18. Edward was committed to my special care and instruction by Sister Priest. He is now studying Arithmetic, Geography, Grammar, and the Scriptures in English, which he speaks fluently and writes with ease. I much need suitable books for him. He is among those who are seeking the way of life, aged 16.

The children constituting the Sabbath school at Culpepper C.H., Va., have resolved to support one child, reserving to themselves the privilege of naming it. This plan was suggested to them by F.M. Laibam, Esq., an able and pious lawyer of that place. How many Sunday school teachers will go and do likewise? The plan is successfully practiced among English Missionaries. Twenty-five or thirty dollars is sufficient for one child. Individuals as well as Sunday schools can support a child. Many children are thus sustained in English Missions. I was much interested in a letter of yours in the Index. Like you, I think Georgia will do her duty. I am glad to see that the Georgia Baptists are so much interested in [Colperiage]. I hope they may adopt the plan of Virginia, given by the zealous and active brother Dickenson, since it has been so successful in that state to the discomfiture of the enemies of Baptist principles, and to the edification of ignorant Christians, and the salvation of many precious souls.

Yours, affectionately,
R.H. Stone

Liverpool Janry 13, 1863
I T Smith Esq
New York

My Dear Brother,

I now find myself a stranger in a strange land. Fearing to keep my wife another dry season in Africa we sailed for Liverpool on the 10th of last month, and arrived here yesterday evening. When we left Lagos, we were both feeling very badly, but we already feel much benefited by the change. We left things in quite a disordered state. The Egbas were becoming very troublesome to the English by interrupting the trade on the river, and when we arrived at Lagos, we learned that the Governor of that place had ordered all persons who placed themselves under the protection of the English to leave Abeokuta. The merchants had done so, but the missionaries declined doing so, for very evident reasons. Before I left however, there were many signs of a general peace. The Egbas were endeavoring to make restitution to the English for their robberies, and Negotiations were going on between them and their native enemies the Ibadans. The King of Dahomey intended attacking

Abeokuta, but I think that the English commander of the Coast will most likely dissuade him from it. We are very anxious to get to America but do not wish to come until there is peace or an armistice. I do not know where my parents are, but I suppose they have remained in Alabama for Culpeper County—I hear is a desert, and I suppose he has removed. Mrs. Stone is deeply anxious to see her aged parents.

I can only commit my way to the Lord. We will be compelled to seek employment of some kind if we stay here long, and to make a loan if we can be able to leave for America, for nearly all my money was consumed in the passage, though I sold everything I could.

We are also almost laughably bad off for clothes, Mrs. Stone having but one decent dress, and I but one decent suit. You must know therefore, we have to be very particular to keep them dry and clean. I have not yet made the acquaintance of many who will be likely to assist me but Aaron Brown. May the Lord grant that the war may soon cease. I hear that the Board has funds in hand if they could only get them to their missionaries. But even if they were to get some money to us, I would not like to eat the bread of idleness, if I had to stay here on account of the war. The weather here is not so cold as I expected, I do not suffer at all, but rather enjoy it. I have never yet worn an overcoat.

Our united regards to Sister Smith and self.

Yours Sincerely
R.H. Stone

P.S. If you feel disposed to write to me please address to the care of Aaron Brown 32 Chapel Street. Before closing I would again like to thank you for your great kindness to us and to every member of our mission. Yours/ R.H. Stone

Liverpool, Janry 14th 1863
Wm Crane Esq.
Baltimore

My Dear Brother,

Thinking it inadvisable to remain in Africa another dry season I have come to England, though we were both feeling quite indisposed when we left. We already feel much benefited by the change. I do not suffer from cold as I expected. I yet have no overcoat. We are in very poor circumstances having spent nearly all our money in getting here. Though it is my intention to seek employment here, I would like much to get to Baltimore, if I could find a comfortable maintenance there.

I do not wish to be dependent or eat the bread of idleness, and if the Lord helps me, I will not be so. I should be deeply obliged if any party or parties in Baltimore would advance me [Twenty or Thirty Pounds 20 or 30]. Bro. Taylor has informed us that they have money in hand for us but that they have no way to send it. My passage money and part of my usual supplies are due me from the Board. I have disposed of everything I could in Africa. We might effect a loan here, but Bro. Taylor when he wrote authorizing us to do so, neglected to send the proper security. I commit my way to the Lord, I can do no more, I live only for him, I have little else to live for now. Mrs. Stone sends her love to sister C and family. With our united Christian regards I remain yours in the Lord.

R.H. Stone

P.S. Address to the care of Aaron Brown 32 Chapel Street

Letter to Mission Board
Liverpool, England
Jan. 15, 1863

"Fearing to pass through another dry season without giving my wife a change of climate, I came down to Lagos. The Egbas were then on the river demanding tribute from every canoe that passed. By making them a small present I was permitted to pass in safety, until I came to a party which had no leader. We there had a narrow escape of our lives; but dissension having arisen among them, used the opportunity to push off our canoe and escape down the river. By running all night we entirely escaped them. On arriving at Lagos, not being able to get accommodations, after three weeks' stay, I took the steamer for this city. When leaving we felt very badly in health, but are already much improved by the change. We are in very poor circumstances, though I sold everything I could in Africa. I hope to get employment here until funds sufficient reach me to enable me to come to America. I can only commit my way to the Lord."

Culpeper, July 15, 1863

My dear Bro. Taylor,

Enclosed you will find two letters which I hope you will be able to forward to their proper destination via the blockade.

We all feel quite gloomy here to the news of the surrender of

Vicksburg and Port Henderson. If you can conveniently communicate with me before Saturday I would be glad to hear from you. I have abandoned the idea of taking Mrs. Stone with me when I go to Georgia. She does not seem willing to leave her father under present circumstances.

When do you desire that I shall go?

With our united regards,
Yrs. Sincerely
R.H. Stone

Sparta, GA, Sept. 2, 1863

Dear Bro. Taylor,

I received your letter of the 22nd ult. I was very glad to hear that the Dahomians had abandoned their design upon Abeokuta, and that there was a probability of reconciliation between the authorities of Lagos and that town. Before this, I suppose, you have received my letter mentioning some incidents attending my visit to Macon during the session of the Central Association. The success which attended my visit there, disposes me to attend the session of other Associations in this state. If I had not been present not a cent would have been contributed to foreign missions. The anti-foreign missionary men were in the ascendancy and one prominent brother Bro. Kendrick formerly of Charleston, admitted that foreign missions had passed out of his mind. After the statements I had made, however, in regard to our foreign missions the brethren generally seemed very much stirred up, and resolved to divide the contributions to general mission purposes, equally between foreign and domestic missions and passed resolutions that they would give more to the former than they had been doing in the past.

I have just been plunged in the deepest grief by the loss of my second and last brother. His body was found in a mill pond in Fauquier after the enemy had left. Gen. Stewart for some reason always kept him in a post of the most unusual peril as he did my other brother. Thus have both been sacrificed.

Yours affectionately
R.H. Stone

Sparta, Sept. 29, 1863
Rev. James B. Taylor
Richmond

Dear Bro. Taylor,

Your letter bringing the news of the accident to my wife is to hand. Truly afflictions do not come upon me single handed. Added to the death of my last brother, I now hear that my wife is wounded and probably killed. As there is no possibility of my getting to see her for the present I am willing to remain and visit the other associations in the capacity of an agent, but this suspense, you must feel, is dreadful. I hope therefore that you will endeavor to get as much information about my wife as possible. Probably Bro. Dickenson or someone else you know may be able while visiting the army to see someone who has escaped from Culpeper C.H. and is acquainted with the particulars. Persons frequently escaped from there while Pope was in possession and came into our lines. Please write immediately on receiving any information and don't conceal the worst from me. I read in the papers a few days ago that three ladies were killed in the town by shells and my heart sickens at the thought that my wife may be one among them. Can't you send me the paper in which you saw the notice, or any other Richmond paper which contains any details of the fight the day the town was occupied? If you can see anyone that knows anything about the accident to my wife, please inquire whether she was wounded by a shell or shot and in what part of the person. I have just returned from the session of Washington association. I do not yet know what is the amt. of the contributions to the African mission. It will be paid over to me in a few days. I expect to visit a small association near here next Saturday and then attend the session of the Georgia.

Yrs. Affectionately,
R.H. Stone

Culpeper, C.H. Va.
Oct. 20. 1863

Dear Bro. Taylor,

During my trip in Georgia I collected $3611.95. My traveling expenses were over $150 leaving a balance to the credit of the Board of $3461.95. As I supposed that you would compensate me for my services in Ga. I left a package containing $3370.00 with Sister Taylor, and appropriated the remainder $91.95 to my fut. expenses untill we have an opportunity for a settlement.

While standing in the porch with her father and sister, my wife was wounded in the thigh by a Minnie ball. They seemed to have drawn the fire of the enemies' sharpshooters through mistake. Eight balls struck close to them and a shell burst over their heads. They escaped almost through a miracle. The house and furniture were considerably injured by the shell and the balls.

Gen. Lee has fallen back behind the Rappahannoc after pursuing the enemy to their entrenchments at Bentonville or Warrenton. Gen. Hill is said to be under arrest for tardiness and allowing men to escape.

With united kind regards to all.

I remain
Yrs. affectionately
R.H. Stone

P.S. I forgot to say that Mrs. Stone is nearly well.

Culpeper CH
Oct 18 1864

Dear Bro. Taylor,

I do not feel well qualified to give information on the subject of your last letter.

Bro. Phillips was very kindly received by the immediate friends and relations of those English missionaries whose acquaintance he had made while in Africa. He was encouraged by several prominent Baptist ministers to make an effort to obtain either a donation or loan from the Bapt. Ex. Comm. For—located at London, but entirely failed. Before leaving the country, however, he collected from private individuals the sum of seventy pounds sterling. Some seemed to take a considerable interest in our African mission, especially, schools.

My reception in England by the relations of our missionary acquaintances in Africa was equally kind as that given to Bro. Phillips. I made no effort to collect funds except the small sum of five pounds for a little boy in Lagos. Through the kindness of Rev. H.S. Brown of Liverpool, I readily obtained this sum.

In England, a southern man has to contend with many difficulties and discouragements. As a general thing, the people have been educated to regard slavery as the "sum of all villainies," and think it heresy in a Christian to give "aid and comfort" to anyone who sympathizes or is connected with this institution in any way. Some who might be disposed to render us assistance are afraid of public opinion. I suppose, however, that the latter has much changed since I was in England, and enough funds might be collected there to warrant the expense of sending someone for that purpose.

It might be well, however, to first communicate with some prominent Bapt. Minister there. If you should conclude to do this, I would recommend the name of Rev. Hugh Stowel Brown of Liverpool, a man of enlarged sympathies and views, whose understanding soars far above national prejudices. He is one of the most influential Bapt. Ministers of England and might render us a good deal of service. If you should write to him, you will doubtless receive a prompt and candid but courteous reply.

In regard to a postage account I know of no one who would be more likely to accommodate you than Aaron Brown Esq., provision merchant, Liverpool. He is no relation to Rev. H. S. B. but is a Bapt. and an excellent man. He once consented to act as agent for us if we should establish an agency in England.

We would all be glad to have you to services. An ambulance nearly always awaits passengers at Orange C.H.

Very Sincerely.

R.H. Stone

Culpeper CH

July 4th, 1865

Dear Bro. Taylor,

I take advantage of the opportunity allowed me by the P. Marshal at this place to inquire after you all, and to inform you of my own safety.

The magazine blew up just as I was leaving the city stunning me considerably. A cry that the enemy's horse[s] were immediately behind us kept the party into which I had fallen in this quick step untill we reached "Flint-pump" where we retired into the woods and took a little rest. We camped the first night about 2 miles this side of Rockville having come a distance of 22 or 25 miles. We reached Louisa CH in the afternoon of the third day, walking all the way. As I held onto all my baggage you may know that I was quite rejoiced to find a train of cars there to take us to Gordonsville on the same day. By traveling in the night we reached Culpeper CH the next day, and found Mr. Broadus very ill. He lived a short time longer then entered into that rest prepared for the people of God. I am now teaching in a small school, but the scarcity of money here as elsewhere, make[s] it a hard struggle to get both ends to meet. Providence permitting I continue to try to preach. I am quite anxious to know if my friends Capt. Duggan and Lts. Latiner and Jourdan recovered from their wounds, and whether they are still in Richmond. What became of yr. son Charles after leaving me? Have you all been kindly treated by the authorities.

I am also quite anxious to learn whether you have had any communication with our brethren in Africa, or rather if you have heard from them since the fall of Richmond?

We are quite well excepting my little girl. We are suffering much anxiety on her account at this time.

With our united kind regards to Sister T, family and self.
I remain
Affectionately yrs.
R H Stone

To the Brethren of the
Washington Association, Georgia
Culpeper C.H., V., Dec 6, 1865.

Dear Brethren: After several abortive attempts to obtain communication with you through private channels, I have adopted the present mode. I regret that the condition of the country and the absence of so many of the brethren in the summer of '63, prevented me from having more conference with you at that time. Since then, I saw several of the absent members in the army, and though they were surrounded by all the circumstances of war, they were as warm-hearted and as devoted to the cause of Christ as ever. Two of them, brothers Duggan and Latiner, I left dangerously wounded in Richmond, just before its fall, but they endured their sufferings like Christian heroes. I have since learned that they died. Peace to their ashes. They were gentle as lambs, but brave as lions.

My object in writing this letter is to inform you that I do not purpose returning to Africa for the present; and for the sake of the mission, I desire to plainly state my reasons for not returning.

First of all, I would impress upon your minds that it is not because I suspect the practicability or success of the mission. The fact that white men can live in Africa has been fully demonstrated. So well am I persuaded of this fact that I would have been willing last summer to return to Africa for several years without my wife, if it had been allowable. The success of this like all other missions, depends entirely upon our faith. If I could be persuaded that we have no sincere and earnest Christians among the converts of our Yoruban Mission then I

could believe that none could be found in the world. We often have to
contend with the same propensities among some of the converts over
which the Apostle Paul so often lamented. What church has not had its
corrupt members? Should we expect more of heathen than enlightened
converts?

Again it is not because I doubt that the Lord called me to the work.
If I was a subject of delusion in this matter when you sent me forth in
'58, I still remain one and expect to remain so as long as I live, whether I
return to Africa or not. Nor is it because I dread the dangers, afflictions
and privations attending the work. As the Lord knows my heart, I can
truly say, "None of these things move me, neither count I my life dear
unto myself, so that I might finish my course with joy, and the ministry
which I have received of the Lord Jesus, to satisfy the Gospel of the
grace of God." Beds of languishing and of pain, days of care and
sorrow, and nights of terror and peril, your very memory is sacred.

It is not because I do not love my missionary brethren, the native
Christians, and the cause. Whether it will ever be my privilege to return
to Africa or not, will always be, I hope, as it has heretofore been, one of
my chief pleasures to think of and pray for them.

Distressing changes which have occurred in my family since my
return from Georgia, in '63, have brought me to this conclusion: All
my brothers perished in the late civil war. My father's plantation was
swept with the besom of destruction, and a recent destructive fire has
left him, my mother and two sisters homeless and destitute for the
present. The health of my wife, who, with two sisters, has recently
become an orphan, also offers a very serious impediment. Under
such circumstances, it seems my duty to remain in this country for
the present. This decision has cost me many an earnest prayer and
anxious thought, and though I here resign the commission which in the
providence of God you gave me, I hope you will not cease to pray for
me, that I may know the will of the Lord in all things, and have grace to
do it. I propose opening in this place a female school, but I hope I shall
never forget that my principal mission is to win souls to Christ.

Why does not brother Jennings write to this wandering sheep of his
flock? Why does not brother Reed let me know where he is?

Yours in Christ,
R.H. Stone

P.S.-The sum of fourteen hundred and forty-two dollars, which I
received from the Association in '63, was transferred to brother J.B.
Taylor with the other money received for Foreign Missions. I have

drawn no salary since returning from Africa. I made a complete report of the sums received from individuals, churches and associations to the Corresponding Secretary of the Board, Brother Taylor. I would have sent a copy of this report to the INDEX at the time, but the disturbed state of the country prevented me from doing so. I will yet do so.

R.H.S.

Culp. C.H., July 9th. 66

Dear Bro. Taylor,

Enclosed you will find a very important letter to Bro. Phillips. It is concerning a little boy whom we left at Lagos and who is now much neglected. This we have learned in a letter just received from Bro. Phillips. The Sunday School here have agreed to raise the money to support him and to place it in your hands to be included in the appropriations for the school at Abeokuta. I have written to Bro. Phillips to take him immediately to Abeokuta, and place him in the school there. I hope the Board will make a liberal appropriation for the school at Abeokuta, for I am fast coming to the conviction, that schools for the rising generation must be the basis of all missions among barbarous and savage heathen. The gospel should be preached regularly and steadily, faithfully and prayerfully; but, through the children, we get at the root of idolatry, and leaven the whole belief. This letter encloses one from Sue to the little boy. I intend to mail a copy of it direct, so that one or the other may be sure to reach him. But I place most dependence in this.

All well. Remember us to your family.
Affectionately-yrs.
R.H. Stone

Culpeper C.H.
Jany 8, '67

Dear Bro. Taylor,

I return Bro. P's letters with many thanks. I received a letter from him addressed to myself, a short time ago.

I do not know how he obtained the idea that I expected to come out without Sue but on this subject he need not give himself any uneasiness.

I hope you will not give much attention to Bro. P's rash remark in regard to Bro. Reid. Having been associated with him for several years, I perhaps know Bro. P. better than any man living does, and I think he has never lacked that encouragement in his missionary life, which springs from a proper appreciation of his own abilities and labors. I certainly think we need men of "great abilities" in our Yoruban mission [yourself, Dr. Jeter, Bro. Poindexter, or Dr. Burrows for instance] if we cd. by any means persuade them to go out there, but as they will not, Bro. Reid and myself desire to do so, hoping and believing that the grace of our Lord will be sufficient for us, that in our weakness we will be made strong.

We are quite well.

With our united regards to family and self,
I remain
Affectionately. Yrs.
R.H. Stone

Lagos West Africa,
January 25th, 1868
An appeal to the colored Baptists in the South

In the year 1858, when much concerned to know in what way I could most acceptably serve the Lord, I was led by a series of events which left me in no doubt about my duty, to leave my native state of Virginia, and come as a missionary of the Southern Baptist Convention, to this country. For four years, I lived and labored here with other brethren of our Board and the English and German missionaries in the interior of the country; but failing health compelled me to return to America during the war. There, I was detained untill the month of October last. I have again landed at this town and found that great changes have taken place in it and the surrounding country since my departure four years ago. Some of these changes are for the better, but others are apparently for the worse.

The gospel has greatly prevailed in this and other towns during that time; but the inhabitants of a very large town in the interior called Abeokuta, where I formerly lived, have risen up in defense of their idols of wood and stone, broken down the missionary dwellings and houses of worship, and driven the missionaries themselves down to this place on the coast. Not being permitted just yet to go up to Abeokuta again, I am here in this town with a very important field before me, for multitudes of its inhabitants continue to worship idols. To these, we must preach that gospel which alone will turn them away from such vanities to the true and living God. But this is not all we should do. Thousands of children are here, and millions in the towns around and beyond us, who know nothing of the Bible, and who will grow up to be worshippers of idols like their parents, unless they are instructed while they are young and know nothing of these things. You know what the Bible teaches, and how very important it is for them to know it. If they should remain in ignorance of these blessed truths which alone bring salvation, do you think our Master will hold you blameless when he has committed His word to you with a command in it to send it to them? To these children, I desire to call the attention of all colored Baptists in the South; but I would especially address myself to those who live in Va., D. Columbia and Maryland.

Previous to the late war, our board at Richmond made very liberal appropriations for this part of our work here; but they can now do very little, if anything in that way. I shall feel very thankful if they can maintain us in our preaching labors among the people, for our support and traveling expenses, together with the building of dwellings and houses of worship, entails a very heavy expense on them.

Must these children be allowed to grow up ignorant heathens without any effort on my and your part to impart to them the knowledge of God and such useful and important knowledge as will make them intelligent and useful men and women? I can get good teachers in Sierra Leone, who are colored men trained especially for the work, but they cannot work for nothing, and I must give them what others do. The widow of our late colored missionary, Rev. J.M. Harden, is still living here, and is willing to again engage in the work of teaching if suitable arrangements can be made. Previous to her husband's death, she had the training of all the girls at our mission station in this town.

It will be necessary to fit up a house convenient for the purpose, obtaining one colored male and one colored female teacher, and send to England for books adapted to the capacities of the children. Now, I ask if you cannot raise at once for this object, eight hundred or one thousand dollars? To whom else can I so properly apply but to you? They are of your race, and many of them are your immediate relations. You are now enjoying the privileges and advantages of freemen, and hold in your hands that precious Book which has brought "life and immortality to light," and through the knowledge of which you daily rejoice "in the hope of the glory of God." You must then feel an earnest desire to be the means of communicating these glorious truths to your benighted race in the land of your fore fathers, else all your professions and rejoicings are solemn mockery and an abomination in the sight of God. Christians in England contributed most liberally to this work when we had no one else to whom we could go for aid during the past troubles; but they may well feel surprised that I now come to them when there are tens of thousands of intelligent colored Baptists in the land whence I came, who have as yet done nothing for the enlightenment and salvation of their unhappy race and kindred in this country. To you, then, I must come now for aid in this all-important work; and having written this appeal, my hands are free from blood so far as you are concerned. See, brethren, that your hands are free from the blood of souls in this matter, for you know that no idolater can enter the kingdom of God, and that there is only one way for all men in all the world in all ages to be saved—through an humble trust in the atoning blood of Jesus alone.

If your hearts are in this matter, you can easily communicate with me. Any letter addressed to this place, marked "Via England," and prepaid thirty three cents, will reach me in safety. Money deposited with S.G. & G.C. Ward, agents for Baring, Brothers and Co, Wall St., New York, will be in my hands as soon as a letter can come from them informing me of the fact; for these gentlemen will send me a letter of credit on their house in London, and I can sell a draft for the amount here in Lagos for cash. Thus all the risks of transportation will be avoided. For any sum thus sent me, I will render a faithful account to anyone who may be selected for the purpose. In the manner of collection, and place and person for depositing the small sums untill they can be collected in a whole, I hope you will exercise your own prudence and pleasure. As the distance is so great, I cannot communicate readily with these gentlemen on the subject and am compelled to use their names without their knowledge or consent, but I am persuaded that Rev. J.W.M. Williams D.D., Baltimore, Rev. G.W. Samson D.D., Washington, D.C., and Rev. J.B. Taylor D.D. and Rev. Robt. Ryland D.D., Richmond, Va., would take pleasure in receiving and forwarding anything that may be placed in their hands for this purpose.

In conclusion, brethren, allow me to affectionately say that I hope the day is not far distant when you will be less concerned about the things of this vain life, and more interested in those things which pertain to the Kingdom of our blessed Redeemer, and that you will soon cooperate with some missionary board in sending out good and faithful men of your own number who will unite with us in preaching "the unsearchable riches of Christ" among their idolatrous brethren in this country. I feel persuaded that when we all meet at "the judgment seat of Christ," and when that judgment shall "first begin at the house of God," you will not be held guilty while the heathen here go weeping and gnashing their teeth down to Hell, if you deliberately neglect to hear this voice from Africa.

R.H. Stone

Lagos, West Africa, January 25th 1868
Rev. J.B. Taylor, D.D.
Richmond, Va.

My dear Bro:

Yours of 29th came to hand, and I thank you for the words of sympathy it contained. I need other letters of similar import for which I feel thankful. By the enclosed appeal, I hope to raise some funds for our school here about on the same place that we have been collecting them in England for the same purpose—while I will render an account to any man whom the contributions may be pleased to appoint for that purpose, I will also notify the board of the receipts of any money received in this way, accompanying the acknowledgement with an account of the manner of its expenditure. In this way I hope to draw the most pious and kindly disposed of our Colored brethren into cooperation with us in our work out here. I have endeavored to draw a very distinct line between their contributions and the peculiar work of the board, only hinting as plainly as I dare do for the present, that their cooperation with our board would be a very appropriate thing in regard to our African mission. I have endeavored to write it in the fear of the Lord, and I humbly trust that He will add his blessing to it.

That it will receive no opposition is not to be hoped as every enterprise begun for the extension of Christ's kingdom in the world must necessarily be opposed by the devil who too often uses Christians themselves as his deceived agents. I send a copy of this appeal to Drs. Lawson & Williams, requesting them, as I do you and Dr. Ryland, to excuse the unauthorized use of their names in it. I have another thought. I suppose the So. B. C. will soon meet at Balt. and that some kindly disposed northern brethren will be present. What do you think of a union of the northern & southern boards in this African mission? I hear that they contemplate beginning a mission in Africa. It may be that the boards could work harmoniously and efficiently together, allowing Southern men to be responsible alone to the southern board and northern men to the northern board; yet in consideration of the opening we have made, they might advance sufficient funds to restore the material part of our operations, and begin the work with new vigor.

This is a very delicate subject, I know, and I cautiously turn it over into your more experienced hands as I wd. a loaded bombshell. If an attempt is ever made to open it, I hope it will be done by old gunners who know what they are about, or else it might explode and somebody [will] get hurt. This talk is intended only for your ears and those of the board. It may be that you have previously considered it, though I have never heard the subject mentioned by anyone, or received a communication about it. Whatever you may do, it is very important that we should immediately place the material part of our missionary operations here on a more solid basis, or people here friendly to the cause generally, will render us no aid; for they will lose confidence in a mission in which the churches which we represent apparently feel neither confidence nor interest. It is hard for them to realize the poverty of our people, when they look on the large operations of other societies in the town. In addition to this, unless they are moved by personal esteem, people will not attend our little bamboo chapel; neither will children come to our school if they think we will always go on in this feebly, flickering, uncertain way. This is entirely natural and quite reasonable. It wd. be so at home and anywhere else. We do not like to be connected with anything that fails, or looks like failing.

While talking about this part of our work, I will mention that the promised remittance of L100 has arrived; but we are almost as much disturbed about the way to dispose of it as we were for the want of it. Bro. Phillips refuses to go to England untill his debt with Carns & Brown is paid, and I am obliged to send one portion to England for the most necessary articles of household & kitchen furniture, while reserving a portion for necessary expenses here such as house-rent & c. Besides we had to borrow some money which we repaid. Under such circumstances, Bro. Phillips has determined to remain untill another remittance arrives sufficient to carry him home and leave enough to carry on the work here.

Sister Harden is a great treasure to us, and I would like to have her employed. If I can raise the money, I want to have a good school house with proper seats, & c. We are still living in the rented house, but will have to leave soon, and I don't yet know where we will find a place to lay our heads; for houses are hard to find at any price. I can't think of turning Sister Harden out, though I know she would go without saying a word of objection; but it wd. be as difficult for her to find a house for herself and two little boys and our girls, as it is for us. Besides, it is a miserable structure with leaky roof and only two habitable rooms. The bedroom has no ceiling and the ceiling poles are about as high as the floor ought to be. I would run serious risk for my life if I were to stay in it a month during the rainy season. Unless it is repaired for Mrs. Harden as our teacher, the best thing that can be done with it is to tear it down, and take the ground for a better house.

Though I am living harder than I ever did in my life (except when I was in the army) I find that I will gradually become deeper in debt to the Board unless my salary is increased beyond $500 per annum. Everything in the way of provisions, having either to be bought from foreign countries or from a considerable distance in the country is very dear. The great numbers of European residents and civilized residents has much to do with this. As a specimen, I will mention the price of two staples in the way of food. Meat is eighteen cents per pound, and yams 50 cents per dozen (specie). What milk and butter we eat is imported, and though not so pleasant to the taste as our fresh, Abeokutan luxuries in this line, very far excel no milk and butter. Butter 50 cts per. pound & milk [desiccated] 40 & 50 cts per vial.

Some of the merchants and officers at this place are disposed to be very friendly with us, and some are in to breakfast or tea with us very frequently. As their chief complaint against us here is that the missionaries will have nothing to do with them, but treat them as if they were outcasts and villains, I am very careful to be pleasant with them, and never fail to invite them to take a cup of tea with us if they are in at the time. In this way an astonishing hole is made in our flour, sugar, tea, milk, butter, coffee, & any foreign provisions we may happen to have. You see I am giving you all the points. Besides, I must have comparatively nice clothes here. I can't wear old shoes with my toe sticking out, and old sagged coats & pants as I sometimes did in Abeokuta & Ijaye. I must live and dress exactly as I would in Richmond or Culpeper C.H.; for any apparently eccentric departure from the social customs here would cause as much remark, and be attended with the same consequence as they would in the above mentioned places. Unless it could be proved that he was forced to it from the direct necessity, it would never do for a missionary to engage in secular business here, for competition rides very high in all departments of business and if a missionary were to enter the list, they would probably unite to ruin him. Many of the men who came out on the steamer with me, thought that I was secretly connected with some secular enterprise, as they could not see why a man would leave his wife & children behind and come way out here to this inhospitable climate without a secret design to make money. Money is their God, and they thought it was mine also.

They are exceed'ly suspicious and jealous on this subject. One man said before I left him that he would not be surprised to hear very soon that I was a merchant. My only reply was, "I don't know what I may have to do." I say all these things to give you a reason for saying what I think the salary which should be allowed to single missionaries in this place is that which is allowed to European single missionaries at Abeokuta and other places in the interior—about twice the amount which you have always allowed single missionaries. You see how I blot out and scratch when writing about money; or I don't like to do it, and I don't know hardly what to say when it affects myself. It almost frightens me to say that L200 or $1000 is necessary to support single missionaries here, but in justice to the missionary who may live here with European customs, I am compelled to say it. He may live on less but I imagine that concern about his private affairs would occupy his mind almost as much as the affairs of the mission. I am afraid that he would be thinking more about the way in which he would pay his washer woman's, cook's, and butcher's bills than about the preparation of his Yoruba sermon. I am trying to live as economical as I can, and will give myself no concern on this subject.

We will try very hard to make the last remittance last untill we receive another. 57 pounds had to go as soon as it arrived—forty pounds to England to pay Bro. P's debt with Carns & Brown & purchase the most necessary things and 11 pounds for debts contracted here. We only allow six and three pence per week for the children whom we are supporting, and wd. not allow that but they are orphaned and interior children.

I now conclude by alluding to a subject which excepting my duty to my Master, gives me more concern than any other. Whatever you may conclude to do in reference to my support out here, don't forget my wife and children [for I suppose I have two children by this time]. I hope the $250 allowed to herself and the $80 each for my children, will be paid over to her in stated installments regularly; for I know that nothing but the direst necessity will ever make her mention the subject to you. Our earthly patrimony has been wrecked by the war, and without my presence to recover and improve what is left, very little if anything will ever be available to us. Though she may not, therefore, need all of her allowance at the time when it is paid, the time may come when as a helpless and dependent widow, she will need it all and more. I cd. not conclude this better without relieving my mind on this subject. I sometimes fear that I may have done wrong in leaving her; for it is said that if a man provideth not for his own household, he hath denied the faith and is worse than an infidel. Such thoughts may be sinful, but they are natural. The Lord directs me in all this.

I am quite well; so is Bro Phillips.

Affectionately yrs.
R.H. Stone

Culpeper, Va., April 14th, 1888
Rev. H.A. Tupper
Corresponding Sec. 7n Missions
Richmond, Va.

Dear Bro:

After many years, Yoruba is again freely open to white missionaries and it is of the utmost importance to our work there that the centers of influence and population in that country should again be occupied as soon as practicable by our white missionaries. From Yorubans and their descendants at Lagos, our flourishing church in that place derives much of its strength, and it is among refugees and visitors from Yoruba, the missionary at Abeokuta will find the most successful work. The C.M.S. has done much towards civilizing the people of Lagos and Abeokuta, but it is chiefly to the Southern Baptists, the Yorubans will have to look for the saving doctrines and wholesome discipline of the gospel. If we would not have our work circumscribed and even strangled at Lagos and Abeokuta, we must not lose any time in sending experienced white men to Ogbomiso, Awyaw and Ibadan, but especially to Ogbomiso. Yet in all the country of Yoruba, since Hanson—has left the work, we have not even a native agent unless one has gone there very recently.

Breth. David and Smith will probably return to this country this summer and there will be no one in the field who can go. Besides this, such pioneer work is hardly suited to men who have wives and infant children. They would be very far from the conveniences and medical assistance of the coast and traveling backwards and forwards would be attended with considerable risk. In view of these facts, I feel it my duty to offer to go again to Yoruba as the missionary of the S.B. Convention upon the condition, however, that the Board will allow me to draw a married man's salary while my wife remains at home with our three younger children. I feel some hesitation in making such an application, but as the case is urgent and it is the best I can do, I hope the Board will ignore its seeming immodesty. As lady missionaries are not specially needed in the interior now and the expense of transportation and outfit, not to mention doctor's bills, will be saved, I think this would be the most economical arrangement at this time and will be in the end, and I obtained her consent to make this offer last summer. I have a comfortable home, but no income except my salary, and my wife and at least two of my children will be dependent on what is allowed them from my salary. I have, however, an insurance of $2000 on my life which I have carried for many years and which will not be vitiated, I am informed, by my going to Africa. If I am allowed to return for six or eight months at the end of every fourth year, I have reason to hope that, if this application meets with a favorable reception, I may be able to perform fifteen or twenty years of good service.

I am just fifty and in reasonably good health, being entirely free, so far as I know from any disease. Mr. Seyes—with whom I first went out remained at work there until he was over eighty. I have seen several old men and women in Africa on the coast enjoying good health so far as I could see. I have not only talked freely with my wife on this subject but I have conferred with Bro. James our pastor. While declining to give any advice one way or the other, Bro James thinks that I do well in making this application.

If the Board thinks what I have written is worthy of their consideration, but prefers to talk with me before committing themselves, I will come to Richmond at any time they may be pleased to appoint. I hope they will reach some conclusion by the beginning of summer.

It is an open secret in my family that I have long desired to resume my work in Yoruba, but I do not want to leave in such haste as to make my children think that I am deficient in affection for them. I would like to make things comfortable at home before leaving and make such arrangements that my family will feel that my going to Africa is in no sense deserting them. Government officers, explorers and merchants, leave their families for several years at a time without being thought unfeeling. I have never forgotten the language; the people have never forgotten me and wish me to return. I feel better qualified for the work than I was when I first went out and the work in the interior demands services such as I hope to be able to render. Under these circumstances I feel that I should test the matter at once by making this application. May the Holy Spirit direct you in your decision.

Fraternally,
R.H. Stone

P.S. If I should be appointed, I would prefer not to be appointed for any particular city in the interior. I think it would be best to refer the matter to the brethren now in the field after I arrive at Lagos.

Yrs, in C.
R.H. Stone

Culpeper, Va.
May 19, 1888
Rev. H.A. Tupper, D.D.
Richmond, Va.

My dear brother:

Please accept my thanks for your prompt reply. I am glad to know that there is a time fixed for coming to some decision in the matter. May the Holy Spirit prompt them what to do. I am deadly in earnest. Some missionary of experience ought to enter Yoruba at once and, if possible, occupy Ogbomishaw. I feel it my duty to go, if the Board will accept me under the conditions mentioned in my application. I have long prayed that I might be willing to do my duty in the matter and that if it was the Lord's will that I should go, that I might have the sympathy of my wife and children, the approval of my brethren and the favor and blessing of God. I have also had a strong presentiment that I am yet to be a greater blessing to the people of Yoruba than I have ever been before, and that eventually I am to end my life among the people to whom in youth I was called to preach the gospel.

Sincerely yours,
R.H. Stone

June 2nd, 1888
Culpeper, Va.

Dear Brother Tupper,

I suppose that you have received by this time the statements and resolutions mentioned in the enclosed letter, and I enclose the latter that you may compare it with those statements before coming to any conclusion in regard to this very serious affair. I had never suspected so serious a state of things, though Rev. Mr. Ladejo, who regards me as his spiritual father, has frequently made complaints that the "rules" of the mission were too stringent upon him. I was rather of this opinion myself, but I either exhorted him to be submissive to the instruction and guidance of the missionaries or I did not notice his complaints at all. I have not answered his two last letters at all because I could not do so without saying something about his trouble in regard to this matter. But he persists in writing to me, nevertheless. That such people as Mrs. S.M. Harden and Mr. Vaughn should be included among the disaffected is not only a very serious thing for the mission, but seems to imply that Mr. Ladejo may have some grounds for complaint. Possibly the "rules" of Mr. David are too strict, but as it is not proper for me to interfere in anyway I send the letter to you. I have great influence with Mr. Ladejo, if I am to take his word for it, but I feel some delicacy in corresponding with him under the present circumstances. Were I on the field, I believe I could soon arrange the matter without compromising Bro. David's authority & influence and without humiliating Mr. Ladejo and the native church; but I am afraid to open a correspondence with Ladejo but it might be misunderstood by Bro. David as impertinent meddling; and I don't like to write to Bro. David in regard to the matter untill he first writes to me. I hope, however, that he may see his way here to give Ladejo a better support and to do something to bring the native church back to their home and then duty. Mr. Ladejo is a native of Ogbomishaw, a man of some influence with the natives, and I think he is a man of undoubted piety and ability. He thought proper to assume my name, like many of the native converts, when I baptized them, but his does not prejudice me in his favor more than the other native agents. He is the only one who has been ordained, I think, and this seems to imply that he is superior to the rest. Besides, the church seems to be wholly devoted to him. I hope something can be done to keep him in the mission without weakening Bro. David's influence or without seeming to condemn his cause in the matter. Rev. Moses L. Stone may possibly be too ambitious, and may need to be restrained, but I think a little better support would not only not hurt him, but add to his usefulness. But I suppose Bro. David will tell you all about it. I only send this letter that you may compare it with the one he has written to you. I wish I was there now, and then we could talk it all over in a brotherly manner. But I will not say more. I would be glad to get this letter when you are done with it.

Very sincerely,
RH Stone

Index